Electric Traction

Electric Traction

J. Upadhyay

Formerly Member Electrical Railway Board
Indian Railways & Presently
Visiting Professor
Department of Electrical Engineering
Institute of Technology
Banaras Hindu University
Varanasi

S. N. Mahendra

Professor
Department of Electrical Engineering
Institute of Technology
Banaras Hindu University
Varanasi

ALLIED PUBLISHERS LTD.

New Delhi • Mumbai • Kolkata • Lucknow • Chennai
Nagpur • Bangalore • Hyderabad • Ahmedabad

ALLIED PUBLISHERS PRIVATE LIMITED
D-5, Sector-2, **Noida**–201301
Ph.: 0120-4320295, 2542557, 4352866
• E-mail: delhi.books@alliedpublishers.com

17 Chittaranjan Avenue, **Kolkata**–700072
Ph.: 033-22129618 • E-mail: cal.books@alliedpublishers.com

15 J.N. Heredia Marg, Ballard Estate, **Mumbai**–400001
Ph.: 022-42126969 • E-mail: mumbai.books@alliedpublishers.com

No. 25/10, Commander-in-Chief Road, Ethiraj Lane (Next to Post Office)
Egmore, **Chennai**–600008, Ph.: 044-28223938
• E-mail: chennai.books@alliedpublishers.com

P.B.9932, 1st Floor, Sunkada Chickkana Complex,
Loop Lane Off Race Course Road, Next to Hotel Maurya, Gandhi Nagar,
Bangalore - 560009
Ph.: 080-22262081 • E-Mail: bngl.books@alliedpublishers.com

Sri Jayalakshmi Nilayam, No. 3-4-510, 3rd Floor (Opp. State Bank of India)
Barkatpura, Telangana, **Hyderabad**–500027
Ph.: 040-27551811, 040-27551812 • E-mail: hyd.books@alliedpublishers.com

Website: www.alliedpublishers.com

Fifth Impression, 2012
Reprint, 2022

ISBN : 81-7764-005-4

Published by Sunil Sachdev and printed by Ravi Sachdev at Allied Publishers Private Limited, Printing Division, D-5, Sector - 2, Noida - 201301 (U.P.)

This book is dedicated to the memory of

Late Professor M. Sengupta
Principal
Erstwhile Benares Engineering College
(BENCO)

Foreword

It is an honour for me to have been requested by the authors of the book to record my views on their work in the form of a foreword. The reasons for this feeling are manifold. Firstly, as an old student of Electric Traction and Utilization and a Professor in Electrical Engineering in the specialized area of Electric Drives and Traction, I have been in continuous touch with the momentous developments which have come about in contemporary technology in these areas over the years. Although development of support text materials for students and practising engineers in the area of Electric Drive Systems has received considerable attention in recent years, the same cannot be said about the area of Electric Traction and Utilization with an equal degree of conviction. Even today, the books available follow the style and pattern set by E. Openshaw Taylor and A.T. Starr and little attempt has been made by contemporary authors in the area to incorporate latest state-of-art technologies. This book is a welcome exception from this trend.

I was privileged to have been closely associated with the authors during the preparation of the manuscript of the book. This has given me the opportunity to be acquainted with the chronology and coverage of the materials in the book quite intimately. It was a pleasure for me to interact with Professor J. Upadhyaya, my one-time teacher and then Member (Electrical) Railway Board, Govt. of India, and one of the chief architects of modern electric traction in India on the one hand, and Professor S.N. Mahendra, my able student whom I can claim to have introduced to the fascinating world of linear electric machines. It is only natural that the vast field experience of Professor Upadhyaya, coupled with the backup of sound theoretical and analytical capabilities of Professor S.N. Mahendra, has found expression in the form of a balanced mix of practice and theory in the text and has resulted in the first book of its kind in the field of Electric Traction.

Electric traction, as a course of study at the undergraduate engineering curriculum, has been continuing as a specialized elective subject in many technical institutions of the country. In view of the growing importance and technological developments, which have come about in this area in the recent past, certain institutions have actively considered the possibility of introducing a compulsory course on this subject at final undergraduate level. Majority of the books available today concentrate on train mechanics, traction motors and their control, and elements of accessories but conspicuously underplay important constituent aspects like protection, signalling systems, computer applications in management of electric traction system, condition monitoring and futuristic trends in traction propulsion. The present book has made an effort in overcoming the above shortcomings and is, therefore, a more comprehensive coverage of electric traction systems. It is hoped that the book, in its present form, will not only be received well by students and practising engineers devoted to the area of electric traction but will be of significant help in initiating engineers into this important area which requires large manpower input, especially as newer challenges are being faced in the field of rapid transit and other mass transportation systems with the enormous growth of urban population in the cities.

M. Bhattacharyya
Vice-Chancellor,
Silchar Central University

Preface

Electric Traction and Utilisation of Electrical Energy, with the former constituting approximately two thirds of the course, is an elective subject prescribed in electrical engineering syllabus of most engineering colleges. While there is a growing demand for making this subject compulsory, most students complain about non-availability of books dealing with all elements of electric traction featuring in the syllabus.

To bridge this gap and present the subject in a lucid manner, this book was conceived by the authors with the following broad objectives:

(i) To present electric traction as a complete system.

(ii) To combine knowledge of fundamentals with an eye on practical orientation.

(iii) To give a glimpse of the present state-of-the-art.

The books currently available on the subject mostly deal elaborately with train mechanics, traction motor and its control gears, but miss certain key aspects that are essential for appreciation of the subject as a system of transportation.

The book has sixteen chapters dealing with different aspects of electric traction. The unique feature of this book is that it includes chapters dealing with such aspects as Linear Induction Motor Propulsion, Railway Signalling, Protection of Electric Locomotive Equipment and Circuits, Preventive/Corrective Maintenance and Application of Computers for Management of Electric Traction System. Illustrative worked out examples and unsolved numerical exercises taken from question papers of different universities and competitive examinations are designed to impart sufficient clarity and grasp of the fundamentals. The practising engineer in the field, in most cases, pick up the subject in bits and pieces over a rather long time frame. A complete view of the entire subject in the beginning itself may generate better understanding leading to innovativeness and efficiency at work.

The authors hope that the book will be helpful to graduate level students as well as practising engineers in the field. Suggestions for further improvements in subsequent editions will be most welcome.

J. Upadhyay
S.N. Mahendra

Contents

Foreword *vii*

Preface *ix*

1. Electric Traction Principal and History **1**

   Introduction *1*

   Systems of Traction *1*

   Others Systems of Traction *2*

   The Indian Scenario vis-a-vis Electric Traction *2*

   Present-Day State-of-Art *3*

   Electric Traction as a Viable Transport Strategy for the 21st Century *4*

   Advantages of Electric Traction over other Systems of Traction, Break-even Point for Electrification; Comparison of Diesel-Electric and Electric Traction *5*

   Choice of Traction System: Diesel-Electric or Electric *6*

2. Mechanics of Train Movement **9**

   Introduction *9*

   Speed-Time Curve for Train Movement *9*

   Train Resistance *11*

   Requirement of Tractive Effort and T-N Curve of a Typical Train Load *14*

   Specific Energy Consumption *16*

   Factors Affecting Specific Energy Consumption *18*

3. Adhesion, Types of Suspension and Mechanism of Torque Transmission **19**

   Adhesion *19*

Coefficient of Adhesion *21*

Suspension and Mechanism of Torque Transmission *22*

Weight Transfer *24*

Effect of Unsprung Mass and Wheel Diameter *26*

4. Traction Motor **27**

Introduction *27*

Type of Traction Motor Best Suited for Traction Duties *27*

Available Motor Characteristics and Their Suitability for Traction Duties *29*

Rating and Specification of Key Parameters *32*

Optimisation of Design and Constructional Features for Improved Power-to-Weight Ratio *35*

Three-Phase Induction Drives *39*

5. Traction Motor Control: Principles and Gear **44**

Introduction *44*

Traction Control of D.C. Locomotives and EMU's *45*

Traction Control System of A.C. Locomotives *51*

Control Gear *54*

PWM Control of Induction Motors *56*

6. Braking--Mechanical and Dynamic: Principles and Gear **60**

Introduction *60*

Types of Braking Systems *61*

Essential Requirements of a Good Braking System *61*

Important Characteristics of Friction Braking *62*

Systems for Generating Breaking Pressure: Vacuum, Air Brake (Automatic or EM Type) *64*

Dynamic Braking Systems *67*

Conclusion *73*

7. Electric Traction Sub-Systems: Overhead Equipment **74**

Introduction *74*

Overhead Equipment (OHE) *77*

Sectionalising *80*
Bonding of Rails and Masts *81*
Materials Employed in OHE *82*

8. Power Supply Arrangement including Remote Control and Tariff **83**

Power Supply Arrangement for 25 kV Traction System *83*
Unbalance on the Grid System *83*
Spacing of Substations *85*
Strategy to Reduce Voltage Drop by Improving Power Factor *87*
Protection of Traction Power Supply System *88*
Remote Control Concept: Significance of Auto Reclosing Feature *90*
Tariff Strategy *93*

9. Current Collection Gear, Power and Auxiliary Equipment **95**

Current Collection Gear *95*
Power Circuit Equipments (Other than Traction Motors) *100*
Auxiliary Circuit Equipment of a Locomotive *102*

10. Protection of Electric Locomotive Equipment and Circuits: Safety Considerations and Monitoring **108**

Introduction *108*
Broad Strategy for Protection *108*
Surge Protection *109*
Overload Protection of Main Power Ciruits *113*
Earth Fault Protection of Power of Auxiliary Circuits *113*
Protection from Overvoltage and Undervoltage *116*
Differential Current Protection of Traction Circuits *116*
Protection Against High and Low Air Pressure in the Compressed Air Circuit *116*
Temperature Monitoring *117*
Protection of Transformer by Bucholz Relay *117*
Protection Against Accidental Contact with H.T. Equipment *118*
Protection Against Fires *118*

11. Preventive/Corrective Maintenance of Electric Locomotives and OHE; Reliability Aspects, Application of Condition Monitoring Techniques **120**

Introduction *120*

Types of Maintenance and Their Objectives and Maintaibability *120*

Special Features of Electric Traction Assets Having Bearing on Maintenance Strategy *122*

Attention to Maintainability Aspects at Design/Construction Stage *123*

Maintenance of Overhead Equipments *124*

Maintenance of Electric Locomotives *126*

Condition Monitoring to Achieve Need-Based Maintenance *128*

Human Resource Development: Training of Artisans and Supervisors *131*

12. Railway Signalling **133**

Introduction *133*

Block Section Concept: Automatic Block Signalling *133*

Track Circuits *133*

Colour Light/Semaphore Signals and Interlocking Principle *137*

Train Speed and Signalling *138*

Solid State Interlocking *138*

Automatic Warning Systems *139*

CAB Signalling *139*

Signalling Level Crossings *139*

13. Diesel Electric Traction and Excitation Control **140**

Introduction *140*

Characteristics of Diesel Engine *140*

Use of Diesel Engine for Traction Duty *143*

Electrical Torque-Converter or Power Transmission System *143*

Electrical Transmission Utilizing 3-phase Alternator in Conjunction with a Silicon Diode Rectifier *146*

Electrical Transmission using GTO Converter-Inverter Supplying Induction Motors 147

14. LEM-Propelled Traction: Recent Trends **148**

Introduction *148*

Linear Electric Motor *148*

Linear Induction-Based Traction System *149*

Strengths/Weaknesses of LIM-Propelled Railway Traction *151*

Practical Possibilities of LIM-Propelled Transportation *153*

Inputs/Modifications for Adoption of LIM Propulsion in the Existing System *153*

LIM-Propelled Underground Metro Rail System *156*

Wheel-Less Traction *161*

Present Scenario *162*

15. Application of Computers in Management of Electric Traction **165**

Introduction *165*

Computers' Capability Relevant to Electric Traction Management? *165*

Areas of Computer Application in Traction System Management *166*

Possible Other Areas for Computer-Controlled Monitoring *171*

Conclusion *172*

16. Numerical Exercises (Illustrative) **173**

Illustrative Worked Out Examples *173*

Exercises for Practice *182*

Bibliography **185**

CHAPTER 1

Electric Traction Principles and History

INTRODUCTION

The term electric traction implies a wheeled transport system using electrical energy and electric motors.

The different transport needs of a community are:

(a) Transport of goods and passengers within a city.
(b) Transport of goods and passengers from suburbs to the business centres in the city.
(c) Transport of goods and passengers between different cities.
(d) Transport of goods and passengers between different countries/nations

To cope up with the above needs of the community, the following types of electric traction systems were evolved over the years:

(a) Tramcars moving on rails, trolley buses with rubber tyres moving on roads for transport within a city and battery-operated cars for personal use.
(b) Electrical Multiple Units (EMU's) moving on standard rail tracks for suburban services and in underground metro tunnels for suburban movement as well as within the city.
(c) Electric locomotive-hauled trains moving between cities and adjacent countries.

SYSTEMS OF TRACTION

Historically D.C. traction systems were developed earlier than A.C. traction systems.

The following table gives a brief account of the development of different systems of electric traction:

Year	System
1890	Tramcar supplied directly from a D.C. power plant at low voltage.
1900	Railway with substations supplied from a central A.C. power plant by means of high-voltage transmission lines and converting A.C. to D.C. at 600 V by means of motor generator sets and rotary-converters.
1905-1910	Technical improvements of D.C. machines (including rotary converters) enabled D.C. supply voltage to be increased to 1500 V and 3000 V Experimental scale development of 3-phase and single-phase systems using 25 and 16 2/3 Hz A.C. in-conjunction with A.C. series motor.
1920	Perfection of the mercury arc rectifier simplified and improved the supply of high voltage D.C.
1930	Diesel-electric system with powerpack mounted on the engine itself developed.
1950	25 kV A.C. traction system at industrial frequency developed with mercury arc rectifiers of ignitron and excitron type.
1960	Silicon-diode rectifiers were introduced in lieu of mercury arc rectifiers.
1970-1975	Thyristor rectifiers were introduced for step-less voltage control.
1980-1985	GTO thyristers coupled with development in control and power electronics enabled use of 3 phase induction motors in lieu of D.C. series motors employed hitherto. Development of 2 × 25 kV system. High speed trains with 3-phase drive. Linear Electric Motor systems.

OTHER SYSTEMS OF TRACTION

Historically steam engine was the first motive power used for railway traction. The reciprocating steam engine, as invented, swept the mass-transport scenario almost in every country in the nineteenth century and earlier part of twentieth century. This engine carried its own coal on a tender and had a boiler to generate steam. Due to poor efficiency (approx. 5%) and need for a complicated infrastructure for maintenance and operation, this system of traction has now been abandoned almost everywhere giving its place to more efficient and financially viable diesel and electric traction systems.

THE INDIAN SCENARIO VIS-A-VIS ELECTRIC TRACTION

In India, first electrification was undertaken between 1925 and 1932, when

304 Rkm on Central Railway between Bombay VT and Igatpuri and Bombay VT and Pune, and 62 Rkm on Western Railway between Churchgate and Virar and 32 Rkm (metre-gauge) between Madras Beach and Tambaram were electrified on 1500 V D.C.

In 1954-1958 electrification on 3000 V D.C. was completed in West-Bengal between Howrah and Burdwan and Sheoraphuli and Trarkeswar totalling 142 Rkm. The use of 3000 V D.C. system was adopted for improved transmission efficiency.

1960 onwards 25 kV 50 Hz A.C. electrification was started. This has become the universal system of electrification now in this country as elsewhere abroad due to its greater transport potential and better economics. As of today, approx. 13000 Rkm have been electrified catering to the main trunk routes and dense freight sections.

1995 saw introduction of 2 × 25 kV traction system on Bina-Katni section of Central Railway on an experimental scale.

Tram cars running on 650 V D.C. were introduced in Bombay and Calcutta and continue to run in Calcutta on a reduced scale.

Underground Metro-rail on 600 V D.C. has been fully commissioned in 1996 in Calcutta on Dum Dum-Tollygunj section catering to traffic on a busy arterial route.

Delhi is likely to have high-speed trams on elevated track as a part of an integrated metropolitan transport network, which will have underground metros in high population density areas.

Battery operated motor cars are being developed by Bharat Heavy Electricals Ltd. (BHEL) on an experimental scale to cater for traffic on roads.

PRESENT-DAY STATE-OF-ART

25 kV A.C. at industrial frequency is being universally adopted for all new railway electrification projects almost universally.

There is selective use of 2 × 25 kV system on high speed and heavy traffic density sections as it enhances transport capability with larger spacing of feeding points on graded routes without calling for any alteration to the 25 kV rolling stock. Besides, interference with communication lines is totally eliminated without employment of booster transformers.

For underground Metro systems, use of 1500 V D.C. with overhead conductor-bar and specially designed pantographs instead of third-rail system is being increasingly adopted.

Use of three-phase A.C. induction motor in conjunction with variable-voltage-variable-frequency (VVVF) converter-inverter system is becoming the universal state-of-the-art due to its superior traction characteristics, reduced maintenance cost and improved energy efficiency through regenerative braking.

ELECTRIC TRACTION AS A VIABLE TRANSPORT STRATEGY FOR THE 21ST CENTURY

While approaching the 21st century, there is a lingering doubt about the availability of fossil fuels to cater to the growing needs of industrialisation and human civilisation. While there are different estimates for the probable longevity of petroleum, coal and natural gas reserves, it is universally accepted that the future will have to find some other form of energy for sustenance of the human civilisation as fossil fuels generated and conserved by Nature over centuries may not last for more than half a century hence.

Besides, pollution caused by fossil fuels is becoming a grave issue. There is a general perception that the pollution caused by diesel/petroleum vehicles is making the atmosphere unacceptable for healthy living.

Electric traction offers a technically sound alternative both from the point of view of energy conservation as well as environment friendliness. It uses electricity which can be transported to any point with great ease and can be produced by alternative primary energy sources such as: hydroelectric power, nuclear power, solar/wind power etc. Even fossil-fuel power can be generated at more convenient places with greater efficiency and environment friendliness.

Recent evolution of traction systems using three-phase induction motors has made high-speed transportation at speeds of the order of 300-350 kmph possible which can bridge distances up to 3000 km in a time frame comparable to air transport. This has been adequately established by Shinkansen trains in Japan, TGV in France/Switzerland, ICE in Germany and X-2000 in Swedish Railways. These services are financially viable and self-sustaining due to fare structure comparable to air travel.

ADVANTAGES OF ELECTRIC TRACTION OVER OTHER SYSTEMS OF TRACTION, BREAK-EVEN POINT FOR ELECTRIFICATION; COMPARISON OF DIESEL-ELECTRIC AND ELECTRIC TRACTION

Advantages of Electric Traction over Other Systems of Traction

The following plus points of electric traction are universally accepted:

(a) High horse power only limited by the size of traction motor. The overhead distribution line fed from the grid forms an enormous reservoir of power.
(b) High overload capacity.
(c) Increased trailing loads and speeds. This is on account of availability of high horse power and use of three-phase drives which dispense with limitations imposed by commutator.
(d) Capacity to negotiate steep grades.
(e) Increased track loading and capacity utilisation.
(f) Improved signalling due to availability of electric power all along the track through auxiliary transformers.
(g) Ability to utilise hydro-electric power, low grade fuel in central power stations and atomic energy.
(h) Lower cost of maintenance. This gets further cut down due to use of three phase. Induction motor as traction motor.
(i) Greater fuel efficiency and reduced overall line-haul cost.
(j) Environment friendliness with regard to pollution and noise. However, there is a recent perception about electromagnetic field associated with HT lines being injurious to public health. To date research on this subject has not validated this perception. Even in heavily populated Indian cities no ill effects have come to light.
(k) Railway electrification encourages rural electrification along the electrified route as no new transmission line need be run and power could also be tapped off from the traction feeder line.
(l) EMU's built on modular concept can be adjusted to suit variable traffic pattern of peak and off peak periods.

Disadvantages/Drawbacks

However, it would be incorrect to project that there are no disadvantages. The main drawbacks are:

(a) High capital cost. It takes approximately 25 lakhs per track-km to electrify a route at present day cost level.

(b) Power failure for a few minutes can cause heavy dislocation. With frequent grid failures in India, this aspect assumes importance.
(c) During accidents when traction lines have to be switched off, relief operations require assistance of diesel traction.
(d) Uncertainties of electric tariff have bearing on traction economics.
(e) There is a possibility of interference with communication lines. This calls for provision of booster transformers in sensitive areas or else use of 2 × 25 kV system, both adding to the capital cost.

Comparison of Diesel-Electric and Electric Systems of Traction

Although the global level diesel-electric traction came into existence in 1930, in India diesel locomotives were introduced in 1945 for shunting services and 1955 onwards for main-line haulage.

Diesel-electric traction while retaining quite a few advantages of electric traction listed before does away with the most conspicuous disadvantage of track electrification. The diesel motive power is a self-contained unit having its own diesel-engine which drives a generator.

However the diesel-electric traction has the following disadvantages:

(a) It is not free from pollution nuisance.
(b) Life of diesel engine is limited: approximately 15 years.
(c) It is a fixed torque engine: maximum H.P. is reached at the rated speed. Hence this system has limited overload capacity. This does not match with the basic traction requirement of high starting torque and substantial short time (one-hour) rating for negotiating grades.
(d) Diesel-oil sources are monopolised by a few countries and are limited (exhaustible).
(e) Due to power pack being placed in the locomotive itself, the maximum horsepower available from a given locomotive weight is approximately 2/3rd of an electric engine.
(f) Thermal efficiency is lower than that of electric traction system. In electric traction, it is possible to have an overall system efficiency of 40% or more whereas in diesel the best possibility is around 30%.
(g) It is not possible to recover all the energy during regenerative braking.

CHOICE OF TRACTION SYSTEM: DIESEL-ELECTRIC OR ELECTRIC

From the foregoing discussions it would appear that there are certain situations where electric traction is a must. These are:

(a) Busy suburbs and metros where pollution control is of utmost importance.
(b) High speed systems with speeds above 150 kmph where higher horse power and improved signalling become essential.
(c) Sections with heavy gradients where high horsepower coupled with regenerative braking is a must.

However, bulk of the main-line routes in any railway network could be catered by either system of traction. It would therefore, boil down to traction economics. Basically countries where diesel-oil is freely available have been slow in switching over to electric traction. On the other hand, countries where diesel-oil is fully imported or hydroelectric power is available in plenty have switched over to electric traction in a predominant manner e.g. Switzerland and Japan.

For comparison of economic viability of electric and diesel traction systems where either of them can meet the traffic needs, following aspects need critical analysis:

(a) The capital cost of electrification and additional maintenance of overhead and power supply equipment.
(b) The limited life of a diesel engine (approximately 15 years) corresponding to the life of diesel power pack vis-a-vis life of an electric engine which could be 40 years or more.
(c) The running cost of an electric engine is lower due to better thermal efficiency and regenerative braking. However, the exact costs based on electricity tariff and diesel oil selling rates have to be critically compared.
(d) The maintenance/cost of an electric engine is lower than that of a diesel engine. Maintenance of power pack imposes an added burden.
(e) Availability of electric engines and flexibility in use is better. Due to high horsepower, the size of the fleet for a given throughput is much smaller.

These factors are evaluated financially over a life cycle period of 10 to 15 years by bringing down all the costs to a common time frame using Discounted Cash Flow (DCF) technique.

It is obvious that there would exist a break-even point related to traffic density. However, these comparisons often get vitiated due to subsidies. Presence of a strong road-transport lobby and irrational electricity tariffs in developing countries are factors that tend to influence the decision in this regard.

The predominant trend is that most countries are resorting to electrification in a phased manner to spread out the financial burden, in anticipation of a possible paucity of diesel-oil and to avail the benefits of pollution free high-speed transportation. Hence the concept of break-even point is fast disappearing. It is becoming a function of available financial resources and emphasis on modernisation of the transport system. From a long-term point of view all community transportation systems must get based on electric-power which is bound to become the only practical source of energy in days to come.

CHAPTER 2

Mechanics of Train Movement

INTRODUCTION

The various phases through which a traction load passes in the course of its transportation from one point to another and the behaviour of load resistance during these phases must be studied closely to evaluate the requirement of tractive-effort, horsepower and energy. These aspects will be covered in this chapter.

SPEED-TIME CURVE FOR TRAIN MOVEMENT

The actual movement of a train between two successive stoppages can be represented graphically by a speed-time curve. A typical speed-time curve is shown in Fig. 2.1. The curve can be divided into the following segments:

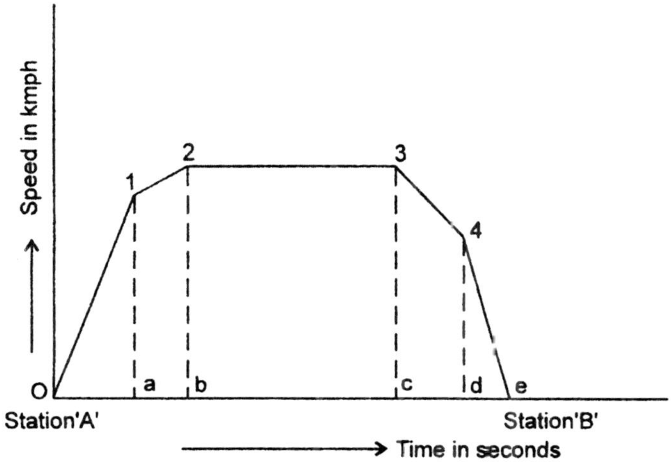

Fig. 2.1 Typical speed-time curve

0a: During this period the load is accelerated from rest. The tractive effort is kept at a high level, which is practically constant.

ab: Notching up stops. The torque gradually falls as the speed increases according to the torque-speed characteristic of the traction motors. A balancing speed is achieved at which the tractive effort equals the train resistance.

bc: Free running period during which the train runs at constant speed with constant torque and horse power input.

cd: Power is cut off, the train coasts and its speed falls gradually due to train resistance.

de: Brakes are applied to bring the train to a stop at the next station.

The speed-time curve is different for different types of services by way acceleration and retardation, maximum speed attained, the period of free running and coasting. Table 2.1 shows typical values of these parameters for some representative services.

Table 2.1 Typical Characteristics and Parameters of Different Types of Services

Type of service	Sub-urban (passenger)	Main-line (passenger)	Main-line (goods)	Main-line (parcel)
Accleration	1 to 4 kmph/sec	0.5 to 1 kmph/sec	0.2 to 0.4 kmph/sec	0.3 to 0.5 kmph/sec
Retardation	3 to 4 kmph/sec	1.5 to 2 kmph/sec	0.3 to 0.5 kmph/sec	0.3 to 0.5 kmph/sec
Maximum speed	60 to 80 kmph	100 to 160 kmph	60 to 100 kmph	80 to 100 kmph
Distance between stoppages	1 to 3 kms	10 to 15 kms for passenger and 100 kms or more for express.	50 to 100 kms	50 to 100 kms
Special features	Free running period is small & some times, Nil.	Free running time is large	Free running time is large	Free running time is large

The basic criteria for selecting the various parameters of speed-time curve for a particular service are linked to the desired average speed or time of running between the two stations A and B and the maximum permissible speed. While acceleration and retardation are linked to the available tractive-effort or braking-effort, their values are also limited by considerations of passenger comfort in case of passenger services.

The areas of various segments of speed-time curve being $\int v.dt$ represents the distance travelled; hence the total area of speed-time curve represents the distance between stations A and B. It follows that the time taken will be minimum if the load is accelerated to the maximum speed (V_m) quickly, runs at the maximum speed all the time before braking at the maximum permissible retardation. The speed-time curve in this case would be a trapezium, as shown in Fig. 2.2.

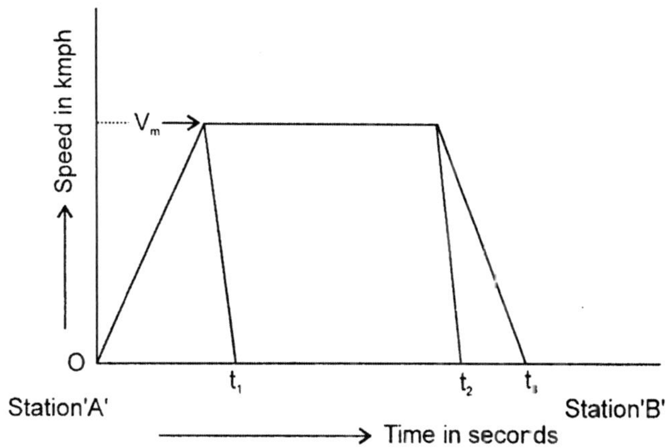

Fig. 2.2 Trapezoidal speed-time curve

The distance (D) covered is given by the following equation (t_1, t_2 and t_3 being as shown in Fig. 2.2):

$$D = \frac{1}{2}\frac{t_1 V_m}{3600} + \frac{t_2 V_m}{3600} + \frac{1}{2}\frac{t_3 V_m}{3600} \text{ km}$$

TRAIN RESISTANCE

Train resistance consists of all forces that oppose the motion of the train.

Resistance on Level and Straight Track

On a level and straight track, train resistance could arise due to factors internal and external to the rolling stock.

The internal factors are: friction at the axle bearings and guides; bogie-pivots; friction at the motor bearings and gearing in case of locomotive or EMU's running through wheel-rail interaction based on adhesion.

The external factors are friction between wheel and rail; flange-friction; resistance due to temporary deflection of the track; aerodynamic drag.

The running train resistance, whether internal or external is a function of track and rolling stock characteristics as well as speed. At higher speed, the aerodynamic drag and flange resistance increase while the frictional resistance of the axle-bearings decreases.

A typical equation for running train resistance per tonne weight of the load is as under:

$$r = a + b.v + c.v^2$$

where v is speed in kmph and a, b and c are constants which differ from country to country and are determined experimentally.

In Indian Railways the running train resistance formulae usually adopted are:

(a) For locomotives

$$R \text{ in kg} = 0.65\ W + 13\ n + 0.01\ W.v + 0.52\ W.v^2$$

where W = is the locomotive weight in tonnes
v = is speed in kmph
n = is number of axles

(b) For coaching-stock:

$$r \text{ in kg/tonne} = 1.425 + 0.0054\ v + 0.0025\ v^2$$

(c) For loaded box wagons:

$$r \text{ in kg/tonne} = 0.87 + 0.0103\ v + 0.000056\ v^2$$

For a comparison, the running train resistance formula adopted by French National Railways (SNCF) is given below:

$$r \text{ in kg/tonne} = 1.5\sqrt{\frac{10}{axle\,load}} + \frac{v^2}{120.axle\,load}$$

Starting Friction

The train resistance at starting is high due to static friction at the bearings. This drops sharply as the train rolls but subsequently, as the speed increases, the train resistance rises again due to speed-related components.

The starting train resistance is also a function of train coupling. If all the couplings are in tension, the starting resistance is high. The starting resistance is usually 4.5 to 5.0 kg/tonne on a level track.

A typical train resistance curve would be as shown in Fig. 2.3.

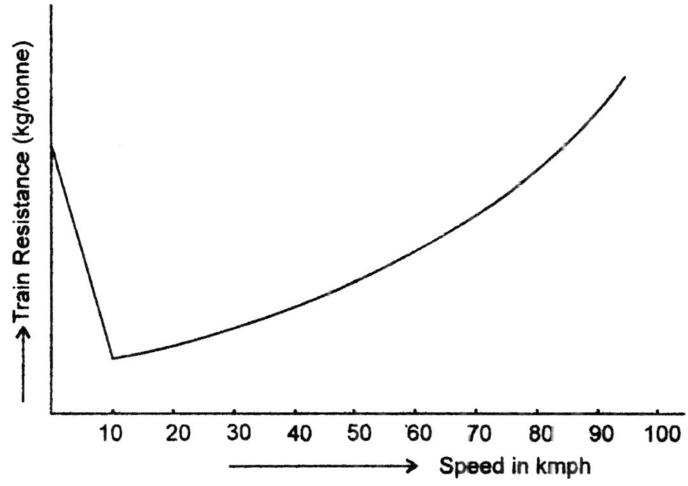

Fig. 2.3 Typical train resistance curve

Train Resistance Due to Gradient

On gradients, a component of the train-load would either oppose the train movement or assist it. If the gradient opposes the train movement, it is called up-gradient. In the opposite case, it is called down-gradient.

Railway gradients are expressed by the height through which the track level rises in 100 or 1000 units of distance. An up-gradient of 1 in 100 would mean that the track level rises by one unit in a distance of 100 units.

Hence for h in 100 gradient the component of load W opposing train movement is $W.\sin \phi = w.h/100$.

Curve Resistance

Curve resistance arises due to the wheel-flange rubbing against the railhead on curves. It is given by the following empirical formula.

$$R \text{ (curve)} = 700 \times W \text{ (tonnes)/Radius of curvature in metres}$$

In Railway practice, the track curvature is expressed in degrees rather than radius. 1° curve is defined as one in which 100 ft length of the curve turns through 1° or (1/360)th of a circle or 100-metre track turns through 3.27°.

Hence 1° curvature would mean a radius of (5730/3.27) or $C°$ would mean (5730/3.27) C metres.

Hence curve resistance per degree of curvature would be $(700 \times W)/(5730/3.27C)$ or 0.4 $C.W.$ kg (approximately).

In traction mechanics it is sometimes convenient to express curve resistance as equivalent gradient resistance. Thus,

$$\text{Equivalent gradient per thousand} = 0.4\ C$$

Total train resistance is the summation of starting or running resistance, grade resistance and curve resistance.

REQUIREMENT OF TRACTIVE EFFORT AND T-N CURVE OF A TYPICAL TRAIN LOAD

The tractive effort (TE) required to haul a train load consists of two components, viz.

(i) T.E. to overcome train resistance
(ii) T.E. to impart acceleration to the load up to the desired running speed.

It would, therefore, appear that maximum tractive effort from a motive power would be required at start when the train resistance is maximum due to static-friction and the need for acceleration is also there. It is the usual practice to maintain the tractive effort during starting (accelerating) segment of the speed-time curve at a level that would give almost uniform acceleration.

T.E. for Acceleration

Consider a train having a weight of W tonnes.

Mass of the train is 1000 W kg-force/g

$$= 1000\ W.g/g = 1000\ W \text{ kg.}$$

To impart this mass an acceleration of α kmphps or α.1000/3600 m/sec^2

The T.E. required would be 1000 W (1000/3600).α

This is equal to 277.8 $W.\alpha$ Newton or (277.8/9.81) $W.\alpha$ kg.

Usually a train consists of a number of rotating parts that also have to accelerate. Such parts in case of coaches and wagons are wheels and axles and in case of locomotives or motor coaches, the traction motor armature and gears, additionally. The existence of these components of the accelerating train increases the effective weight of the train by 8 to 15 per cent. For an approximate estimation, effective mass is assumed as $W_e = 1.1\ W$.

Tractive Effort Required by a Typical Train Load

From the foregoing deliberations, it is possible to assess the tractive effort (T.E.) required by a typical train load at start, during acceleration and free running on power.

The T.E. at start has to be approximately 5% more than the static train resistance such that the load can move at a slow acceleration. As the train moves and picks up speed of about 5 kmph, the train resistance drops sharp. If the tractive effort is maintained at the same level, a higher acceleration will be realised which will quickly accelerate the train.

The higher tractive effort at start and during initial acceleration is achieved due to existence of a short-time rating in case of electric motor. However, the tractive effort has to drop to continuous rating level or lower to avoid thermal overloading of motors.

Considering the above aspects, a typical torque-speed curve for a traction load may be derived. This is shown in Fig. 2.4.

The tractive effort obtained at the drawbar is a function of traction motor torque, gear ratio and wheel diameter.

If the torque developed by the motor is T, overall gear ratio viz. (speed of motor/speed of driving axle) γ_G, radius of driving wheel R_w, and efficiency of transmission η, then

$$\text{T.E.} = \eta.T.\gamma_G/R_w$$

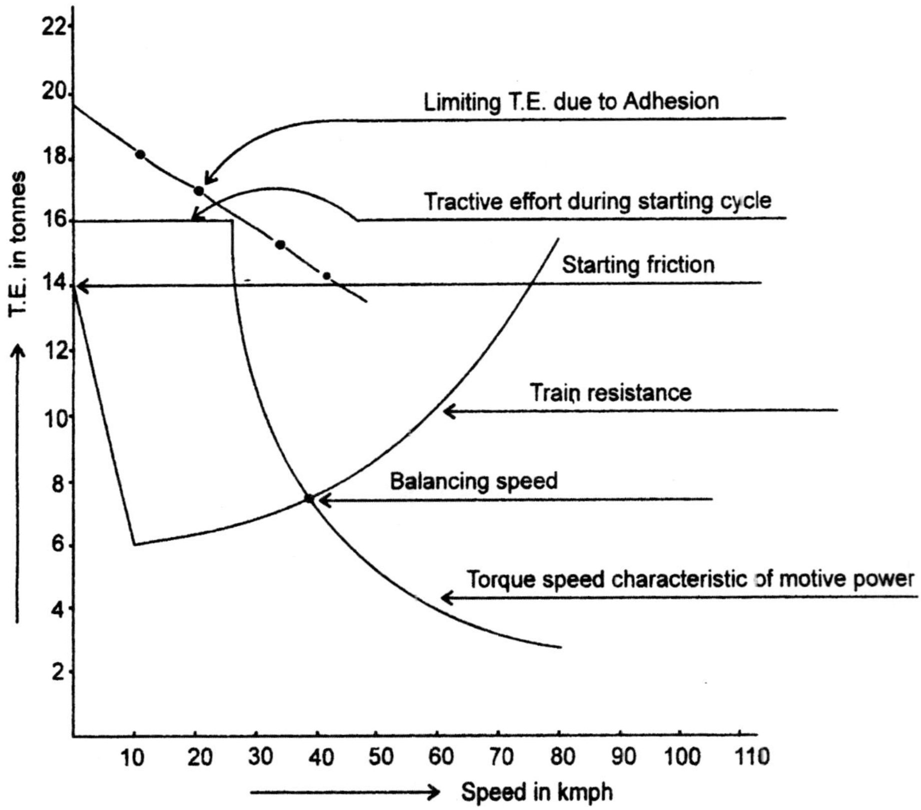

Fig. 2.4 Typical torque-speed curve for a traction load

SPECIFIC ENERGY CONSUMPTION

Specific energy consumption is defined as the watt-hours consumed per tonne-km transportation. This, in turn, is equal to the energy required for covering the acceleration and free-running portions of the speed-time curve divided by overall efficiency of energy conversion, viz. combined efficiency of traction motors and transmission gear.

Assessment of Specific Energy Consumption

Assuming a trapezoidal speed-time curve as shown in Fig. 2.5 the energy output from the motive power can be assessed as follows.

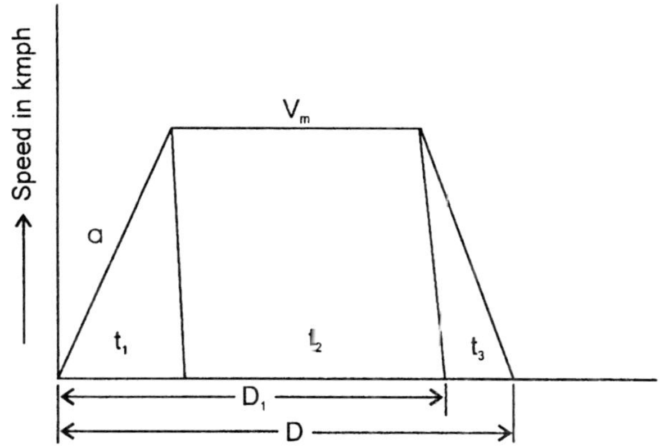

Fig. 2.5 Assumed trapezoidal speed-time curve for calculation of specific energy consumption

(a) Energy required for acceleration to maximum speed V_m

$$= 277.8\ W_e\alpha \cdot \left(\frac{1}{2}\,\frac{V_m \cdot 1000}{3600} \cdot \frac{V_m}{\alpha}\right) \text{ watt-hour.}$$

Where W_e = effective weight of train including rotating masses

α = acceleration in kmph per sec.

Therefore, $E_{(\text{accln.})} = 0.01072\ V_m^2 \cdot W_e$ watt-hours

(b) Energy required to overcome gradient

Assuming the distance covered during acceleration and free-running periods to be D_1 km, the energy spent in overcoming gradient is

$$E_g = 9.81\ W.G.\ 1000\ D_1 \text{ Joules or W-sec.}$$

where G is gradient in ‰. (i.e. rise in track level in meters for every 1000 m distance) and W is the train load in tonnes.

$$E_g = \pm\ 9.81\ W.G.D_1/3.6 \text{ W-hr.}$$
$$= \pm\ 2.725\ W.G.D_1 \text{ W-hr.}$$

N.B. In down gradients, the gradient helps train movement.

(c) Energy required to overcome frictional train resistance

= (Tractive effort for overcoming train resistance on level) × (D_1 . 1000) Joules

$= W \cdot r D_1/36$ W-hr.
$= 0.27778\ W. r. D_1$ W-hr.

where r is train resistance on level in Newton per tonne.

Total energy output required at the driving axles is: (a) + (b) + (c)

$$E = 0.01072\ V_m^2 . W_e \pm 2.725\ W G D_1 + 0.27778\ W r D_1$$

Hence specific energy output = $E/W \cdot D$

$= (0.01072\ V_m^2/D) \cdot (W_e/W) \pm 2.725\ G D_1/D + 0.27778\ r D_1/D$ W-hr/tonne-km

Specific energy consumption = Specific energy input
= Specific Energy output/overall transmission efficiency

FACTORS AFFECTING SPECIFIC ENERGY CONSUMPTION

From the relationship derived above it would appear that:

(i) Specific energy consumption reduces as the distance D between stoppages increases.
(ii) Specific energy consumption reduces as the maximum speed between stoppages is reduced.
(iii) Specific energy consumption reduces as the effectives weight due to rotating masses gets reduced.
(iv) For a given schedule speed, greater acceleration and retardation help to reduce the power-ON period and enable greater coasting. Hence specific energy consumption would reduce due to shortening of the distance D_1.
(v) Higher overall efficiency of the system reduces specific energy consumption.

In suburban services where the distance between stoppages is small, the specific energy consumption tends to rise sharply. It becomes necessary to give proper consideration to fixing of maximum permissible speeds, acceleration and retardation. Higher values of acceleration and retardation consistent with passenger comfort get adopted and the maximum speed is limited to about 80 kmph.

CHAPTER 3

Adhesion, Types of Suspension and Mechanism of Torque Transmission

ADHESION

Unlike most other forms of power machinery, the mechanism of locomotive or a motor coach is completed by a friction drive between the wheels and the rail. The maximum force that can be transmitted by this drive is dependent on the load carried by the driving wheels and the coefficient of friction between the rail and the wheel. In railway terminology this is usually called adhesion.

Figure 3.1 (a & b) illustrates schematically how the torque produced by the traction motor gets converted into tractive effort or pull by which the locomotive pulls the trailing load through a draw-bar and coupling mechanism.

If T is the torque exerted by the motor,

F = the tractive effort exerted by the driving wheel

γ_g = overall gear ratio = speed of motor pinion in rpm (N_1)/speed of driving axle rpm (N_2)

η = efficiency of transmission of power from motor to driving axle

R_w = radius of the driving wheel

then output at the driving wheel = input at the motor pinion η

$$\therefore\ F.R_w.N_2 = h\ T.N_1$$

$$\text{i.e. } F = (\eta\ T.\ \gamma_g)/R_w$$

It would be seen that as the torque produced is increased, the tractive effort gets increased. But there is a limit to it, which is imposed by the grip of the wheel on the rail as provided by the friction existing between the two. When this limit is exceeded, the wheel loses the grip and begins to slip.

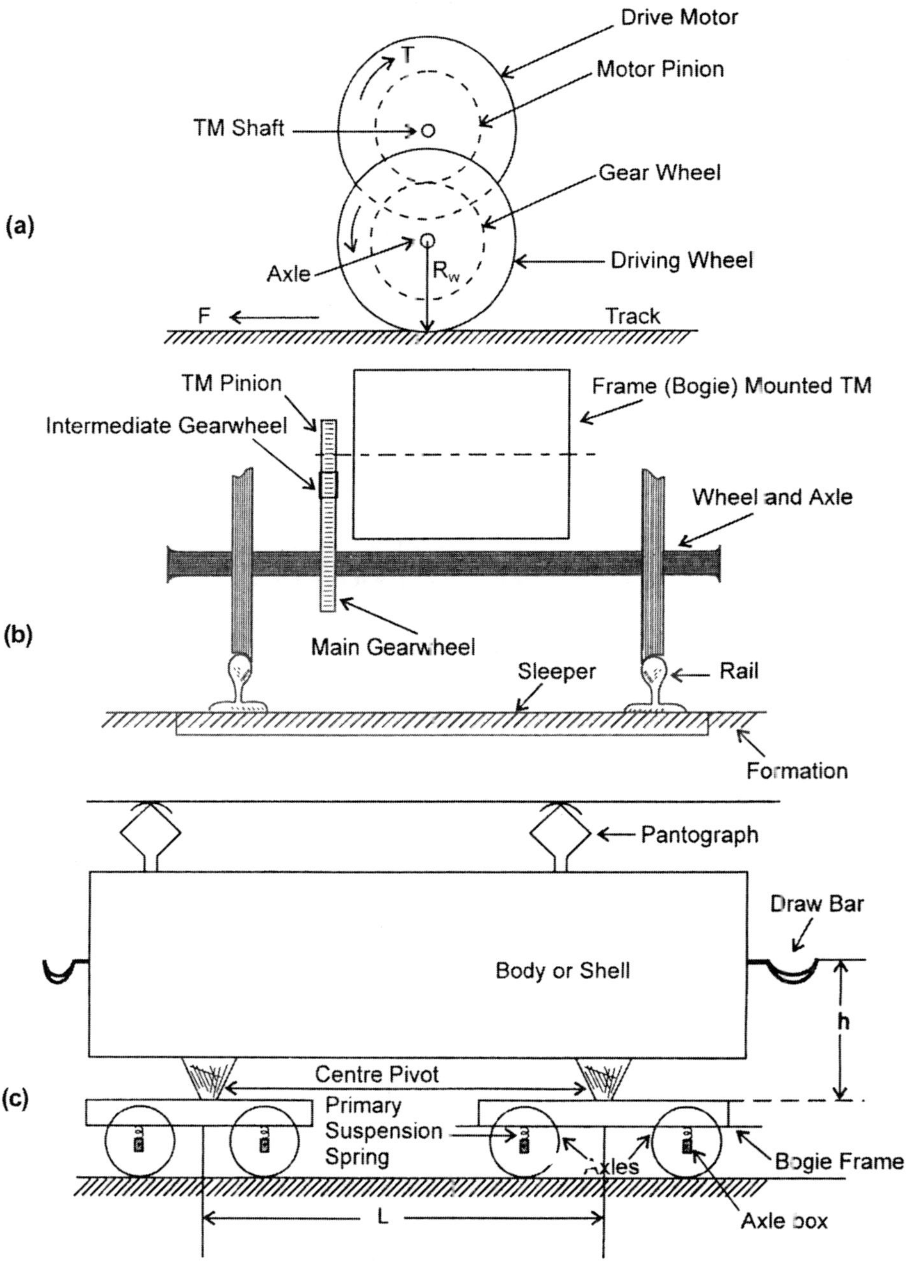

Fig. 3.1 Schematic diagrams illustrating how the torque produced by the traction motor gets converted into tractive effort

Adhesive Weight of Locomotive

The total weight of a locomotive carried on the driving wheels is called adhesive weight. If all wheels in locomotive are driving wheels, i.e. there are no dummy wheels, the weight of the locomotive will equal the adhesive weight.

***Coefficient of adhesion*:** The proportion of adhesive weight that can be made available as tractive effort is called coefficient of adhesion, viz.

$$\mu = \text{Coefficient of adhesion} = \frac{\text{Tractive effort at which wheel-slip occurs}}{\text{Adhesive weight}}$$

Adhesion also plays an important role in braking. The total braking effort permissible gets restricted by μ similar to T.E. to avoid skid.

Under traction conditions, the adhesive weight gets reduced due to weight transfer from one bogie or axle to the other on account of the mechanism of suspension. We will discuss this aspect in greater detail at a later stage.

The normal value of μ with clean dry rails is approximately 0.25 and maximum achievable with sand is approximately 0.3-0.35.

It will, therefore, be seen that adhesion and suspension are inter-related subjects in the context of hauling or braking capability of motive power.

COEFFICIENT OF ADHESION

At the beginning of Railway era, it was apprehended by scientists that the coefficient of friction between steel wheels and steel rails might not be sufficient to enable a locomotive to exert any practical value of tractive effort. Hence at the initial stages, locomotives were driven by a toothed wheel engaging with a series of horizontal projections from the rails. It was George Stevension, the inventor of steam locomotive, who for the first time got convinced that the frictional force could be adequate and permit haulage by a locomotive. This was around 1814, i.e. the beginning of 19th century. In steam locomotives, a number of driving wheels get coupled together to produce the required tractive effort.

Since full weight of the locomotive gets employed as adhesive weight in all new designs of electric and diesel electric locomotives, coefficient of adhesion has become a very important parameter in traction technology. Since the axle load of locomotives is limited by the track structure, the availability of maximum possible tractive effort from a given weight of locomotive could be made possible only by the best use of the available adhesion and optimisation of the same to the extent possible.

Factors Affecting Coefficient of Adhesion

Detailed studies have revealed that the adhesion varies widely under different conditions of the rail surface. The rail surface itself is seldom clean and more often carries a thin layer of oil of the order of 10^{-6} g/cm^2 corresponding to a thickness of about five molecules on the surface.

However, there are certain general conclusions, which can be summed up as follows.

(i) The coefficient of adhesion on wet rail is lower than that on dry rail.
(ii) Presence of oil on rail reduces adhesion.
(iii) Use of sanding on the rail surface improves adhesion.
(iv) The adhesion in stationary condition of the wheel on the rail is maximum and it drops as the wheel rolls.
(v) Application of tractive effort in a gradual manner improves adhesion.

Hence to obtain best result out of a design in terms of minimum locomotive weight for a given horsepower output, the improvements incorporated have been broadly based on:

(i) Mechanisms to clean the rail surface
(ii) Effective sanding gear.
(iii) Stepless control of traction force through use of thyristors with gate control.
(iv) Mechanisms to detect wheel slip in very initial stages and triggering corrective action by reducing the tractive effort.

Modern locomotives incorporating latest techniques can have an adhesion coefficient of the order of 0.4 to 0.45.

SUSPENSION AND MECHANISM OF TORQUE TRANSMISSION

Suspension

The locomotive consists of a body or shell which houses all the equipment except traction motors and brake gear which rests on two bogies with two axles each (B - B or Bo - Bo design) or three axles with 6 wheels each (C - C or Co - Co) design. When each axle is independently driven and there is no coupling between any two axles, the suffix 'o' is used on 'B' representing two axles per bogie or on 'C' representing 3 axles per bogie.

The traction motors are mounted on the bogies, either fully sprung or partly borne on the axle through nose-suspension.

While individual designs may have their own special features, the term suspension implies the way weight of the body is passed on to the bogies and the manner in which traction motors are placed on the bogie and drive the wheels.

Suspension of Body on Bogie

The basic approach is to place body on the bogie in such a manner that the point at which the weight is transferred is as low and close to the track as possible and yet provide adequate spring cushion to isolate the body-borne equipment placed in the shell from shocks generated by the track. The arrangement is schematically illustrated in Fig. 3.1 (c).

There are two alternative arrangements possible:

(i) Either the body is placed directly on the bogie frame through a center pivot and side bearers, or
(ii) An intervening loading bolster is employed which is supported on to the bogie frame through another set of springs giving a two-stage spring suspension and therefore better cushioning.

The bogie frame may rest on the axle boxes through primary suspension springs either directly or through an equaliser beam for better weight distribution.

Modern state-of-art designs dispense with equaliser beams and bolsters and aim at a lighter bogie frame with body weight being transferred to the axle boxes directly through Flexi-coil helical springs.

Suspension of Traction Motor in the Bogie

Two arrangements are usually adopted.

(i) Fully Suspended Motor is mounted on the bogie frame; hence the motor weight is fully spring borne.

Due to increased distance between the axle and the motor shaft, an intermediate gear between the motor pinion and axle mounted main gear becomes necessary. Besides, the intermediate gear ought to have resilience to cater for the relative movement between the bogie frame and the axles due to spring action.

(ii) The Traction Motor is suspended in the bogie frame at one end (nose-end) and borne on the axle at the other end through a sleeve or roller bearing arrangement.

In this arrangement, the motor-weight is only partly spring-borne. However, this arrangement is simple from the point of view of gear arrangement. The motor pinion, being closer to the axle, meshes directly with the main gear that is mounted on the axle.

Nose suspension, though very simple and popular, has limitation of speed due to increased unspring mass. With the advent of 3-phase induction motor traction where the motor weight gets reduced due to elimination of commutator, nose suspension has become possible up to speeds of the order of 150 km/h with roller bearing suspension at the axle-sleeve.

Mono-motor Drives

Some designs use single motor of double the horse power with motor fully suspended in the central part of the bogie frame and driving either axle through a chain of gears. This arrangement is available on WAG_1, WAG_2 and $WAG_{3/4}$ class of locomotives of Indian Railways. It gives better adhesion coefficient. This arrangement, however, was not found very successful due to longer chain of gears and overstressing of gears under wheel-slip conditions.

WEIGHT TRANSFER

When a locomotive is standing still on a level track, its weight is normally shared equally by each driving axle. During condition of traction, turning moments due to reaction disturb the axle load. While some axles get additional load, others may get unloaded. This phenomenon is called weight transfer. It is clear that the unloaded axles will become critical from the point of view of adhesion and will govern the capability of the locomotive for exerting tractive effort. Hence this phenomenon merits closer scrutiny in the context of adhesion.

Broadly speaking, there are two types of weight transfer, viz.

(i) Body weight transfer between bogies,
(ii) Weight transfer within the bogies.

Body Weight Transfer

Referring to Fig. 3.1 (c) if the horizontal pull applied to the trailing load at the drawbar is P and the height difference between the drawbar and the central pivot where the body weight is transferred to the bogie is h, then the turning moment acting on the body under condition of traction would be $P.h$. If the distance between bogie centres is L, the unloading of the rear bogie and added loading of the front bogie would be $P.h./L$. This is called 'body-weight transfer'.

It follows that the body weight transfer will get reduced if the height difference between the drawbar and the pivot gets reduced. Thus a careful design of the system of suspension can help towards reducing the weight transfer or even eliminating it.

Bogie Weight Transfer

This takes places due to the torque exerted by the traction motor through its pinion on the main gear mounted on the axle. If the pinion is pressing the main gear wheel downwards, weight is added to the axle. On the other hand, if the pinion is pushing the main gear wheel teeth upwards, there will be unloading of the axle. Since the locomotive may move in either direction, there is bound to be a reversal of pushing force. The magnitude of this force is equal to Torque/ Radius of main gear wheel.

It is obvious that Bogie weight transfer can never be eliminated as long as the mechanism of torque transmission is through gear wheels. What is possible, at best, is to make the body weight transfer and bogie weight transfer for a particular direction of motion to act against each other. This will reduce the net effect of weight transfer.

This can be achieved by mounting traction motors on the same side of the axles.

To eliminate adverse effect of weight transfer on the *Adhesion,* usually the torque generated by a traction motor is reduced electrically such that optimum results are obtained. However, when Linear Electric Motor drive system is adopted, the dependence on adhesion and complications arising out of weight transfer are eliminated altogether.

EFFECT OF UNSPRUNG MASS AND WHEEL DIAMETER

Effect of Extent of Impulse Loading

Unsprung mass has adverse effect on the track and the resultant shock loading also affects various components of the locomotive, inducing fatigue. Carter made an assessment of the shock-load in terms of momentum as under:

$$\text{Impulse load} = 2\, M_u\, V \sqrt{\frac{h}{D_w}}$$

where M_u = Unsprung mass
V = Velocity of wheel parallel to the rail surface
h = Irregularity or step in the track such as may occur at a rail joint
D_w = Diameter of the wheel.

The effect of unsprung mass and wheel diameter on the extent of impulse loading may be appreciated from the above relationship.

Apart from the aspect of impulse loading, wheel diameter has direct bearing on the stresses generated on the rail as well as wheel tyre. A bigger diameter wheel is flatter at the point of contact with the rail and results in reduced stresses due to bigger area of contact. A smaller diameter wheel, on the other hand, results in higher stress.

Hence although a smaller wheel diameter is preferable from the point of view of conversion of torque into tractive effort as well as its own unsprung mass, a larger wheel diameter of the order of 1100 mm has been preferred all along. It is only of late with greater stress on unsprung mass to achieve higher speed and availability of better rail or tyre materials that wheel diameters of the order of 900 mm have become possible.

CHAPTER 4

Traction Motor

INTRODUCTION

Traction motor is the most important sub-system of an electric locomotive. The rating of a locomotive is governed by the rating of the traction motors and ratings of all other equipment in the traction circuit get matched with this.

Over the past fifty years or so, the progress made in the design of traction motors has been considerable. While the initial stages were marked by improvements in constructional features, type of insulation, speeds and design innovations giving better capability to withstand ripple contents of the rectified D.C., the last two decades have witnessed development of new technologies, viz. 3-phase induction motor drives and use of LEM for traction purposes.

After developing acquaintance with the dynamical requirements involved in the movement of trains and vehicles, the stage now is set to investigate the best suited traction motor and determine criteria for defining its rating. These aspects will be dealt with in this chapter in greater detail.

TYPE OF TRACTION MOTOR BEST SUITED FOR TRACTION DUTIES

Specific Requirements of Traction Duty

At first, it is necessary to appreciate the specific requirements of traction duty, which the traction motor is required to cater. These requirements can be summarised as follows.

(a) Traction loads require a high torque at start to meet the train resistance and acceleration effort. Such requirement may be for two to four minutes for suburban trains but may extend over fifteen minutes or more for goods trains and main line passenger trains. Since torque produced by a traction motor is a function of current drawn from the overhead system, a motor that draws lesser current which does not vitiate its continuous rating capability will be better suited for traction duty.

(b) *Self-governing and protection against overloading*: Usually the terrain over which a train moves has undulating gradients. It should not need frequent manipulation of the control system and traction motor should be capable of looking after itself to a certain extent. Thus when an up-gradient is encountered, the speed may reduce such that the kilowatt loading gets controlled. A traction motor with this in-built feature in its characteristic will be better suited for traction duty.

(c) *Load sharing with unequal wheel diameters*: To cater to the full requirement of load, locomotives may have 4 or 6 traction motors mounted on different axles of a Bo-Bo or Co-Co design. These motors operate in parallel. Since the wheel diameters of different axles are bound to be different, the motors should be able to share load with minimum variation or else a very strict control on wheel diameters may be required which may not be practical.

(d) *Behaviour under conditions of sudden voltage rise*: One of special features of a traction power supply is sudden fluctuations in the voltage. While regulations call for controlling voltage fluctuations within 5% for normal industrial supply, the voltage available at the catenary may vary by well over 20%. A motor which can withstand these variations without flashing over or incurring abnormal current rush will be better suited for traction duty.

(e) *Interruptions to supply*: Since the power is collected from the overhead catenary through a pantograph and there are inevitable irregularities on the track, there are bound to be brief interruptions to power supply even in the best designs of pantograph and overhead system. Such interruptions should not cause distress to the Traction Motor by way of current rush and its associated ill-effects.

(f) *Suitability for dynamic braking including possibility of regenerative braking*: The motor should be capable of dynamic braking—rheostatic or regenerative. This capability arising out of the possibility of running the motor as generator can impart considerable advantage to electric traction by way of saving wear and tear of wheels and brake gear which is inherent in friction braking. It should be possible to achieve this with minimum addition to control gear. Besides regenerative braking offers a unique advantage to electric traction by way of energy saving as the regenerated power in most situations can be consumed within the system.

(g) *Vibration and Impacts*: All traction motors in general and nose-suspended ones in particular get subjected to vibration and impacts arising out of the movement of the vehicle on rails. The passage of the axle over rail joints, points and crossings gives rise to violent shaking. These vibrations and impacts, apart from affecting bearings and gears, have a significant effect on the brush gear and commutation. In case of nose-suspended motors, vertical acceleration of the order of 14 g and transverse acceleration of the order of 7 g have been recorded at speeds of the order of 120 kmph.

AVAILABLE MOTOR CHARACTERISTICS AND THEIR SUITABILITY FOR TRACTION DUTIES

The most important criterion on for selecting a motor for any load is matching of the speed-torque characteristic.

Practically all electric motors exhibit drop in speed as the torque rises. However, the degree by which speed changes with change in torque differs for various kinds of motors, viz. series, shunt, compound motors of D.C. type and induction, synchronous, commutator motors of A.C. type.

Electric Motor Speed-torque Characteristics

These may be classified under three main categories, viz.

(a) Absolutely hard speed-torque characteristic in which there is no change in speed with torque. Synchronous motors fall in this category.

(b) Hard speed-torque characteristic in which there is slight drop in speed with rise in torque. D.C. Shunt motors and to some extent induction motors (over working portion of the characteristic) fall in this category.

(c) Soft speed-torque characteristic in which there is considerable drop in speed with rise in torque. This is the type of characteristic exhibited by a D.C. series motor or D.C. compound motor depending upon the degree of compounding.

Figure 4.1. illustrates the three types of characteristics described above.

To restore balance between driving torque and resisting torque, non-electric prime-movers usually employ a governor which regulates the flow of the energy to match the load requirement. In electric motors, this function is performed by back e.m.f. of the motor. This property of electric motors is very valuable.

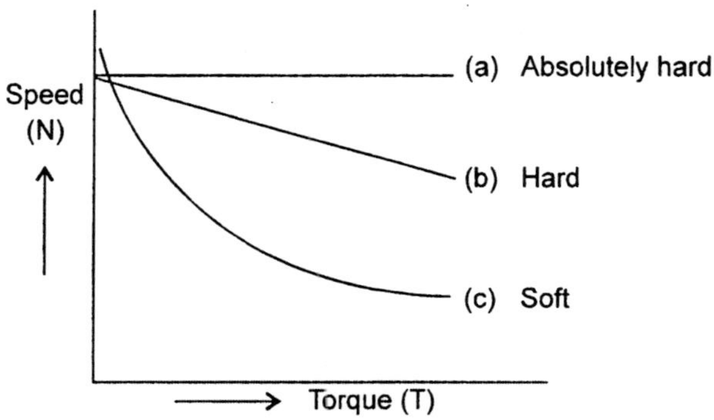

Fig. 4.1 Three types of speed-torque characteristics of electric motors

A reference to the characteristics of traction loads outlined earlier may indicate that a D.C. series motor with a soft speed-torque characteristic may be best suited for traction duty due to its ability to drop speed with increased requirement of torque and thereby save itself from overloading. It may, therefore, be most pertinent to compare D.C. series and shunt motors in respect of other requirements of traction duty to arrive at a conclusion.

Comparison of D.C. Series and Shunt Motors for Traction Duty

The comparative performances of D.C. series and shunt motors vis-a-vis specific requirements of traction duty, outlined earlier, are detailed in the following:

(a) *Starting Duty*: The series motor is capable of exerting a large torque at starting which is proportional to the square of current and independent of fluctuations in line voltage.

(b) *Self-governing and Protection Against Overloading*: In a series motor, the increase in torque requirement automatically decreases the speed and protects the motor against overloading. On the other hand, the shunt motor possesses a rather stiff speed-torque characteristic and is prone to overloading unless control mechanism is actuated to assist self governing.

(c) *Load Sharing with Unequal Wheel Diameters*: Different wheel diameters would result in different speeds of motors coupled to different axles through gearing. A 10% smaller wheel diameter would mean 10% higher speed of the traction motor such that longitudinal distance travelled remains the same. From the characteristic curves shown in Fig. 4.2 it would be seen that the difference in the torques exerted in the case of series motor is marginal (i.e. t_1, t_2) whereas in the case of shunt motor it is substantially large (T_1, T_2). Hence shunt motors would not share load properly and the overall traction capacity would get reduced if overloading is to be avoided.

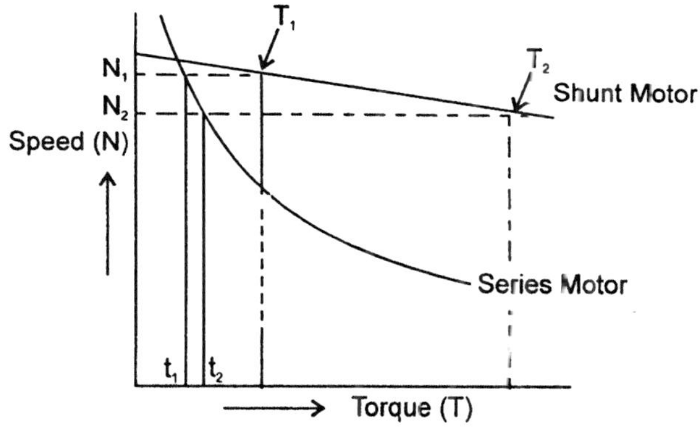

Fig. 4.2 Difference in torque exerted in series and shunt motors due to small changes in speed

(d) *Behaviour Under Voltage Jumps*: A sudden voltage rise, as is commonly encountered in traction duty, would cause a rush of current in the traction motor. The magnitude of this current rush would depend upon the impedance of motor circuit and its duration on the rate of build-up of counter EMF. In a series motor, the impedance of the motor circuit is larger due to addition of armature (Z_a) and field impedances (Z_f). Hence the current rush is of a lower order than in a shunt motor. Besides, the current rush in the field helps to build up the counter EMF faster, thereby reducing its overall duration.

(e) *Temporary Interruptions in Supply Voltage* : Temporary interruptions in supply voltage due to pantograph losing contact are quite common in traction duty. In a series motor, the field dies down with fall of current to zero. Hence upon restoration of the voltage, there is a current rush whose value is determined by $V/(Z_a + Z_f)$ ratio. In case of a shunt machine, the field does not die down so fast due to availability of a closed circuit for the field through the armature. Hence there is a counter EMF present which helps to minimise the current rush. However, the current rush in this case is given by $\frac{V-e}{Z_a}$.

Addition of field impedance Z_f in series motor to the armature impedance Z_a partly overcomes the deficiency of back EMF.

(f) *Suitability for Dynamic Braking*: To enable dynamic braking, the motor has to act as a generator. In a series motor, if self-excitation is to be availed, this would call for reversal of the field connection with respect to the armature such that the magnetic circuit of the field does not get disturbed due to reversal of current flowing due to the counter EMF. However, during dynamic braking, control over the braking force through manipulation of the field excitation is of utmost importance. Hence during dynamic braking, the field is separately excited.

In shunt motors too, a similar strategy, i.e. separate excitation, has to be resorted to as supply voltage fluctuations would otherwise make the braking process unstable.

(g) *Vibrations and Impacts*: This would call for special care in mechanical design irrespective of the type of motor, i.e. series or shunt.

From the foregoing deliberations, it is amply clear that a D.C. series motor is ideally suited for traction duty. It is for these inherent advantages that a D.C. series motor was so far being universally adopted for traction purposes.

RATING AND SPECIFICATION OF KEY PARAMETERS

For determining the key parameters of a traction motor for a given service, it is necessary to specify the trailing load, the booked and maximum speeds and the geographical terrain. While bulk of a railway track is laid on a level gradient, there are stretches of up or down gradients which are kept within the ruling gradient. When a train running at the booked speed encounters an upgradient, its speed falls following the torque-speed characteristic of the motor. However, the speed so attained may be too low to cater for the required running schedule and section capacity. Hence a higher rating for the traction motor may be called for than the continuous rating for a brief period.

It would therefore, be seen that traction motor must be assigned a "*Continuous Rating*" and a "*One-hour Rating*". This is the internationally adopted practice. One-hour rating is defined as the output at normal voltage which, when starting from cold, would cause a temperature rise consistent with the class of insulation during a one-hour run. Continuous rating under similar conditions pertains to running for an unlimited period without exceeding the temperature rise limits.

The load, ruling gradient, terrain, booked speed, maximum speed etc. are specified by the customer. The designer determines the maximum tractive effort at starting, the tractive effort required at the continuous rating speed and tractive effort required under one hour rating speed. From these, the continuous H.P. rating and one-hour ratings get determined.

Weak Field Operation

Weakening of the series field is a common practice adopted to improve the rating of a traction motor and realise its optimum capability.

After achieving stable working speed with the full field, if the field is weakened by introducing a diverter resistance, the current taken by the motor increases due to a reduction in the back E.M.F. Consequently, the motor speeds up to re-establish its relationship with the applied voltage. The extra current input also passes partly through the field giving higher output while catering to the required torque.

Field weakening can be done in two ways:

(i) By connecting a diverter resistance across the series field.
(ii) By cutting out some of the series field turns.

The former method is more commonly used.

The extent of field weakening could be as high as 60% leaving behind 40% field strength only. However as the field gets weakened, its distortion by the armature reaction becomes prominent and this affects commutation adversely. Hence a compromised level of field weakening is arrived at giving due consideration to commutation aspect.

Power Output of Traction Motor

The power output of a traction motor (or any motor) is expressed by the following general formula:

$$P = 2\pi.N.B.A.D^2.L.\eta$$

where N = speed in rpm at the reference rating.

B = average flux density in Tesla in the air gap.
A = linear load in ampere conductors per metre length at the periphery of armature.
D = the diameter of the armature in metres.
L = the effective length of armature iron in metres.
η = efficiency (0.9 to 0.95).

The parameters B, A and η in the above equation can be considered as constants. Hence the output becomes a function of $(D.L.N)$.

There has been a continuous improvement in the maximum speed (N) of motors over the years. While the maximum peripheral speed of armatures was of the order of 30 m/sec in 1920s, it is of the order of 80 m/sec as of today. This has become possible through improved construction techniques especially those pertaining to commutator and banding.

As regards the factor $D\ L$, it is basically related to the size of traction motor that can be accommodated in a locomotive bogie. Considering the case of an axle-hung nose-suspended motor, the limitations in different dimensions can be appreciated from Fig. 4.3.

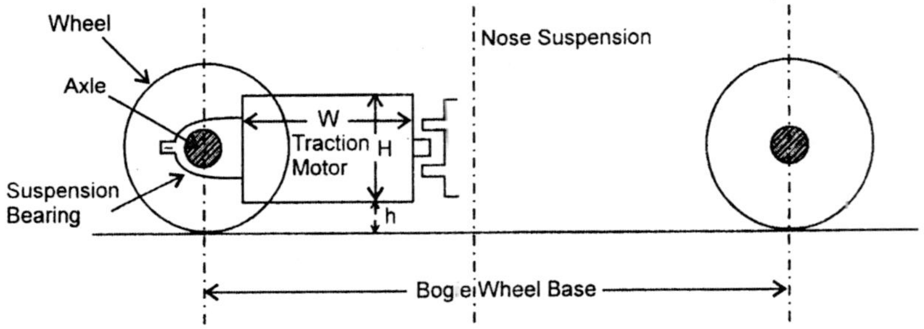

Fig. 4.3 Limitation of nose-suspended traction-motor dimensions

The length of the motor frame is limited by the available space between the two wheels of the same axle, i.e. gauge. The width (W) is restricted by the space available between the suspension bearing and nose support. The height H available gets restricted by the flood water level on the track, i.e. h as specified for a particular system (Fig. 4.3). Of course there has to be a certain clearance from the track even from mechanical considerations.

Hence the diameter D and L of the armature which govern the output get defined in relation to the limitations mentioned above.

OPTIMISATION OF DESIGN AND CONSTRUCTIONAL FEATURES FOR IMPROVED POWER-TO-WEIGHT RATIO

Power-to-Weight Ratio

There has been a very significant improvement in power-to-weight ratio of traction motors (represented by the index kW/kg) over the years. The curve shown in Fig. 4.4 indicates the trend.

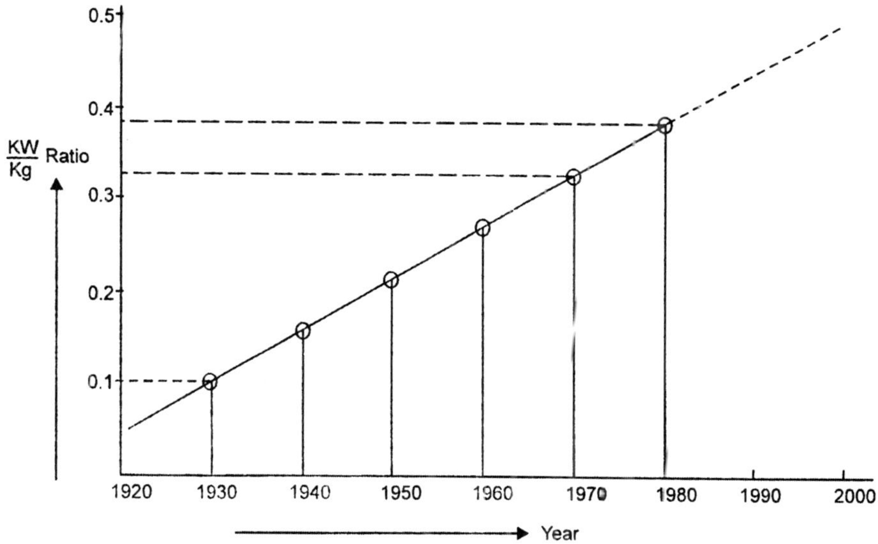

Fig. 4.4 Progressive improvement of the power-to-weight ratio of traction-motors over the years

It may be seen that the power-to-weight ratio has become almost 3.5 times over a 50-year span between 1930 and 1980.

This improvement has come about through optimisation of design as well constructional features by way of materials and techniques. It is proposed to discuss these features in respect of key components of a traction motor.

Stator

For a long time, cast steel casings have been in use. The possibility of existence of casting defects and their effect on flow of flux led to evolution of fabricated stators using steel plate castings or rolled steel plates. This has resulted in weight reduction due to better homogeneity of the magnetic circuit.

Solid stators, however, give rise to higher magnetic losses and retarded flux growth due to eddy currents. Hence to impart better capability to deal with voltage fluctuations and ripples, laminated stator designs have been adopted in critically rated machines. Though initially costlier, these designs yield higher kW/kg ratio and have an element of overall economics on life cycle basis.

Mainpoles and Interpoles

Increasingly, laminated main and interpoles are getting used in all critical designs to enable faster building up of the main and commutating fields with rapidly varying currents. Additionally, the interpoles are provided with higher air gap to ensure proportionality of commutating flux with armature current due to absence of saturation.

Suspension Bearings

In nose-suspended traction motors, sleeve-type suspension bearings which bear approximately 50 percent of the motor weight were used almost universally till early eighties. A recent development is the use of roller bearings for this application which, though costlier initially, has a long term advantage in respect of maintenance/operational cost as well as reliability. Frequent change of bearings due to wear which calls for lifting of the locomotive also gets avoided.

Armature Stack, Winding and Insulation

Greater accuracy in the manufacture of armature stampings with slots for housing conductors has resulted in little need for filing the slots after stacking which avoids iron losses due to shorting of the varnished laminations by burrs and filings.

For designs pertaining to higher speeds, higher flux densities at the tooth or deep slots, the coil sides are made of thin conductors working in parallel. This has become easily possible due to use of Kapton film conductor insulation.

Reduced thickness of insulation which permits use of higher conductor sections has become possible due to universal use of Kapton film insulated conductors. Kapton-film insulation of conductors is almost at par with enamel insulation while giving considerably higher mechanical strength.

Vacuum Pressure Impregnation Using Solventless Epoxy Resins: This is now a universally adopted technique. The solventless varnish does not leave voids or pores upon polymerisation and vacuum pressure impregnation ensures complete filling up of voids and pores prior to impregnation. Apart from eliminating the need for a very high degree of workmanship in conductor or coil insulation, the compact insulation so achieved eliminates incidents of drop of insulation during rainy season and gives an advantage of about 20 to 25°C in terms of temperature rise for identical loading conditions.

Armature Conductor Jointing to Commutator by TIG Welding

The universal technique adopted for this operation till early eighties was soldering. In spite of best possible soldering techniques the joint between the armature conductor and the commutator segment continued to be a weak spot giving frequent occurrence of irregular voltage drop at the commutator joint followed by burn-behind-the-risers (BBCR) and consequent dislocations. In TIG Welding (Tungsten Inert Gast Welding), a tungsten electrode, under a neutral atmosphere, causes the ends of conductor and commutator segment slots to melt with adequate penetration without damaging the conductor or commutator insulation. TIG welding is now universally adopted and incidents of BBCR have become history.

Banding with Resi-glass Tape

Banding with non-magnetic steel wire has now been completely eliminated and replaced by glass tape coated with polyester resin banding. It has been established that compared to steel banding, glass banding does not give rise to greater heating and has the following additional advantages:

(a) It does not give rise to eddy currents and consequent heating
(b) It does not spark in the event of damage to rotor winding
(c) It can be placed directly on the winding without additional insulation
(d) It does not require a smooth surface in order to be applied
(e) On the whole, it is less expensive

Ventilation

It is possible to make substantial gain in power/weight ratio by optimising ventilation. Traction motors used in electrical multiple units are self-ventilated type with the fan being mounted on the armature shaft itself. This is basically due to space limitations on a motor coach. Self ventilation suffers from an inherent disadvantage of low ventilation at lower speeds which includes starting cycle with heavier current inflow. All locomotive traction motors are force-ventilated by a blower motor mounted inside the locomotive body where it has the additional advantage of getting fed by filtered air which avoids dust deposit on the armature and stator windings due to ventilation.

The graph shown in Fig. 4.5, plotted for TAO 646 motor of Alsthom, illustrates the contribution of forced ventilation towards improving continuous rating. It will be seen that the curve becomes asymptotic with respect to the vertical line representing maximum current rating very rapidly.

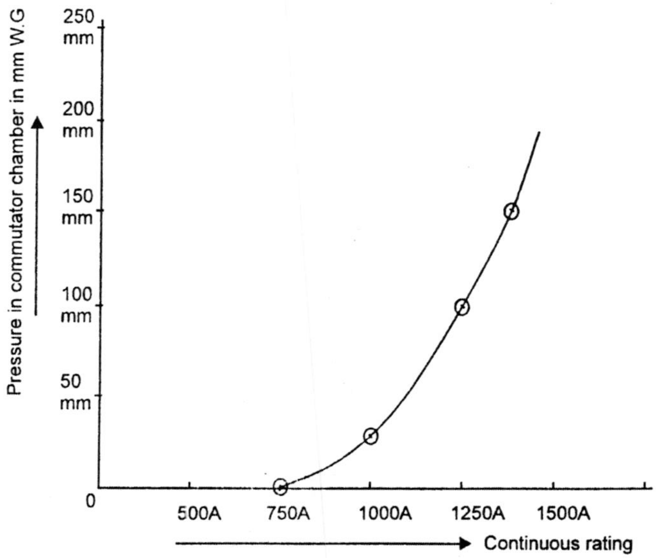

Fig. 4.5 Effect of forced ventilation on continuous rating

Hence rather that laying emphasis on pushing more air through the motor, it is advantageous to improve the efficiency of ventilation by judicious distribution of air inside the motor. This is achieved by making cooling ducts in the armature and exposing greater area of heat-exchange parts to cooling air.

Brush Gear

It should be ensured that the pressure at the brushes does not decrease as they get worn out. To achieve this, spiral springs have been found best and far superior to helical springs for pressing the brushes on to the commutator.

Brush holders must not deform at higher temperatures and be able to dissipate heat generated at the brushes. They should also not melt under arcing conditions occurring during flashovers. These requirements rule out brush holders of arc-resisting insulating materials.

Aluminium bronze brush holders were used for a long time but its arc-resisting property is poor. Recent developments are in favour of using chrome-zirconium-copper brush holders which do not get damaged due to arcing and are wear resistant.

Electro-graphite carbon brushes of appropriate grade for a particular application of split type instead of mono-block type with a silicon rubber plate on the top to damp vibration, are used universally for achieving good commutation. Split brushes in two or three parts are better than mono-block ones as they give better distribution of contact pressure and reduced chances of brush losing contact with commutator due to ovality or impacts.

Measures to Minimise Flashovers

Flashovers in a traction motor are quite common and sometimes cause severe damage to the commutator, brush gear and windings. Good commutation with least sparking is, therefore, an essential requirement.

Use of permanent shunting resistance on the main field helps to shunt out the 100 c/s ripples from the field flux and improves the capability of commutating poles to assist commutation through absence of transformer voltage appearing in the coils undergoing commutation. Apart from above, the voltage between commutator segments is restricted to well below 40 V to minimise flashover proneness. Spark gaps are also provided on the brush holders which break down under conditions of severe sparking and trip the main circuit-breaker through earth faults protection relay. This reduces the period of short circuit due to flashovers and minimises damage.

THREE-PHASE INDUCTION DRIVES

Application of Induction Motors for Traction Puproses

The robustness of induction motors of squirrel cage type and its reduced maintenance and operating cost has all along attracted the traction engineers.

The development of electronics technology both for power and control systems in late 1970s led to application of induction motors for traction purposes. The invention of GTO thyristor which can be turned "ON" or "OFF" by a "gate pulse" coupled with "Microprocessor-actuated PWM control" led to development of "Variable Voltage Variable Frequency (VVVF) inverters" which give VVVF output from a D.C. input. Availability of a VVVF power-supply with greater ease eliminates the main drawbacks of an induction motor, viz. changing of speeds and torque, to cater for the specific requirements of a traction system. In fact the need for an in-built series characteristic for self-regulation as available in a D.C. series motor becomes redundant if an induction motor is fed with VVVF supply.

Under the above conditions the hard characteristic of induction motor which exhibits a sharp drop in torque with slight increase in speed becomes an advantage for realising maximum out of the available adhesion. Should a wheel slip, the torque would drop sharp to a low value which, in turn, would restrict the slipping speed and prevent a run-away situation.

The squirrel cage type induction motor then becomes ideally suited for traction duties. Besides, its initial manufacturing cost is low and absence of commutator enables higher speeds to be attained and reduces the maintenance and operating cost to almost negligible percentage of the total maintenance cost of the locomotive. Apart from the above mentioned advantages, regenerative braking becomes possible with greater ease.

The development of three-phase induction motor traction drives was basically prompted by the following needs:

(i) The need to increase speeds and reduce motor weight.
(ii) The need to minimise maintenance and running cost.
(iii) The need to obtain regenerative braking without complicated control gear to save energy.

Constructional Features of Three-phase Induction Motors Used for Traction

The three-phase induciton motor is a squirrel cage motor, the most robust design of electrical machine. A typical motor consists of a laminated cylindrical rotor carrying the secondary winding as un-insulated copper bars which are shorted by strong copper rings at both ends. Collectors, slip rings, brush devices or other parts subjected to wear do not exist.

The stator consists of laminated steel stampings incorporating the slots for the windings clamped tightly together. The primary winding consists of flat copper wire and is arranged for a three-phase supply with three identical sets of multi-polar winding groups. Large A.C. traction motors are designed with either four or six poles.

Both the rotor and stator cores have axial stamped holes to aid ventilation which is typically by forced air. Thus there are three paths for heat removal, viz. air-gap, holes through stator and holes through rotor. Since the air gap is small and of the order of 2.5 to 3 mm, only a small proportion of heat is conducted through the air gap. The stator windings are more critical component when considering heat build-up; hence they are insulated to class H. The rotor is thermally more robust and able to handle higher temperatures than the stator. Hence, in some designs the laminated stator core is placed in a housing which offers mechanical protection as well as another forced air cooling path to the stator.

An induction motor is able to produce more tractive effort for the same motor volume as compared to a D.C. series motor. This is due to absence of commutator which allows more space for torque producing electromagnetics. In addition, induction motor has a higher thermal limit than the D.C. motor because the only winding having insulation is static and the stator has a larger surface area for heat transfer.

Where traction distribution system is A.C. single phase, the use of capacitor bank for stabilising the D.C. link voltage leads to unity power-factor which has added advantage in terms of tarrif.

Torque at Different Speeds

In general, traction loads require a large torque at start and during low speed range to cater for acceleration. At the working speed the torque required is comparatively smaller as it is only required to overcome the train resistance at that speed. To satisfy these torque-speed characteristics and maximise the utilisation of available inverter voltage, the output voltage of the inverter is varied in relation to the output frequency as in Fig. 4.6.

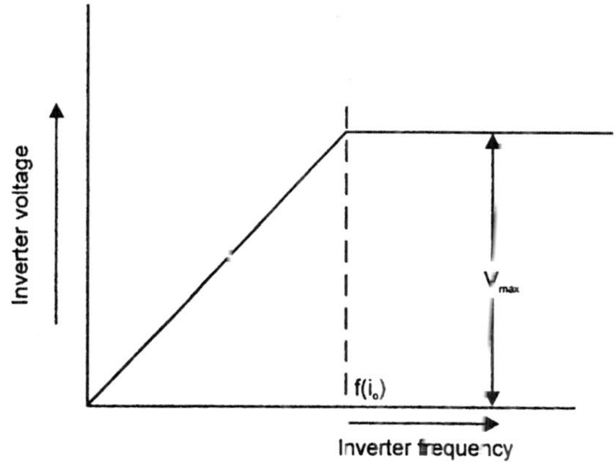

Fig. 4.6 Variation of voltage and frequency to achieve desired speed-torque characteristics for traction loads

In the lower speed range the voltage is controlled in proportion to the frequency upto f(i_0) by PWM control. However, all through higher speed range, the inverter voltage is constant and only the frequency is changed to obtain different speed-torque characteristics (Fig. 4.6).

In this way, the speed-torque characteristic required for traction load is built up of several induction motor characteristics obtained by varying voltage and frequency as stated above. This is illustrated in Fig. 4.7.

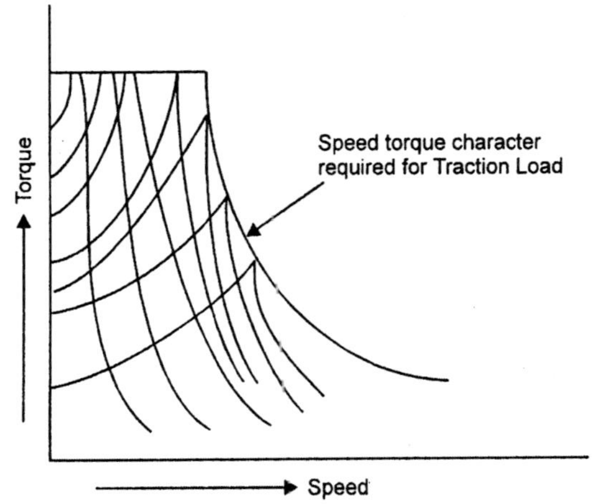

Fig. 4.7 Torque-speed control of induction motor for traction duty

Comparison of A.C. Induction and D.C. Series Motor Traction Systems

System Efficiency: Overall efficiency of A.C. Traction Motor locomotives in terms of ratio of wheel-rail tractive power to rectifier output power is approximately 90 percent as compared to 86 percent of D.C. series motor locomotives. This is based on the findings of Association of American Rail Roads.

Productivity: From the same locomotive weight, it is possible to get distinctly superior hauling capability with A.C. induction motor. This is primarily due to improved adhesion level which could be of the order of 40 percent plus in state-of-the-art designs. Besides, reliability of the electrical system and overall availability of the locomotive is of a much higher order due to elimination of failure-prone control gear and D.C. motors. Hence the traffic offering on a given sections can be managed by a smaller fleet with a reduction of approximately 10 to 20 percent in the fleet size.

Maintenance Requirements: Due to elimination of cummutation gear, tap-changers and failure-prone control gear, the maintenance schedules get distinctly reduced in induction motor locomotives as compared to conventional ones. This saves cost and improves availability of locomotives.

Higher Speed: Induction motors are capable of higher rotational speed and power output. Hence their weight for the same output is much lower. This is ideally suited for higher speeds in freight as well as passenger services.

Sensitivity to Wheel-diameter Differences: Conventional D.C. series motor locomotives are sensitive to wheel diameter variations as this results in an unequal power output distribution which could result in overloading of some motors. Tests by Association of American Rail Roads have established that induction motor locomotives can tolerate wheel diameter differences up to ±15 mm which gives significant latitude in maintenance and interchangeability of wheel-sets.

Short-time Rating and Overloading: Conventional D.C. series motor locomotives have short-time ratings for starting current and one-hour output. Three phase induction motor drives are free from this problem. Each value can be applied continuously.

Reduced Current Loading of the Distribution System: In three-phase induction motor drives, voltage rating of the traction motors is almost two times that of D.C. series motor where maximum voltage gets restricted by bar-to-bar voltage considerations. This feature coupled with unity power-factor gives reduced loading of the distribution system.

Regenerative Breaking: In three-phase induction motor drives, regenerative braking is possible right up to zero speed, in sharp contrast to conventional D.C. motor drives where mechanical brakes are essentially required at lower speeds. This feature has distinct advantage in terms of wear and tear of wheel disc and brake gear components.

Wheel-spinning: Conventional D.C. motor locomotives require reliable slip-detection device to avoid wheel-spinning which destroys wheels as well as rails. In 3-phase induction motor drives, axles can develop spinning of the order of 0.5 kmph at the most as the steep torque/speed characteristic checks runaway speeds.

Direction Reversal: No reversal is required in 3-phase induction motor locomotives. Electric control takes care of reversal through necessary change in phase-sequence.

CHAPTER 5

Traction Motor Control: Principles and Gear

INTRODUCTION

The object of providing a control system for the traction unit is to provide means of connecting traction motors to the supply and thereby control their power output such that:

(a) A smooth acceleration is achieved without shocks that would damage the couplings and cause inconvenience to passengers, and
(b) The traction motor speed can be adjusted as required for the type of service and terrain.

It is obviously not possible to switch motors directly on to the supply. The current flowing through a motor is given by the relationship $V\text{-}E/Ra$ where V is the applied voltage, E is back EMF and R_a is the resistance of armature circuit that also includes the field resistance in a series motor. At standstill E is zero and this builds up gradually as the train accelerates. Since R_a is low, unless either the applied voltage is reduced or an additional resistance is introduced, a very high current will flow which must be avoided. Besides, it should be possible to reach the final balancing speed condition in steps such that the acceleration is smooth and there are no sudden jerks.

It follows that the control system should cater to the need of applying the available voltage in steps either as it is or with the help of a resistance bank. Further, the control system for D.C. and A.C. Traction power supply would be different as the latter has the advantage of transformer mechanism.

We will therefore dwell upon traction control system in two parts, viz.

(a) Control system for D.C. locomotives or EMU's working on 3000 V, 1500 V or 750 V traction power supply; and,

(b) Control system for A.C. locomotives or EMU's working on 25 kV traction power supplies.

Use of thyristors as choppers in D.C. systems or as grid-controlled rectifiers in A.C. system is yet another system of control of a later origin and will also be dwelt upon.

TRACTION CONTROL OF D.C. LOCOMOTIVES AND EMU'S

The simplest control mechanism would consist in introducing a resistance bank from which the resistance is cut out in the desired number of steps as the train speed picks up and the back e.m.f. builds-up. This can be schematically represented by the circuit diagram of Fig. 5.1.

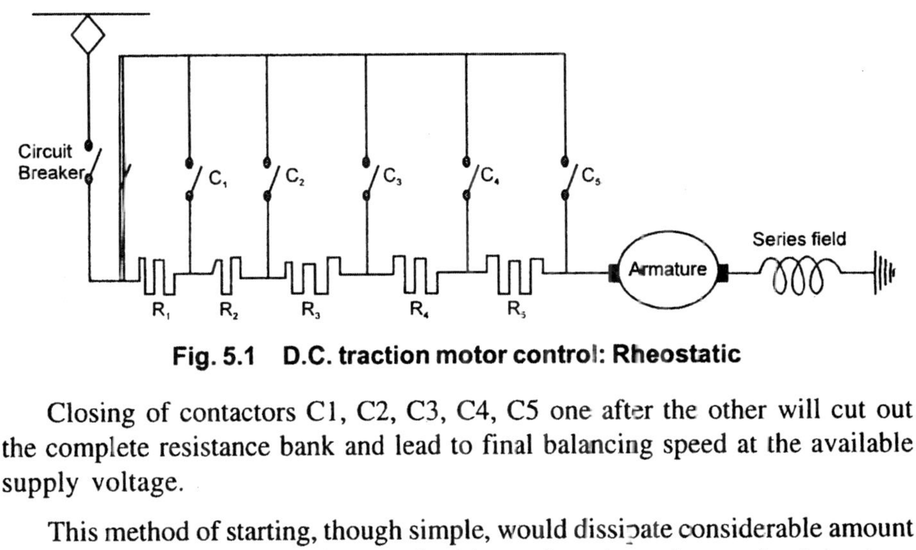

Fig. 5.1 D.C. traction motor control: Rheostatic

Closing of contactors C1, C2, C3, C4, C5 one after the other will cut out the complete resistance bank and lead to final balancing speed at the available supply voltage.

This method of starting, though simple, would dissipate considerable amount of energy in the starting resistance. Besides, unless the resistance bank is given a continuous rating for the highest starting current, there will be only one balancing speed and only one speed-torque characteristic on which the motor can run continuously. These are severe limitations and restrict maneuvreability of the motive power.

Series Parallel Control Combined with Rheostatic Control

Since the locomotive or EMU has two or more motors, it is possible to conceive a number of series parallel combinations which may help to divide the available voltage in two or more steps and thereby permit more than one torque-speed characteristics and balancing speeds. Taking a typical case of motive power with four traction motors, the following series parallel combinations would be possible.

(a) All motors in series with each having 1/4th of available voltage,
(b) Two motors in series with two such groups in parallel with each group having 1/2 of available voltage,
(c) All the four motors in parallel with each having full available voltage.

Assisting the above three combinations with suitable resistance banks, it is possible to have three stable torque-speed characteristics and a larger number of starting steps.

Transition from Series to Parallel Combination

To illustrate the principle, a system consisting of two motor groups will be considered. There are three methods of transition used to achieve changeover from series to parallel combination of motors, viz.

(a) Open circuit transition
(b) Shunt transition
(c) Bridge transition.

Open Circuit Transitioin: In this method, the motors are disconnected from the circuit and regrouped. This has a serious disadvantage of complete loss of torque during transition and severe arcing at the contactors. Hence this method has no practical use.

Shunt Method of Transition: This consists in shunting one of the motors during the transition. The steps involved are illustrated schematically in Fig. 5.2.

Although this method of transition is an improvement over open-circuit method and requires fewer contactors than Bridge Transition method, it suffers from the disadvantage of momentary reduction in torque to approximately 50% of torque achieved after attaining full series position.

Bridge Transition: Step by step bridge transition is illustrated in the schematic circuit shown in Fig. 5.3.

It will be seen that in this method of transition, there is no discontinuity of torque. The bridge contactor does not carry current in an ideal situation and only a small current in most practical situations due to inequality of circuit elements and back EMF.

The bridge transition is the best alternative and ideally suited for automatic control by a current limiting relay (CLR).

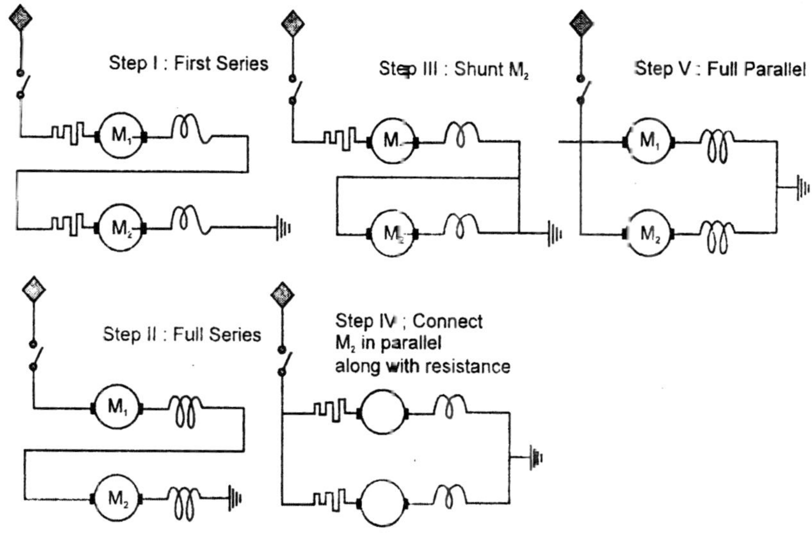

Fig. 5.2 D.C. traction motor control: Shunt transition

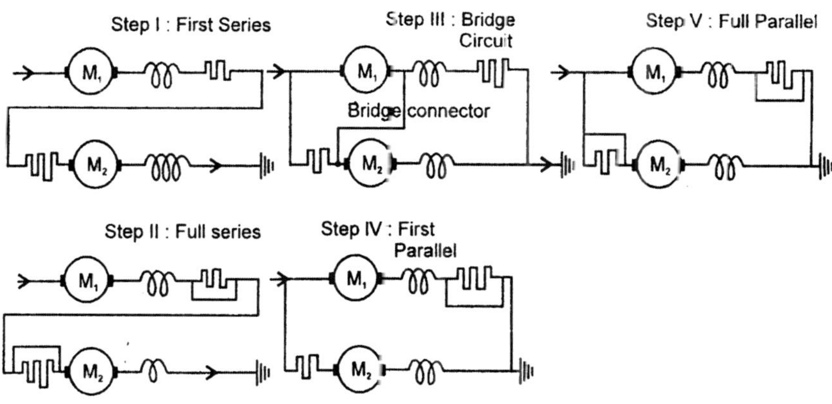

Fig. 5.3 D.C. traction motor control: Bridge transition

Energy Efficiency and Limitations of Series-Parallel-cum-Rheostatic Control Techniques

Series parallel control helps to reduce energy wasted in starting resistance during starting. To appreciate this point, consider the simplest case of two motors being started directly in parallel combination using a rheostat or via series-parallel combination. The supply voltage and current per motor may be assumed to be constant as V and I and starting time taken as t sec. The voltage drop in motor resistance may be assumed to be negligible.

(a) When motors are started directly in parallel the total energy taken from the supply system during starting is $V.2I.t = 2\ VIt$.

Since the voltage at the motor terminals varies from zero to V, the average voltage is $V/2$. Hence the useful power output from motors is $V/2.\ I.\ t \times 2 = VIt$.

Hence energy wasted in starting resistance is 50% of the total energy intake from supply and the energy efficiency during starting is 50%.

(b) In series-parallel control the two motors are first started in series when the voltage rises to ($V/2$) per motor. Then motors are connected in parallel when the voltage would rise from $V/2$ to V per motor. Assuming the series and parallel starting periods to be equal, i.e. $t/2$ each, the total energy taken from the supply system during starting is:

$$V.\ I.t/2 + V.2I\ t/2 = 3/2.\ V.I.t.$$

On the other hand, energy used by the motors to produce useful torque is:

$$[V/2.I.t/2] + (3/4)V \times 2\ I \times t/2 = V.I.t.$$

wherein the average voltage across the motors is $V/2$ in series combination during the starting cycle of $t/2$ sec and 3/4 V during parallel combination for further $t/2$ sec.

Hence energy wasted during starting in resistors is $(3/2)VIt\text{-}VIt = 1/2\ V.I.t.$

The energy efficiency during starting = (useful-energy/total-energy intake) × 100

$$= \frac{VIt}{3/2\,VIt} \times 100 = 66.6\%$$

It will, therefore, be seen that energy efficiency during starting improves from 50% to 66% when series parallel mechanism is used.

Table 5.1 summaries the salient features of series-parallel starting for 2, 4, 6 motors on the motive power.

It is clear that though series-parallel control is an improvement over the pure rheostatic control both in terms of energy efficiency and number of balancing speeds available for continuous working, the starting cycle of D.C.

motors in D.C. supply system invariably entails some loss in the starting resistors which is inescapable.

There is yet another disadvantage of rheostatic control, i.e. keeping two or more motors in series during starting or continuous working. Should one of the motors experience slipping due to adverse track conditions, there is a snowballing effect due to continued rise of back EMF of the slipping motor and corresponding drop of voltage at the resistor or other motors in the circuit due to reduction of series field strength.

Table 5.1 Balancing speeds available and energy efficiency during starting for series-parallel control mechanism using 2, 4 and 6 motors

System of control	No. of balancing speeds available (continuous working)	Overall efficiency during starting (under ideal conditions)
(a) Rheostatic-control of 2-motors in parallel	1	50%
(b) Series-parallel cum rheosatic control of two motors	2	66.6%
(c) Double series-parallel control of 4-motors, viz. all series, two series and two groups in parallel and all four in parallel	3	72.7%
(d) Double series-parallel control of 6-motors viz all motors in series, two parallel groups of 3 in series and 3 parallel groups of 2 in series	3	75%

Hence in D.C. supply systems the assumed adhesion is rather conservative and seldom exceeds 20% even though the available adhesion is much superior.

Chopper Control of Motors in D.C. Traction Systems

Regulation of the average voltage applied to the traction motor can be attained using a thyristor rectifier which connects the supply cyclically to the traction motors. The voltage graph in Fig 5.4 shows the pattern.

The available voltage from the supply is chopped into slices of t_1 duration followed by t_2 periods of no voltage which gives a reduced average voltage which can be varied to suit the starting duty.

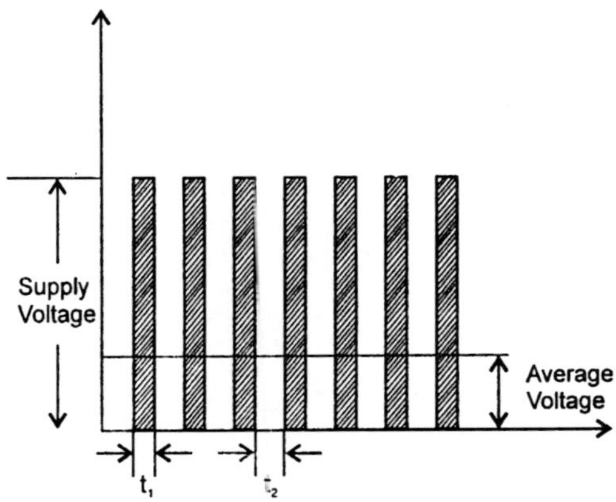

Fig. 5.4 Pattern of voltage applied to the traction motor using thyristor

A thyristor carrying direct current will only switch-off if the current is reduced to zero and the thyristor has a reverse voltage applied for a short time. Many circuits are in use to achieve this, the basic concept being that a charged capacitor is used as a temporary source of current and reverse biasing the thyristor to turn it off. The capacitor is switched into circuit using an auxiliary thyristor. A typical circuit is shown in Fig. 5.5.

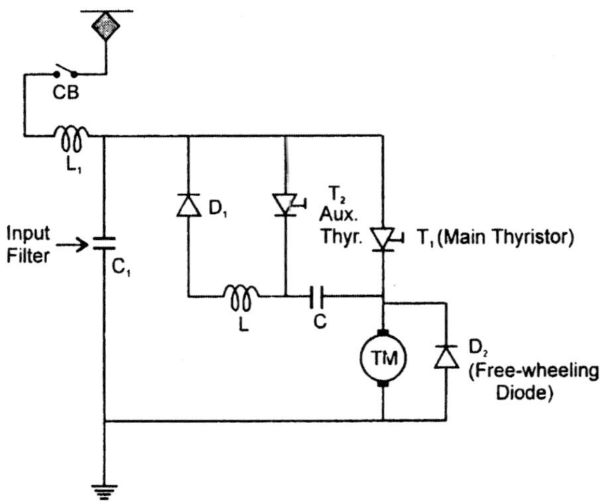

Fig. 5.5 Chopper control in D.C. traction system

When the supply is connected, auxiliary thyristor T_2 is turned 'on' to charge the capacitor C via the motor path. When the capacitor C gets fully charged, the current in T_2 falls to zero and this thyristor gets turned 'off'. Next thyristor T_1 is turned 'on' which applies full supply voltage to the TM. This also allows the capacitor C to oscillate via L and D_1 for half period thereby reversing the polarity across C. Further oscillation cannot occur due to blocking action of T_2 and D_1. When sufficient current has built up in the T_1 circuit, T_2 is again turned 'on'.

Capacitor C applies a reverse bi as to T_1. Further current flows through the TM via T_2 and C till the polarity of C gets reversed conforming to the initial conditions. The TM current thereafter decays via the free-wheeling diode D_2. When TM current has fallen to a pre-determined value, T_1 gets switched 'on' again and the cycle is repeated.

Capacitor C should have adequate capacity to perform its function of re-verse biasing and acting as a current source for the TM. By controlling firing pulses of T_1 and T_2 the mean voltage applied to the motor can be regulated to suit the train speed.

It is customary to fire T_1 at a fixed frequency such that input filter L_1C_1 can be designed to limit the ripple current drawn from the supply and avoid gen-eration of harmonics at track circuit frequency.

This form of control altogether avoids losses of the rheostatic control and can give an output voltage which varies smoothly rather than in steps. This can help to improve adhesion by 5 to 10% if all motors are connected in paral-lel all the time.

Recent development of Gate turn 'off' thyristors gives a simplified control circuit by avoiding the use of an auxiliary thyristor switch to turn-off the main thyristor.

Chopper control, though costlier as a first investment, is cost effective on life cycle basis through energy saving during starting especially for suburban services where frequent starting is involved.

TRACTION CONTROL SYSTEM OF A.C. LOCOMOTIVES

In A.C. supply traction system, the applied voltage to the traction motors can be controlled with greater ease due to availability of transformer mechanism. This would enable motors being connected permanently in parallel and avoid losses of rheostatic control. For this reason, A.C. locomotives have a distinctly superior adhesion performance.

The output of the secondary winding of a given transformer is fixed for a fixed input voltage. Hence to obtain a variable output voltage for supply to the traction motors, one of the following schemes may be employed:

Tappings on Secondary Side

A number of tappings may be made on the secondary winding of the transformer depending upon the number of voltage steps desired. As secondary currents are large, heavy connections are essentially required which limits the number of possible tappings. This system is known as low-voltage tap changing and is illustrated schematically in Fig. 5.6.

High Voltage Tap Changing

As an alternative to tappings on secondary winding the input voltage to the primary may be varied by employing an additional auto-transformer winding which can be, tapped throughout. The output of the auto-transformer is then fed to a fixed ratio traction transformer. All windings are housed in the same oil tank. The arrangement is shown schematically in Fig.5.7.

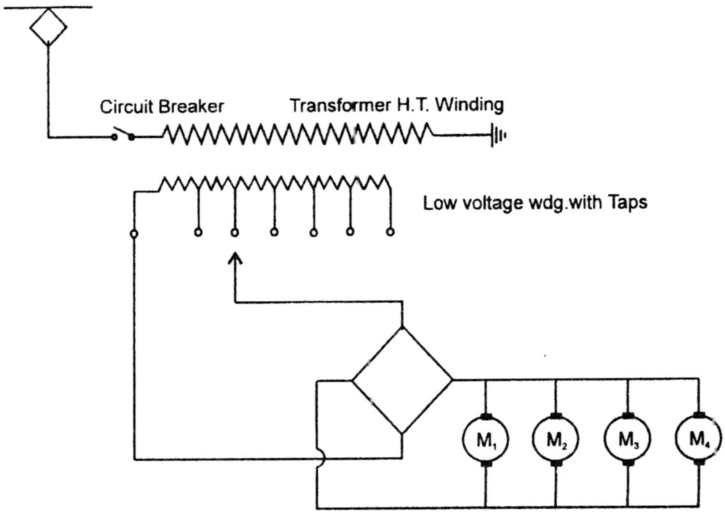

Fig. 5.6 Low voltage tap-changing

The high-voltage tapping with the aid of an additional auto-transformer winding carries a proportionately much lower current as compared to the secondary and can be easily fitted with more tapping points. Also, the tap changing gear handles lesser current and is simpler.

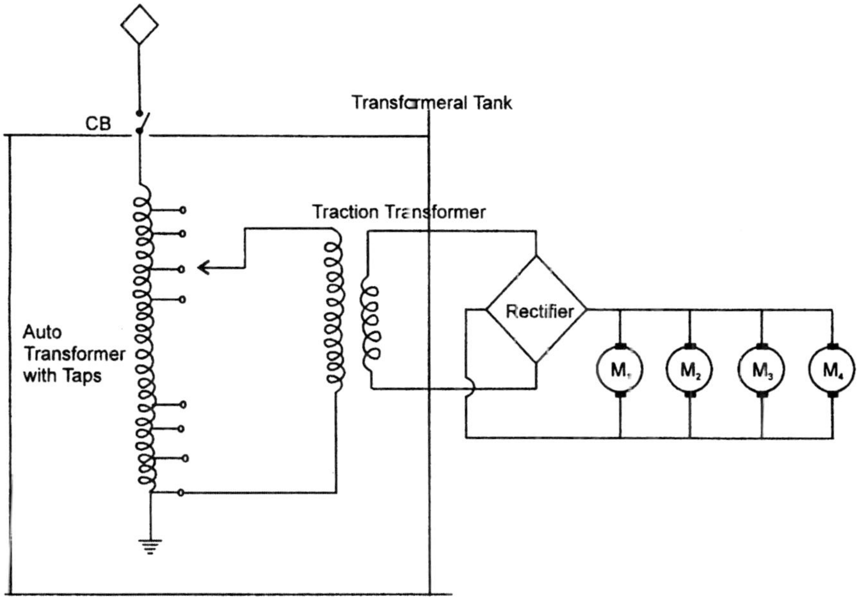

Fig. 5.7 High voltage tap-changing

Tap Changing Gear

There are two possibilities viz.

(a) Tap changing through use of contactors for each tap and a resistor or choke to limit the short circuit current while moving from one tap to another.

(b) Tap changing by a sliding contact tap changer working in conjunction with two cam-operated contactors and a resistance or choke to limit the short-circuit current between two taps while the change occurs. It is ensured that the sliding contacts do not make or break current as their speed being low, severe pitting would occur. They should be capable of carrying current from a pre-selected tap.

When the number of taps is large as in the case of high voltage tap changing which gives smaller voltage steps, it is desirable to adopt sliding-contact tap changing system which assures an overall economics.

Stepless Voltage Control through Use of Thyristors

Developments in power thyristors in 70's offered an attractive alternative for voltage control which is contactless as well as stepless. In A.C. systems, the current drops to zero every half cycle; hence only firing angle to start conduction need be controlled to yield the desired average D.C. voltage.

Suitable choke to smoothen the output current and filters to shunt out the harmonics would be essentially required to avoid adverse effect on track circuits. The harmonics left out must not constitute more than 5% level to avoid harmful effects.

Use of thyristor rectifier eliminates the need for a tap changer and provides stepless control of voltage to the traction motors which helps to improve the adhesion by 3 to 5%

CONTROL GEAR

The control gear for traction motors consists of the following elements:

(i) Master controller with or without dead-man's device.
(ii) Reverser.
(iii) Contactors: Electropneumatic or electromagnetic.
(iv) Current Limiting Relay (CLR) for automatic acceleration.
(v) Field weakening contactors.
(vi) Starting and field weakening resistances.
(vii) Tap changer for A.C. supply systems with associated gear.

Contactors

To carry out switching operations in the traction motor circuit, it is essential to employ some form of contactor. The contactor is a device which incorporates a fixed and a movable contact which are pressed together with a contact force when the circuit is made and separated by a distance of 2 to 2.5 cm when the circuit is broken. Both fixed and moving contacts are spring loaded and mounted on insulated supports. The contacts have a wiping action incorporated which enables contact to be made at the tip and maintained at the heel such that damage to the contact due to arcing action does not vitiate the contact capability.

All power contactors have arc-chutes and blow-out mechanism for blowing out and quenching the arc. The blow out mechanism is a coil carrying the main current and producing a magnetic field perpendicular to the arc which blows out the arc in the forward direction towards the arc-chute.

The operation of closing or opening of the contactor can be carried out by the following means: (a) Electromagnetical, (b) Electro-pneumatical and (c) Cam and roller mechanism.

In electromagnetic contactor, the coil operating the contact mechanism carries a small low voltage current and has several thousand turns to be able to create a magnetic field which can actuate the contact mechanism.

In electropneumatic contactors, the coil is much smaller and actuates a magnet valve which admits air in a cylinder which displaces the contact mechanism through a piston.

In its simplest form, the cam and roller method of actuating the contactor has a moving contact mounted on hinged arm to which a roller running on cam is attached. All cams of different contactors of a group are mounted on a cam shaft. The cam-shaft may be either manually, or electropneumatically or motor operated.

All contactors are accompanied with auxiliary contacts which help their interlocking amongst themselves or with other circuit elements.

The control coil voltage is usually 110 V. The contact pressures may vary from 5 to 10 kg. The rating of the contactors may be as high as 1000 to 1500 A.

Electropneumatic contactors are more popular for higher ratings due to greater compactness and overall economics.

Reverser consists of a multi-contact two-position change-over switch-group operated by a double acting piston in a cylinder fed by compressed air under control of two magnet valves. The motion of the piston is converted to a rotary motion of 45 to 60° by a lever on the rotary shaft.

Reverser is required for reversing the field connection with respect to the armature to ensure reversal of the direction of motion

Master Controller

To ensure different control operations in a proper sequence, a master controller is required which has a number of cam-operated auxiliary switches operated by cams mounted on a shaft which is moved to different positions by a hand wheel. The reverser is also actuated by the master controller through switches mounted on a different shaft.

Master controllers of EMU's are smaller due to use of current limit relay for automatic acceleration. These master controllers incorporate a dead-man's device. The driver is required to maintain a downward pressure on the operating handle/knob whenever the train is in motion failing which the operating handle springs up releasing a switch which trips the circuit breaker and applies brakes to the train.

Current Limiting Relay (CLR)

This is an electromagnetic relay used for automatic acceleration to full-series or full-parallel position in a D.C. unit. The relay should close and open on predetermined current values, thereby cutting out resistance elements one by one.

Starting and Field Weakening Resistances: To ensure compact design these resistances are made of alloy steel strips assembled on porcelain separators.

Tap Changers

For low voltage operation, tap changers are built up through a group of electropneumatic contactors suitably interlocked to prevent incorrect operation through a group cam-shaft.

For high voltage operation, the tap changer is of sliding/rolling contact type. A number of contacts (fixed) corresponding to the number of taps are mounted either on a circular or a longitudinal contact plate. The rolling contact is moved from one tap to the other by an air servo-motor mechanism in which each control pulse moves the mechanism through one step with a degree of precision. This mechanism can also be operated by a stepper motor.

As already mentioned, sliding contact tap changers work in conjunction with cam-operated contactors which break the current during tap changing and enable the sliding contacts only to carry the regular current.

PWM CONTROL OF INDUCTION MOTORS

An induction motor operates economically in the steep-range of torque-speed characteristic curve as shown in Fig. 5.8. The pull-out torque should not be exceeded and operation in the saddle zone is excluded.

Since anyone speed-torque characteristic is not capable of catering to the traction requirement, a series of speed-torque characteristics are required to cater to the speed-torque requirement of the load as shown in Fig. 5.9. The "location curve" of different pull-out torques which caters to the traction or braking requirement is derived from different individual curves as shown in Fig. 5.9 by varying voltage (V) and frequency (f). Upto 40 Hz frequency, V/f is kept constant and thereafter V is kept constant and f is varied which results in pull-out torque getting reduced in proportion to the square of speed. This gives constant tractive effort during starting cycle of the traction load and series characteristic thereafter.

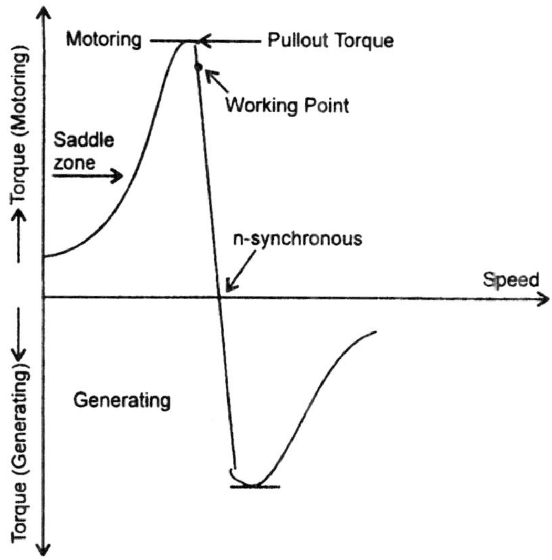

Fig. 5.8 Torque-speed characteristic of induction motor

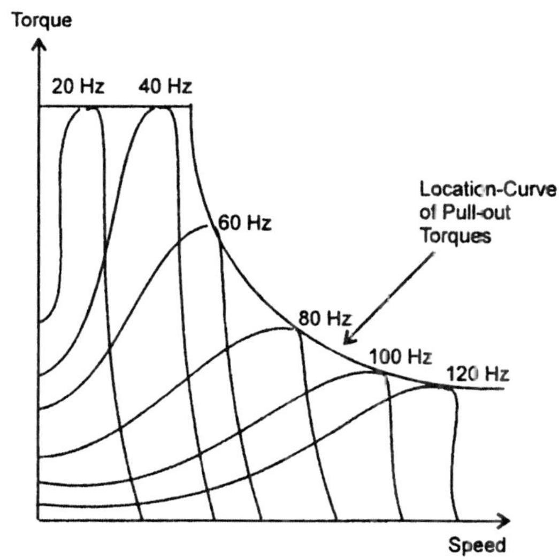

Fig. 5.9 Deriving the location-curve from a series of speed-torque curves obtained by varying 'v' and 'f'

Four Quadrant Controller

Thus the control system is required to give a variable voltage and variable frequency power supply to the traction motor from a fixed catenary voltage. This is achieved by using a voltage-source inverter (VSI) which is fed from the 25 kV catenary power through a converter and D.C. link capacitor. In a VSI the voltage as well as frequency are varied on demand during inversion while the input to the inverter is a fixed D.C. voltage supplied by the controlled converter. To enable movement in either direction and regenerative braking, the power flow must be reversible; hence the converter and invertor are both controlled and function as converter or inverter as required. This is achieved through a four-quadrant controller.

The block diagram (Fig. 5.10) illustrates this point.

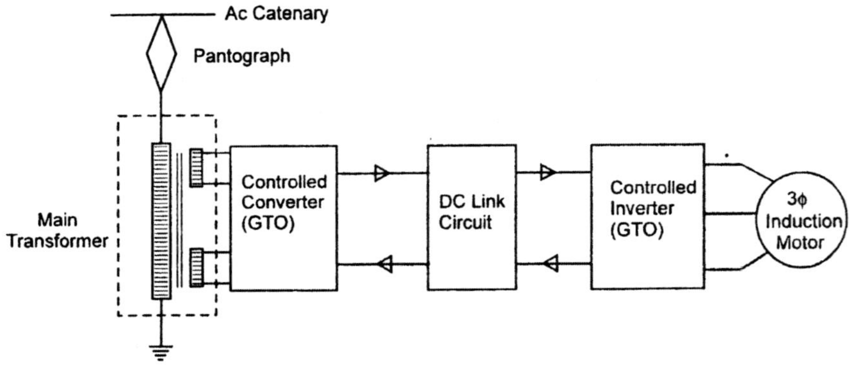

Fig. 5.10 Block diagram of the power circuit of a 3 induction motor. Locomotive with 4-quadrant control

Since the flow of energy is either way, each Gate-turn-off (GTO) thyristor has a diode connected in parallel to enable conduction in the reverse direction. Besides GTO's need *di/dt* and *dv/dt* control through suitable snubber circuits for protection of the silicon junction. The flow of current through the rectifier does not equal that conducted by the inverter at every instant. The difference is either stored or supplied by the D.C. link circuit which has a metallised paper capacitor bank. The capacitor bank also supplies reactive power to transformer for excitation which enables achievement of near unity power factor.

PWM-Control

To achieve an output as close to the sinusoidal waveform as possible such that the harmonic level is kept within an acceptable limit, the technique of Pulse Width Modulated (PWM) control of GTO is adopted.

The control pulses which turn a GTO "on" or "off" several times during a half cycle and for varying durations are obtained by comparing a triangular carrier-wave with a sinusoidal modulation wave.

An alternating voltage with a very small proportion of harmonics is produced if the duration of pulses during a half cycle are varied (modulated) in such a way that pulses in the middle are of longer duration than those of the ends. The larger the number of such pulses during a half cycle, the closer is the output waveform to a sine wave and lesser is the proportion of harmonics.

In order to ensure that the motor operates at its most efficient working points, the rotor speed is constantly monitored by a sensor installed on the motors. This information is fed back to the traction control computer which calculates the correct 3-phase supply frequency for required torque-speed output and executes the same through the four quadrant controller.

It will, therefore, be seen that the four-quadrant controller technique for the 3-phase induction motor is a complex system though highly efficient and reliable.

CHAPTER 6

Braking—Mechanical and Dynamic: Principles and Gear

INTRODUCTION

Braking, in effect, amounts to application of negative tractive effort to the train. Its purpose is to reduce the train speed and if necessary stop it under the following conditions:

(a) To stop a train on a red signal.
(b) To stop a train short of an obstruction in the event of an emergency situation coming to the notice of the crew.
(c) To reduce train speed for observing a speed restriction
(d) To control train speed on a down gradient.

Unlike during acceleration, the train resistance assists braking and a down gradient opposes it.

The *mechanism of adhesion plays* its part in braking process in the same way as it does during acceleration. In fact during friction braking, the maximum permissible braking force that would permit rotation of wheels and avoid skidding of the locked wheel is an additional factor.

An important aspect of *Braking Process* is the limited distance over which it must bring the train to a stop. Assuming that the red aspect of a stop signal gets warned 1 km in advance and the sighting distance of the warning signal under worst condition of visibility is of the order of 250 m, the braking process of the train from the maximum permissible speed at which it may be running must get completed over a distance of 250 m beyond the stop signal. Thus if the train speed is 120 kmph, the average speed during braking assuming uniform deceleration would be 60 kmph or 1 km per minute. Hence the braking process has to get completed with-in 1.5 minutes and the deceleration rate must not be less than 120/90 = 1.33 kmph per sec. In fact a higher deceleration would be preferable to avoid overshooting of the red signal and the train entering the block section overlap.

Hence the rate of retardation to be catered by the braking system is of a much higher order than the acceleration necessitating participation of more vehicles of the train apart from the locomotive itself. In most passenger trains all vehicles apart from locomotive have brake-gear to reduce the burden of individual vehicles from the point of view of adhesion and skidding. In goods trains, the practice is to provide at least 75% active vehicles in respect of brake power.

TYPES OF BRAKING SYSTEMS

The following types of braking systems have been employed:

Friction Based (i) Vacuum Brake
(ii) Air Brake, Electropneumatic or Electromagnetic
(iii) Hand Brake for parking

Electrical: Momentum Based
(iv) Dynamic Brake, Rheostatic or Regenerative
(v) Eddy current Brake.

In general, electrical braking is a supplementary braking and not an alternative to friction braking.

The electrical braking designs in practical use have to depend upon availability of electric power from the overhead system for excitation of the generator and their effectiveness reduces as the speed drops. Hence electrical braking is employed to supplement the friction braking on down gradients and bringing the train speed to around 10 kmph when employed to assist service braking.

ESSENTIAL REQUIREMENTS OF A GOOD BRAKING SYSTEM

A good braking system for a train must meet the following requirements:

(a) The brake system should be continuous over the train such that it is possible for the train guard to apply the brake from the rear in an emergency.
(b) *Every vehicle should*, as far as possible, *be braked* simultaneously to avoid bunching and coupler forces due to un-braked vehicles.
(c) In the event of a coupler failure resulting in parting of the train, *brakes should apply automatically* on both parts of the train.

(d) In the event of *complete failure of the motive power, it should be possible to apply brakes and bring* the train to a halt and park it indefinitely even on the steepest down gradient of the section.

(e) The *braking force should be limited to a value* that does not cause skidding, abnormal coupler forces or discomfort to the passengers in case of a passenger train.

The maximum rate of retardation permitted by British Rail is 1.2 m/sec or 4.3 kmph/sec.

IMPORTANT CHARACTERISTICS OF FRICTION BRAKING

The most predominant system of braking consists in pressing of a cast iron brake block shaped to the circular wheel profile on to the wheel tread. A typical arrangement of "double-acting" brake system is illustrated schematically in Fig. 6.1.

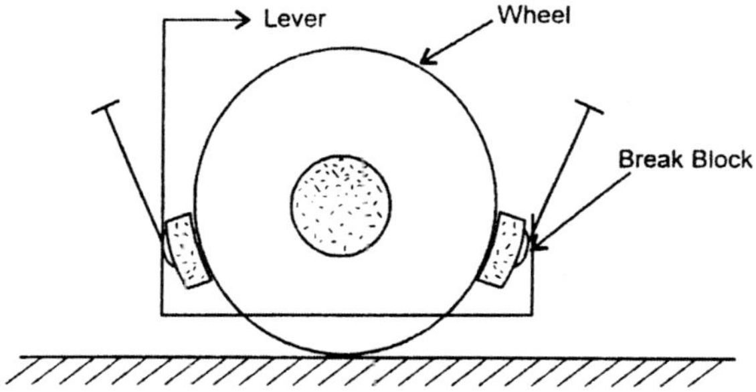

Fig. 6.1 Double acting brake system

Cast iron brake block, as originally conceived, has been most popular due to the following inherent advantages:

(i) Cast iron being much softer than the steel wheel wears itself rather than the wheel.

(ii) The heat generated during rubbing is absorbed both by the wheel and the brake block, which gives larger heat dissipation surface.

(iii) The brake block helps to preserve adhesion by cleaning the wheel surface during braking.

The characteristics of the frictional force available between the brake block and the wheel have been investigated by several research organisations connected with railways and can be broadly stated to be:

(a) The coefficient of friction μ between cast-iron brake block and steel wheel was found by Koffaman to conform to the following formula:

$$\mu = k\sqrt[3]{\frac{1}{v}}$$

where k is a constant, v = velocity/speed and p is the intensity of pressure.

(b) During extended application of braking pressure, Galton found that there is a tendency for the coefficient of friction to get reduced at constant speed due to softening of the brake-block material, which generates lubrication tendency (See Fig. 6.2).

(c) The coefficient of sliding friction between the wheel and the rail (with the wheel locked) at speeds above 20 kmph is of the order of 0.07, Figure 6.2 illustrates this point.

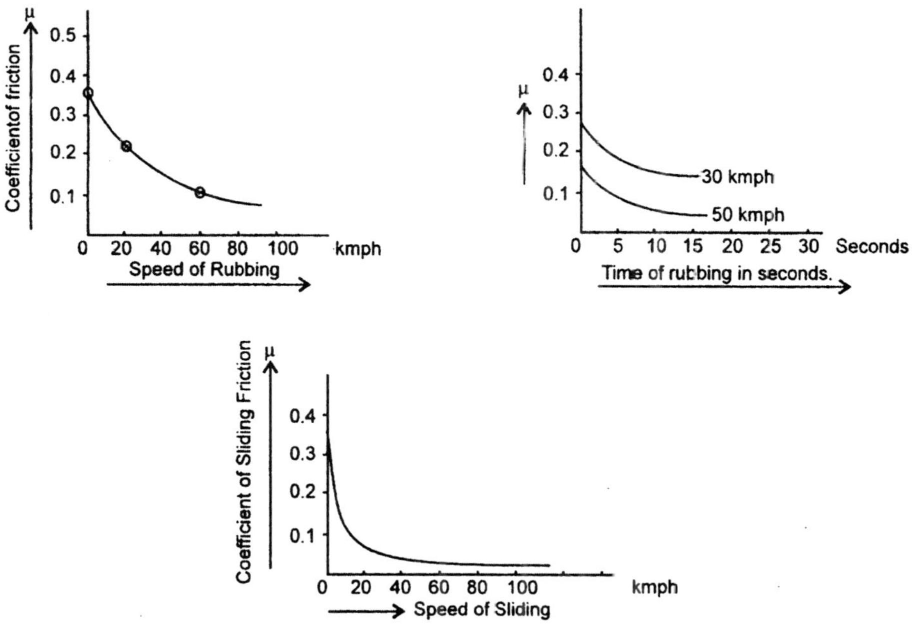

Fig. 6.2 Variations in coefficient of friction with speed and time of rubbing and speed of sliding

It may be appreciated that cast iron brake blocks though used predominantly hitherto have certain inherent weaknesses, viz.:

(a) They wear too fast calling for frequent renewals.

(b) The coefficient of friction is not stable and varies with pressure as well as duration of application.
(c) Brake block dust is produced which is metallic and may get deposited on insulating surfaces etc.

These difficulties get partly overcome through development of composite brake blocks which are made of a mixture of asbestos powder, metallic iron or iron oxide and mineral powders bonded together by resin. There are several compositions which can give any desired property, e.g. constant value of friction upto higher speeds, less tyre wear, non-metallic brake block dust etc.

Disc Brakes

In this arrangement, the braking process is delinked from the wheel tread where wear calls for re-profiling and change of tyres or wheel disc. A separate disc is mounted on the axle and brake pads are applied to this disc from both sides.

SYSTEMS FOR GENERATING BRAKING PRESSURE: VACUUM, AIR BRAKE (AUTOMATIC OR EM TYPE)

Vacuum Brake System

Vacuum brake system at one time was generally employed for freight as well as passenger trains except for Electric Motor Coaches and similar vehicles in which the space is limited. However, due to inherent limitations of this system, it is being eliminated to cater for increasing speeds and trailing loads.

The basic arrangement of a vacuum brake system is illustrated in the schematic diagram shown in Fig. 6.3.

The vacuum exhauster or ejector (in steam locomotives) creates a vacuum of the order of 50 to 55 cm (against 76 cm absolute vacuum level) in the train pipe and brake cylinders. A higher vacuum level than 55 cm is unstable and also undesirable for working of exhausters which require some airflow for cooling. Vacuum relief valve caters to this requirement and limits the maximum vacuum.

The brake cylinders located on individual braked vehicles have a piston which has a top chamber connected through a ball valve. The ball valve permits suction of air from the top chamber but seals it when air is admitted in the bottom chamber for pushing up the piston during brake application.

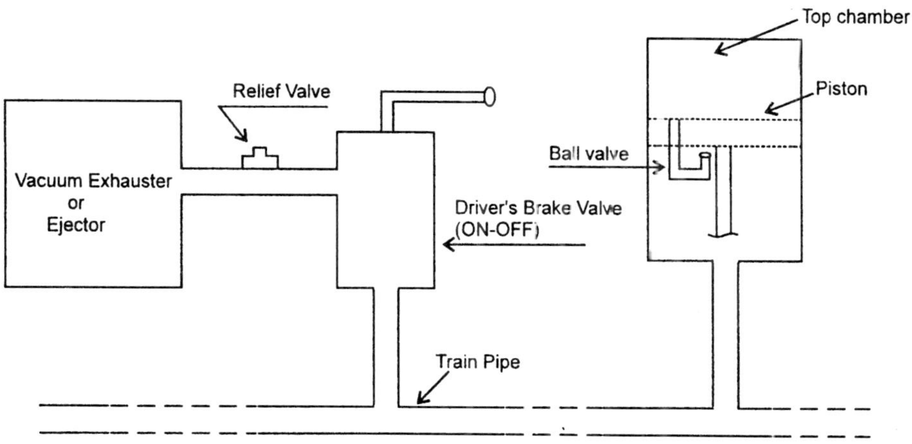

Fig. 6.3 General arrangement of vacuum brake system

The vacuum exhauster or ejector (in steam locomotives) creates a vacuum of the order of 50 to 55 cm (against 76 cm absolute vacuum level) in the train pipe and brake cylinders. A higher vacuum level than 55 cm is unstable and also undesirable for working of exhausters which require some airflow for cooling. Vacuum relief valve caters to this requirement and limits the maximum vacuum.

The brake cylinders located on individual braked vehicles have a piston which has a top chamber connected through a ball valve. The ball valve permits suction of air from the top chamber but seals it when air is admitted in the bottom chamber for pushing up the piston during brake application.

The maximum pressure available for braking is of the order of 2/3rd atmospheric pressure as compared to approximately 2.5 to 3 atmosphere in air brake system. Hence the vacuum cylinders are much larger for generating the same braking force.

Besides the rate of propagation of air from the motive power in the train pipe during brake application is around 65 m/sec in 50 mm dia. train pipe. This results in appreciable time lag between braking of vehicles close to the motive power and further away from it. This causes bunching and coupler forces.

The latter deficiency, however, is overcome in optimised systems through use of *Direct admission valves*, which are sensitive to slight drop of vacuum level in the train pipe and admit air directly into the brake cylinder when activated.

For quick release, two exhausters running at higher speed are provided.

In spite of all possible optimisation, the vacuum brake system has the in built weakness of a lower braking pressure which calls for heavier brake cylinder and brake rigging with greater leverage. Besides the storage of brake power is limited to brake cylinders and just suffices for one application in the event of failure of exhausters. Hence to cater for increasing burden on braking due to higher speeds and trailing loads, Air brake system became a pressing need and vacuum brake system is becoming obsolete.

Air Brake System (Automatic)

A schematic arrangement of automatic air brake system is illustrated in Fig. 6.4.

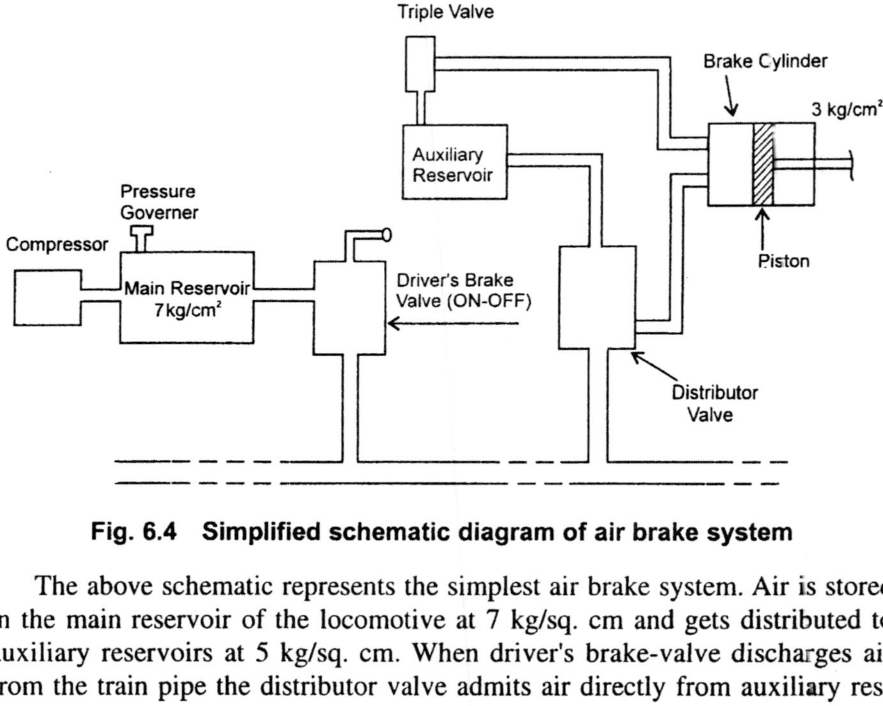

Fig. 6.4 Simplified schematic diagram of air brake system

The above schematic represents the simplest air brake system. Air is stored in the main reservoir of the locomotive at 7 kg/sq. cm and gets distributed to auxiliary reservoirs at 5 kg/sq. cm. When driver's brake-valve discharges air from the train pipe the distributor valve admits air directly from auxiliary reservoir.

A further sophistication consists in use of two train pipes one of which is called main reservoir pipe and the other one brake pipe. The former is used exclusively to charge the auxiliary reservoirs on individual vehicles from the main reservoir located on the motive power and the latter for relaying brake application. Destruction of the air pressure in the brake pipe by the drivers' brake valve actuates the triple valve fitted on individual vehicles which in turn connects the auxiliary reservoir to the brake cylinder which supplies the braking air pressure locally.

The reverse happens during release when the triple valve vents the brake cylinder while re-charging the auxiliary reservoir from the main reservoir.

During train partings, the brake pipe disconnection causes automatic brake application.

EP Brake System: In motor coach trains or similar systems where electrical power is available throughout the train it would be logical to apply the brakes electrically. This is catered by the Electropneumatic (EP) brake system in which magnet valves located on individual vehicles are actuated by the driver from the driving cab and admit air into the brake cylinders from the auxiliary reservoirs locally. The speed of brake application in this system is faster and so is the release.

Mechanical or Hand-operated Brake System

It is possible and necessary to operate a part of the available brake rigging by a hand wheel on every vehicle, locomotive and Guards brake van. Such a provision, apart from being useful in an emergency, is also required for parking any of the vehicles at a station or yard for long duration.

Independent Brake System for Locomotives

Since locomotives have to often work light, they must have an independent brake system of their own which can be actuated without going through the complete train braking system. Such a brake system is also required essentially to permit releasing of the train brakes on a gradient while still holding the train in stationary condition before taking starting notches after full release of the brake on the train and receiving starting signal. The independent locomotive brake system should be specially designed to cater for this requirement, viz. holding the heaviest hauled train on the steepest grade of the section. Usually the independent brake system of the motive power gets synchronised to the train brake application to avoid bunching action.

DYNAMIC BRAKING SYSTEMS

The term "dynamic braking" implies systems in which train momentum is converted into electrical energy and consumed either in braking resistance or returned to the power system. Thus there are two broad classifications of dynamic braking, viz.

(i) Rheostatic
(ii) Regenerative

Rheostatic Braking

The traction motor is made to function either as a self-excited generator or a separately excited one. The kinetic energy of the train thereby gets converted into electrical energy and is dissipated through a braking resistance; hence the name 'rheostatic braking'.

Self-excited System

To enable self-excitation to take place, the field connection is reversed with respect to the armature such that reverse flow of current through the armature circuit under influence of back EMF does not undo the excitation. The arrangement is illustrated schematically in Fig. 6.5.

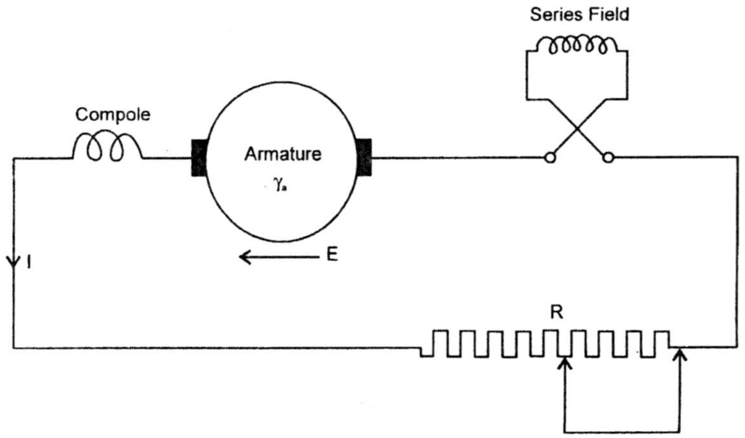

Fig. 6.5 Self-excited rheostatic braking of a series motor

If $(R + r_a)$ is not more than the critical resistance, the self-excitation will build up and get sustained. The current I which results in a dissipation of $I^2(R + r_a)$ power in the resistance, can be regulated by varying the resistance R. This will give rise to a braking torque. Assuming that I is kept near constant at the rating permitted as generator, the braking effort will depend on R. As the speed drops, the generated voltage comes down. Hence to derive maximum braking power, the resistance R would have to be reduced to maintain the current I at the rated value. Thus it can be seen that the braking effort gradually diminishes and the braking becomes ineffective below a certain speed.

Besides, in a self-excited system, the braking resistor is only partly used for most part of the braking cycle. This amounts to uneconomical use of the braking resistance.

Separate Excitation

An alternative arrangement could be to delink the field from the armature circuit and excite it separately. The whole of braking resistance can then be kept in armature circuit all the time and braking current controlled by varying field excitation. This arrangement is more commonly used as it gives better braking effort and enables full use of the braking resistor.

In 25 kV A.C. locomotives, the variable field excitation is provided by a separate transformer and rectifier bridge. The primary of this transformer. is fed from the secondary of main transformer, the voltage control being obtained through the tap changing mechanism used for traction.

Though separate excitation gives better results, the braking effort and speed range in which it is available is limited due to limiting value of braking current and limited possibility of increasing field excitation due to saturation. Hence rheostatic braking is best used either for controlling a train on long gradients or to assist service braking in the higher speed range for economising on brake block wear. On long descending grades, the rheostatic brakes can be designed to hold the train speed at the maximum permissible value at which the mechanical service brakes can bring it to a halt within the stipulated braking distance. This would give better average speed while descending the grade and save brake block as well as tyre wear.

Regenerative Braking

As the name implies, the electrical energy produced by the traction motors working as generator is returned to the overhead system whereby the train momentum gets converted to electrical power and regenerated.

For regenerative braking to take place there are two essential conditions viz.

(a) The generator voltage must be greater than the overhead voltage and
(b) The overhead system must be receptive to the regenerated power.

Before discussing the various aspects of electrical regenerative braking, it may be mentioned that there is a possible way of achieving regenerative braking mechanically. This can be done by grading the track such that the momentum gets converted into potential energy through a rising gradient before the stoppage and reconverted into kinetic energy through a falling grade after re-starting of the train. A typical layout could be as shown in Fig. 6.6.

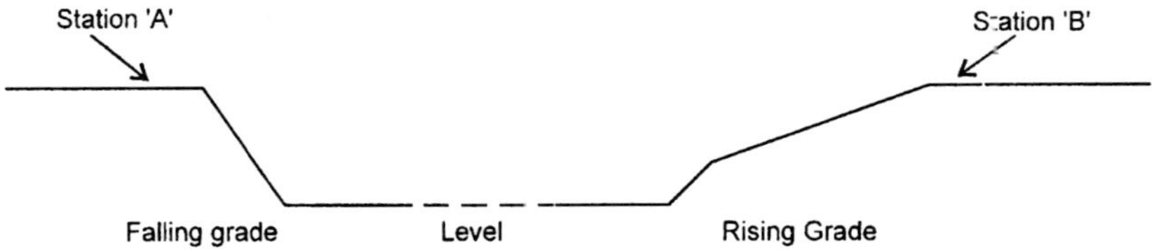

Fig. 6.6 Mechanical regenerative braking through grading of track

This form of regenerative grade was adopted by London tube Railway. However, the application of this system has limited practical application to sections where movement is unidirectional and stoppages of all trains have a fixed pattern.

For electrical regenerative braking, separate excitation of the traction motor while working as generator is a must. This alone can permit higher excitation to give a higher voltage than the overhead system voltage. Besides, the magnetic circuit of the motor must not get saturated, i.e. the magnetic circuit should be designed to work well below saturation level such that higher excitation becomes possible. This would mean heavier motor than otherwise without regenerative braking.

However, the energy saved through regenerative braking on long gradient sections is substantial and offers an overall economical operation.

Circuit Configuration for Stable Regenerative Braking

Since the overhead system voltage undergoes heavy fluctuations in a traction system, there is need for a circuit configuration which will not result in violent variation of regenerated current. The schematic circuit presented in Fig. 6.7 answers this requirement.

The regenerated current I_g and field current produced by the exciter; both flow through a common resistance. Should the overhead system voltage fall, I_g increases. This causes a higher current to flow through R_s. The drop across R_s increases which reduces the excitation current as the exciter voltage does not change. The reduced field strength controls the generator voltage such that I_g gets controlled.

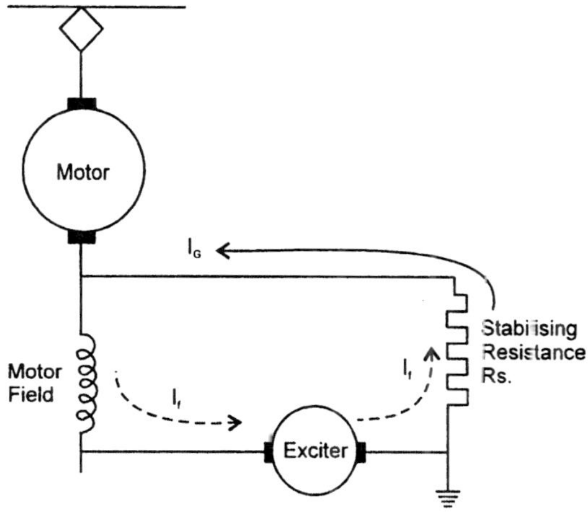

Fig. 6.7 Circuit configuration for stable regenerative braking

With electronic control, excitation current can be adjusted to suit the overhead system voltage by sensing the latter to actuate controls. This would give better control over braking current.

Receptivity of the Overhead System for Regenerated Power

The most serious issue in regenerative braking is receptivity of the regenerated power by the overhead system. As long as there is a net demand within the traction system, there is no problem. However where power has to be returned to the external grid supply system, the traction substation and grid substation system should to be capable of accepting the reverse flow of power.

In D.C. traction system, so long as rotary converter was used for AC-DC conversion, reverse flow of power was easily possible. In rectifier substations, however, reverse flow is not possible. In such systems, a resistance bank is usually provided at the substation which gets switched 'ON' electrically as soon as conditions for reverse flow of power into the grid system arise.

Regenerative Braking with 3-phase Induction Motor

This is the simplest system of regenerative braking with no additional apparatus or equipment being necessary. Since the induction motor operates as a generator when driven at a speed exceeding the synchronous speed, the switchover from motor action to generator action is automatic on a down grade with the tendency of the train to speed up. The system is, however, not self-exciting. In "VVVF" system, the synchronous frequency of the motor can be varied to create the required disparity with respect to the supply frequency which would permit braking even on level section and almost up to zero speed.

Eddy Current Braking

High-speed passenger trains handled by locomotives cannot have dynamic braking in the trailing stock. Where dynamic braking from the locomotive is not enough, it is possible to provide eddy current braking in the trailing stock to avoid extensive use for the friction brakes. Eddy current braking is provided by mounting an ECB DISC on the axle and providing pole shoes on either side as per the schematic arrangement shown in Fig. 6.8.

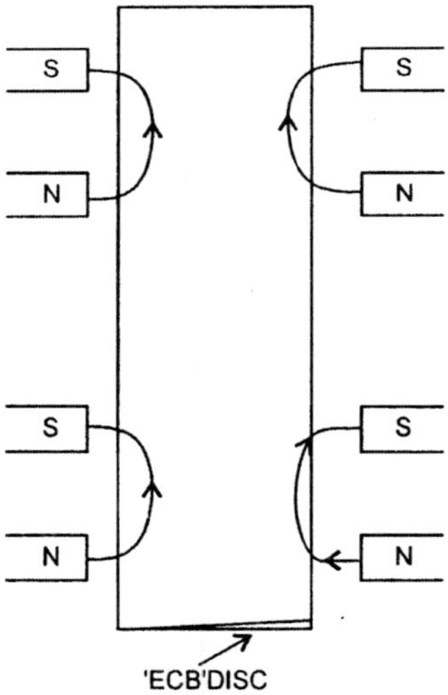

Fig. 6.8 Schematic arrangement of eddy-current braking

It is possible to obtain sufficient braking force by this means to bring down the train speed to around 70 kmph.

CONCLUSION

From the foregoing deliberations it may be appreciated that with D.C. series traction motor dynamic braking is not a primary or exclusive braking system but can be suitably blended with air brakes to reduce the burden of friction braking in high speed ranges as well as on long graded sections. This helps to reduce brake block as well as tyre wear and offers considerable economy in terms of wear and tear and energy saving in case of regenerative braking to justify the cost of additional gear employed. However in three-phase induction motor drives, regenerative braking can be used up to near-zero speed.

CHAPTER 7

Electric Traction Sub-systems: Overhead Equipment

INTRODUCTION

To get an integrated view of electric traction, it is necessary to develop acquaintance with different sub-systems, which with suitable coordination yield electric traction as an end product.

The chart shown in Fig. 7.1 brings out the typical sub-systems in a broad classification signalling, though somewhat different, has a very important bearing

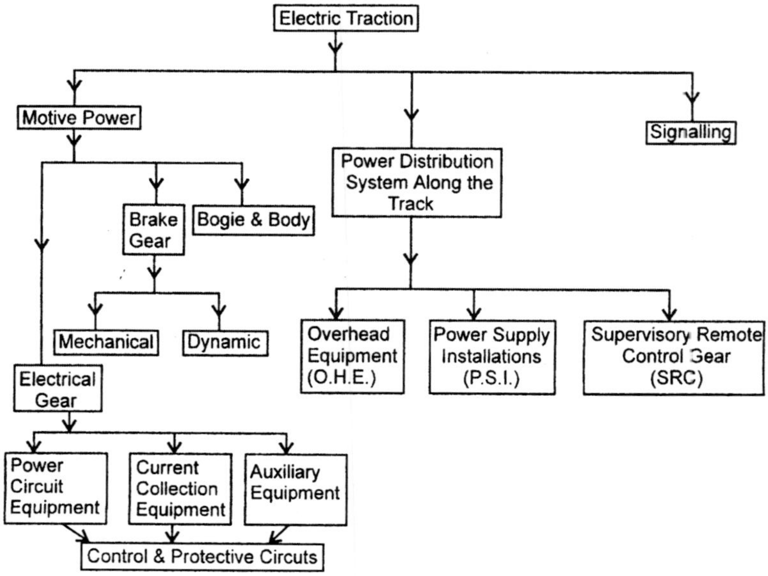

Fig. 7.1 Electric traction sub-systems

on the traction mechanics. Besides, electric traction helps to modernise signalling system to match its own potential. Hence it is a key sub-system. A closer look at each of these sub-systems will enable an integrated view of electric traction.

The electrical gear of the *motive-power* is arranged *in different circuits*, which are broadly classified as *power, auxiliary* and *control circuits*. The current collection is done by a *pantograph* from the overhead equipment laid along the track and is fed to the power circuit. In the case of a 25 kV A.C. locomotive the power is fed to an autotransformer which is mounted on the locomotive and is fitted with a *tap changing* system for voltage control. The output of the autotransformer is fed to the *traction transformer* with a fixed transformation ratio. The output of this transformer is fed to rectifiers for converting A.C. to D.C., which, in turn, is fed to the *traction motors* after passing through a *smoothing reactor*.

For performing *auxiliary functions* such as cooling transformers, traction motors and other power equipment, generating compressed air for locomotive braking and catering to Electro-pneumatic control equipment, creating vacuum for the train brakes etc., a number of auxiliary motors are required which are usually worked at *380 V-3 phase*. The 380 V-3 phase power is obtained through an auxiliary winding magnetically coupled to the main autotransformer and using a *phase converter* for single phase to 3-phase conversion.

Yet another auxiliary winding gives a 110-V supply which, after rectification, charges a battery supplying the control circuits.

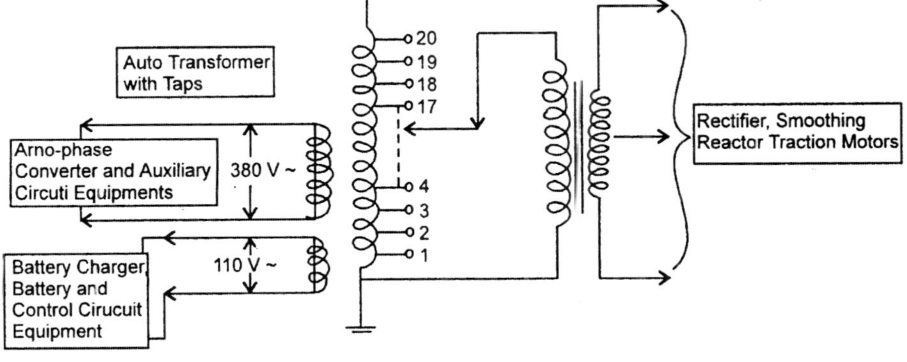

Fig. 7.2 Motive power sub-circuits

An integrated view of these sub-systems can be had from the simplified schematic diagram in Fig. 7.2. The photograph reproduced in Fig. 7.3 illustrates a typical locomotive built by the Chittaranjan Locomotive Works (CLW) for Indian Railways.

Co-Co TYPE WAG-5 CLASS ELECTRIC LOCOMOTIVE

First locomotive of this types was built by CLW to the design of RDSO in 1980. This class of locomotives is currently under series production in CLW and BHEL.

The locomotive is powered by six axle-hungs, nose suspended, ventilated TAO-659 (CLW) or HS-1050/10250 (Hitachi) dc traction motors. Speed control is achieved by connecting the motors in parallel combination. Field weakening of motors was provided in subsequent series of manufacture at CLW.

These locomotives utilise silicon rectifier for conversion of ac power into dc.

This can be used for a multiple operation to a maximum of four locomotives. Compressed air brakes for the locomotive and dual brake for the trains are provided. In addition, these locomotives are provided with rheostatic braking.

Main Data

Type of traction		25 kV ac
Guage		1676 mm
Driving wheel diameter (New)		1092 mm
Bogie wheel base		3810 mm
Total wheel base		15984 mm
Length over couplers		19974 mm
Maximum width		3055 mm
Height with pantograph down		4162 mm
Axle load max.		19.8 t
Weight total		118.8 t
Adhesion in dry condition		33.5%
Maximum T.E.		33.5 t
Continuous T.E.		20.6 t
Continuous speed		50.5 km/h
Horse power		3850 HP
Maximum speed		80 km/h
Continuous transformer rating		3900 kVA
Traction motor continuous rating	Voltage	750 V
	Current	840 A
	Output	585 kW
Auxiliary machines		50 Hz, 3 phase
Gear Ratio		3.61/4.53

Fig. 7.3 A view of a typical electric locomotive built by the Chittaranjan Locomotive Works with its salient specifications

OVERHEAD EQUIPMENT (OHE)

The overhead equipment laid along the track is *the most distinctive and visible feature of electric traction.* This along with the power supply system has to be installed as a pre-requisite before electric traction can take place. This is a capitalintensive exercise and involves an investment of the order of rupees 10 to 15 lakhs per kilometer track at the present-day cost level. Its maintenance and up keep is additional, which distinguishes electric traction from diesel-electric traction placing the former at a disadvantage in financial evaluation. We will have a closer look at the overhead equipment and its distinctive engineering features.

Current collection from third rail, though often used in metro underground systems has its limitations both from the point of view of insulation as well as quality of current collection. Theoretically and experimentally, current collection from an elastic conductor system is best. Hence current collection for most electric traction systems is from an overhead trolley wire.

The simplest form of overhead trolley-wire system would consist of a single solid wire. However, such a system suffers from the problem of sag. Although sometimes employed from the point of view of cost economy, this system calls for more frequent supports and limits the speed to about 30 kmph due to inevitable sag where the pantograph is likely to loose contact at higher speeds. Such a system is usually called Tramway-type overhead system and is used for tramways and yards/sidings in case of main-line traction where speeds are restricted.

The type of overhead conductor system employed for 25 kV traction consists of a stranded catenary from which the trolley-wire or contact-wire is suspended by means of droppers. A typical layout and its main components are illustrated in the sketch shown in Fig. 7.4 . This schematic sketch does not show insulators for the sake of simplicity.

Although the catenary wire has a sag, droppers ensure that the solid contact wire is almost horizontal with respect to the track.

The usual parameters adopted for the 25KV OHE in Indian Railways are as follows.

(i)	Span	:	72 m on straight track
(ii)	Ht. of contact wire above rail level	:	5.5 m
(iii)	Encumbrance at support	:	1.4 m
(iv)	Spacing of droppers	:	9 m
	Cross-section	:	5 sq. mm
(v)	Current density	:	4 A/mm
(vi)	Cross-section of contact-wire	:	107sq. mm

(vii)	Cross-section of catenary wire (Cd-Cu) having 9 strands	: $65 \times 0.8 = 52$ sq. mm
(viii)	Rating of OHE system	: 600 A with 50% overload for 3 min

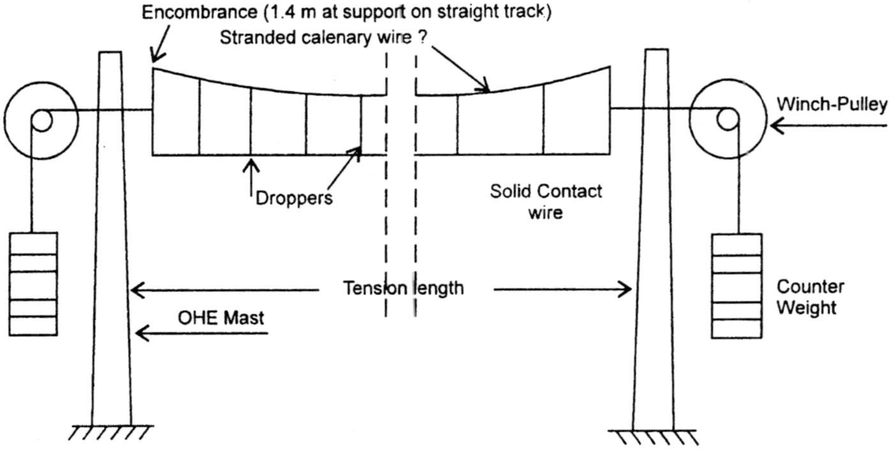

Fig. 7.4 Schematic layout of overhead equipment

The supporting arrangement at a typical mast is illustrated in Figs. 7.5 (a) and (b).

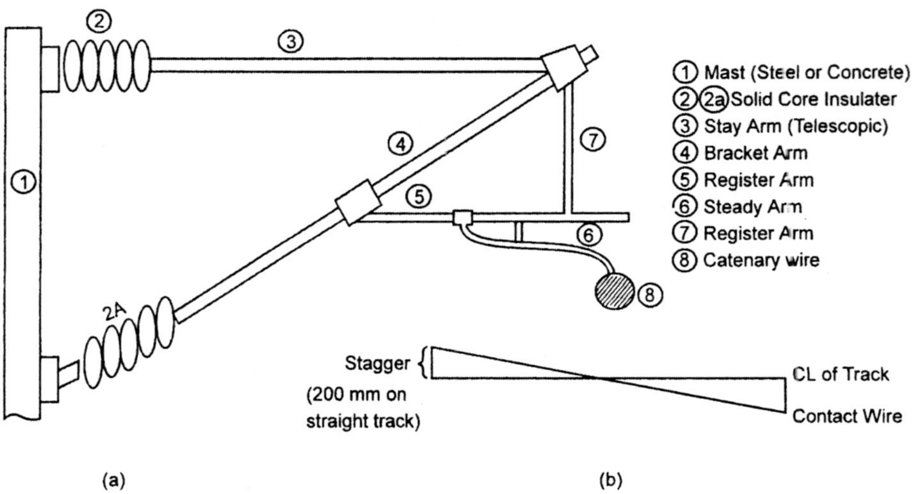

Fig. 7.5 Supporting arrangement at a typical mast and staggers

The suspension arrangement illustrated schematically is capable of horizontal swiveling about the supporting mast; a feature essentially required for auto tensioning of the system.

Stagger of Contact Wire: If the contact wire is kept absolutely centrally between two rails of the track, it will cut a groove in the current collecting strips of the pantograph. Hence a stagger is provided. Maximum stagger of contact wire at support with respect to centre line of the track is 200 mm.

Gradient of Contact Wire: Changes in the height of contact wire would become necessary when passing an over bridge or a level crossing. The rate of change or slope has to be limited to 4 mm/m for permissible speeds up to 100 kmph and 3 mm/m for speeds above 100 kmph.

Automatic Tensioning Device for Regulation of OHE against Sag: Temperature variations due to seasonal effect would cause expansion or contraction of the OHE. Hence it is necessary to provide some arrangement to regulate the sag or hog. This is done by a tensioning weight as per schematic arrangement illustrated in Figs. 7.6 (a) and (b) and the photograph in Fig. 7.7.

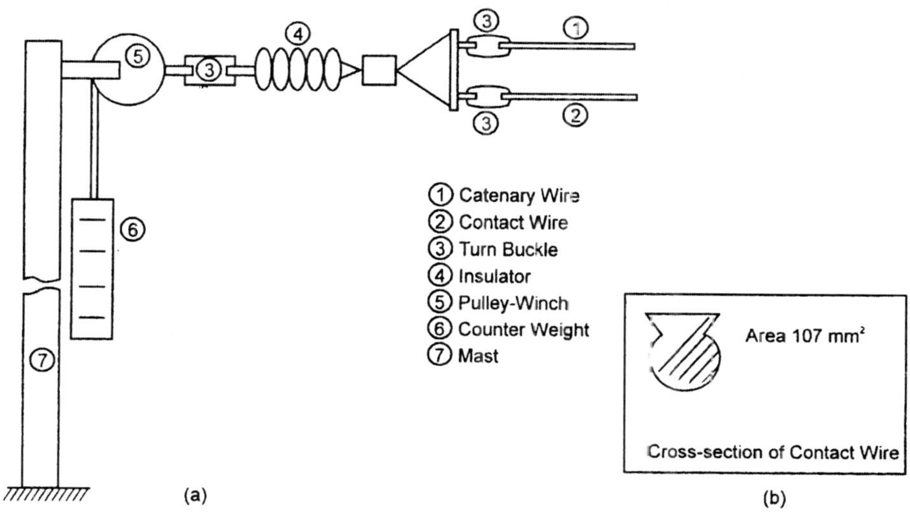

Fig. 7.6 Schematic of the tensioning arrangement (a) and cross-section of the contact wire (b)

Usually a tension of 1000 kg is provided in each, i.e. contact wire and catenary. Hence to produce a pull of 2000 kg with a mechanical advantage of 5 generated by the winch, the counterweight has to be 400 kg or 2×200 kg.

Fig. 7.7 Winch type-regulating equipment

A tension length is usually 1.5 km. The midpoint of the tension length is fixed by an anti-creep arrangement to avoid dragging of OHE system to one side due to a running train.

SECTIONALISING

The OHE has to be sectionalised into smaller elementary sections to permit isolation for maintenance. For this purpose a tension length of 1.5 km is made an elementary section which is electrically bridged by a manually operated isolator switch.

Insulated overlaps are installed between elementary sections at sub-sectioning posts.

These overlaps are bridged by remote controlled interrupters and are intended to help trouble shooting and maintenance. Insulated overlaps are also provided opposite feeding posts.

Between two adjacent feed zones, neutral sections are provided where no power is available. Usually the neutral section spreads over 3 OHE spans and is negotiated by switching-off Locomotive circuit breaker. Recently PTFE neutral sections have got developed which are much smaller and compact and reduce power-OFF duration as shown in Fig. 7.8 . Yet another development is a *Dynamic Neutral*

Section which avoids tripping of the locomotive circuit breaker and eliminates power-OFF duration by switching the neutral section to out going and incoming phases one after the other during passage of a train taking advantage of the fact that the locomotive circuit breaker trips through no-volt sensing relay with a time lag of 0.5 sec. or more.

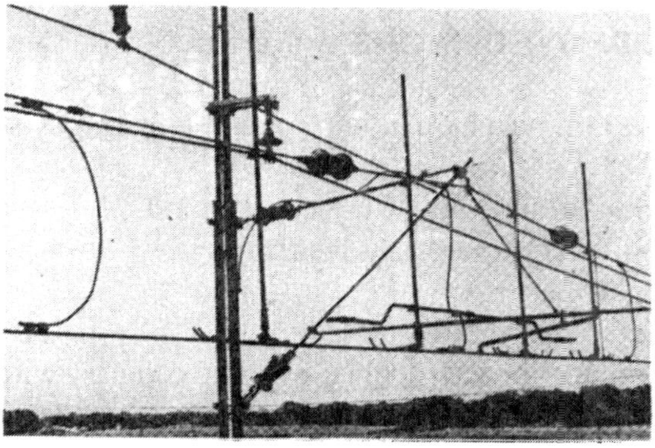

Fig. 7.8 Short neutral section with synthetic resin-bonded glass-fibre contact wire insulator (composite insulator)

BONDING OF RAILS AND MASTS

In D.C. traction systems, practically the entire return current flows through the rail due to location of feed points at close intervals. Hence bonding of rails at the fish-plate joints is essential. In 25 kV A.C. traction system, however, the return current mostly flows through the earth leaving the traction rail except for small zone extending few hundred meter on either side of the electric locomotive and a similar zone in vicinity of the feeding point. Hence bonding of rails is not essential over the entire length; bonding in the vicinity of feeding posts would suffice to spread out flow of return current to earth and onwards to the earthed leg of traction transformer. Since the locomotive is a moving object, the return current which is much smaller than that for D.C. traction gets dispersed to earth after flowing through the rails over a small zone on either side.

All non-current carrying metallic parts of traction masts and track side structures including metallic parts of concrete or wooden masts are connected to the nearest traction rail of a wired track by structure bonds to avoid possibility of their assuming unsafe voltage level.

In this context it may be mentioned that the traction rail of a wired track especially when laid on metallic sleepers provides a reasonably good earth.

In track circuited areas, rails are bonded over the entire track-circuited length with a view to ensure that the A.C. voltage drop due to return currents is within the immunisation level of the D.C. track relay. The bonding also helps to reduce the resistance of the path for D.C. signalling currents than available from rail circuit with fish-plate joints.

MATERIALS EMPLOYED IN OHE

(i) Contact wire: Grooved hard drawn copper with a cross-section as shown in Fig. 7.6 (b).
(ii) Catenary-wire: Stranded Cd-Cu wire (9 strands).
(iii) Insulators: Solid core-porcelain insulators
(iv) Counterweight: Cast iron
(v) Droppers: Solid copper wire
(vi) Mid-span jumpers between contact wire and catenary wire at alternate spans to ensure that the two work as one conductor: Stranded copper wire.
(vii) Mast: Steel, rolled section or fabricated. Sometimes concrete masts are used for economy.
(viii) Wire rope of tension regulating equipment: Stainless Steel (stranded)
(ix) Components of bracket assembly; Tubular steel.

To ensure economical and maintenance-free OHE design, the salient recent trends are:

(a) Use of spun concrete mast in place of rolled or fabricated steel.
(b) Use of alloyed aluminium conductor.
(c) Use of contact wire of higher cross-section, say 150 sq. mm, to enable indefinite life and reduce frequency of renewals. This works out cheaper on life-cycle basis.
(d) Use of concrete counterweights as a measure of cost reduction and to avoid theft proneness.
(e) Use of longer creepage distance insulators, which would not need cleaning between rainy season cycles especially in localities where dust deposits are likely to vitiate creepage distance.
(f) Use of 'fit and forget' type fittings which do not loosen under vibration.
(g) Staggering place of stoppage of locomotives and EMU's through use of stop-boards wherever possible.

CHAPTER 8

Power Supply Arrangement Including Remote Control and Tariff

POWER SUPPLY ARRANGEMENT FOR 25 KV TRACTION SYSTEM

The 25 kV A.C. 50 Hz power for electric traction is derived from the grid system of State Electricity Boards through traction substations (TSS) located along the route of the electrified section at a spacing of the order of 50-80 km. The exact distance between adjacent traction substations is governed by voltage drop at the farthest point which, in turn, is a function of traffic density, gradient, train loads and speeds.

The arrangement at a typical traction substation is illustrated schematically in Fig. 8.1.

UNBALANCE ON THE GRID SYSTEM

The generation and transmission system of supply authority (i.e. grid) is 3-phase whereas the power drawn at any TSS is single phase. This causes unbalance in the supply system and is not desirable. The negative sequence current component produces reverse rotating fields in the generators, which induce heavy currents in the damper windings. Besides voltage unbalance in a system causes unbalance of current all along.

Hence most supply authorities lay down the limits of unbalance. Typical unbalance figures are as under:

Duration	*% Voltage unbalance*
Instantaneous	5
2-hr.	3
Continuous	2

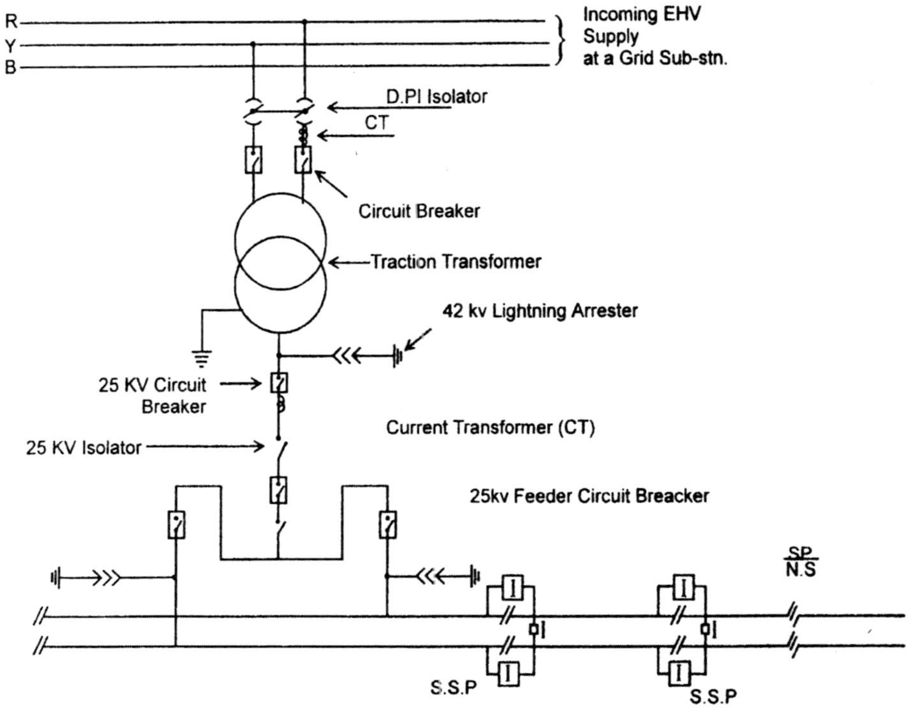

Fig. 8.1 Schematic arrangement at a typical traction sub-station

To keep the unbalance on the grid system within the above limits, power for A.C. single-phase traction is tapped off the grid across different phases at adjacent substations in cyclic order. This would necessitate separation of adjacent feed zones electrically at the junction point through a "neutral section". The "neutral section", as the name implies, is a "Zone of No Power" to enable transition from one phase to another.

Scott Connected Transformers

Where use of all the three phases from the same grid is not possible, use of SCOTT connected transformers for three-phase to two-phase conversion may become necessary to contain the system unbalance in the grid within acceptable limits.

Since the two output phases on the secondary side have 90° phase separation, a neutral section opposite the feeding post also becomes necessary. A schematic diagram of this supply arrangement is presented in Fig. 8.2 (a).

In a Scott connected system of feeding, two single-phase transformers B and H called "the Base" and "Height" elements respectively and having similar secondary windings but primary windings with turn ratio $\sqrt{3}/2:1$ are used as shown in Fig. 8.2 (b).

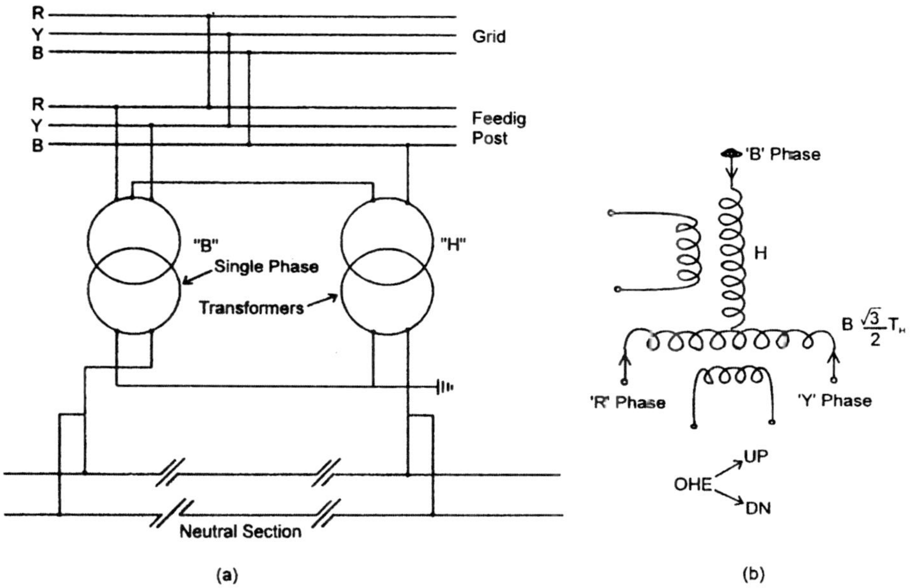

Fig. 8.2 Schematic diagram of Scott connected transformer feeding post

It will be seen that on the primary side all the three phases of the gird are required. In order to enable the use of identical single phase transformers to permit interchangeability the primary winding is given a tapping which permits its use either as "base" or "height" element.

Since there is a 90° phase displacement on the secondary side (LV side) two separate bus bar systems with a neutral section in front of the feeding point are provided. This neutral section is in addition to the one between two adjacent feedpoints.

SPACING OF SUBSTATIONS

The spacing is basically governed by voltage drop considerations. It is therefore necessary to predetermine the voltage drop in the catenary system for a given pattern of traffic.

In 25 kV traction system at industrial frequency, the voltages permitted are:

Nominal 25 kV
Maximum: Opposite feeding points 27.5 kV
Minimum: At the neutral section: 19 kV
Minimum instantaneous: 17.5 kV

In Indian Railways the catenary system consists of:

Cadmium-Cu catenary: 65 mm^2 cross-section and hard drawn copper contact wire of 107 mm^2 cross-section

In stretches where booster transformer and return conductor are not used, the measured values of impedance are:

Single trackoverhead equipment: 0.41 $\angle 70^\circ$ ohm/km
Double track overhead equipment: 0.24 $\angle 70^\circ$ ohm/km

where 70° represents phase angle of the impedance.

The impedance also depends upon soil conductivity. To ensure minimum impedance, the catenary, of adjacent up and down tracks are paralleled at all the switching-stations.

Apart from voltage drop in the catenary, there is also internal voltage drop at the traction transformer, which is not insignificant and increases with a poor power factor of the load.

When booster transformers are used to neutralise effect on communication circuits the return current is made to flow through a return conductor mounted on the same poles close to the catenary system. Very little current then passes through the Earth. In this system, the OHE impedance becomes higher by almost 50% and this increases the voltage drop. A schematic diagram showing booster transformers is given in Fig. 8.3.

2 × 25 kV System of Power Distribution

The problem of voltage drop as well as electromagnetic interference gets overcome in one stroke through adoption of 2 × 25 kV system of power distribution. This enables hauling of heavier loads at higher speeds without reducing sub-station spacing. The principle adopted is illustrated by the schematic diagram in

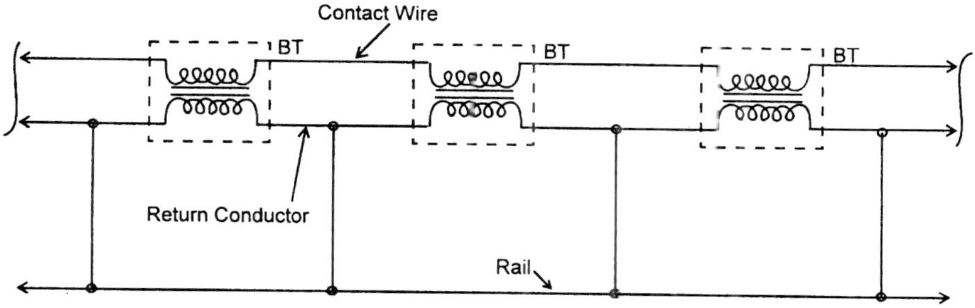

Fig. 8.3 Schematic diagram of return conductor and booster transformer

Fig. 8.4. For running train loads of 5000 t on graded sections with traffic density approaching saturation, 2 × 25 kV system traction becomes inescapable if substation spacing has to be 50 km or more.

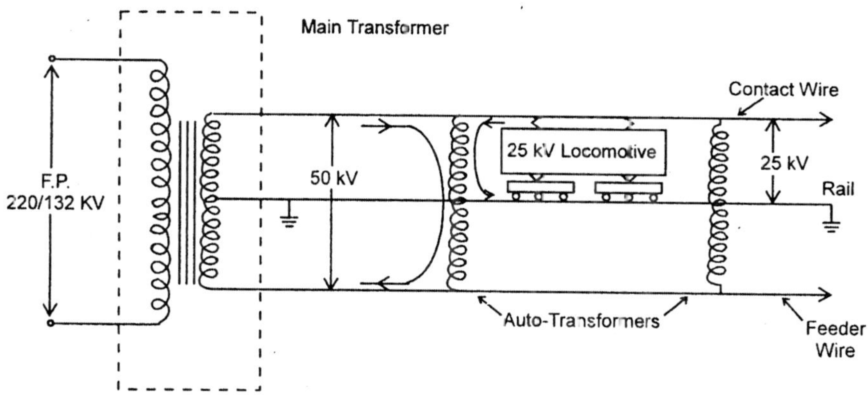

Fig. 8.4 2 × 25 kV system of power distribution

STRATEGY TO REDUCE VOLTAGE DROP BY IMPROVING POWER FACTOR

Equipment like induction motor, power transformers, thyristors etc. have low power factor. Besides electric locos have a poor load factor due to the terrain, which could be of the order of 50%. These result in a poor power factor of the order of 70 to 75%.

Apart from causing higher kVA loading, power factor attracts penalty tariff from some electricity boards, which lay down a minimum power factor clause of 85%.

Both from the point of view of tariff and transmission efficiency (i.e. voltage drop, IR loss etc.) it is economical to think of reactive power compensation. This can be done either by using a shunt capacitor or a series capacitor.

In traction application use of shunt capacitors has been found to be more beneficial. The capacitor bank is usually located at the feeding post from practical considerations. The design of the capacitor bank must ensure that it does not cause voltage surges whenever there is sudden drop in system voltage.

PROTECTION OF TRACTION POWER SUPPLY SYSTEM

The single-phase traction power supply system differs from the usual three-phase power system in some respects, which necessitates a different protection strategy. In three-phase system, earth fault in individual phases can be detected through the flow of zero phase sequence current and three phase short circuit through flow of large currents. On the other hand a single-phase traction system has one terminal earthed. Hence the protection system must discriminate between earth fault current and load current. Besides, earth faults at farthest end of a feed zone may not give enough current to be detected as short circuit.

The traction transformer is protected for:

(a) Overcurrent
(b) Differential protection for earth fault in transformer windings: The differential protection relay is made insensitive to magnetising current in-rush during switching as it does not reflect on secondary side. Luckily such in-rush has a short duration of the order of 10 to 15 μ sec.
(c) Buchholz protection to detect formation of gas in the transformer tank.

For the catenary system the most common faults are:

(a) Earth fault
(b) Overloads
(c) Faults due to incorrect switching
(d) Low voltage protection

Distance-relay Protection: For earth-fault, distance-relay protection is adopted as faults occurring away from the feeding post may not cause sufficient overload in the system to get detected by the overload relay.

Distance-relay protection, being sensitive to power swings and transient currents, calls for special measures to avoid fictitious trippings.

Basically, distance relay or impedance relay is an impedance ohm-meter. Over-type impedance relays operate when the fictitious impedance seen at their terminals exceeds the impedance setting. The under-type impedance relays operate when the impedance seen at their terminal drops below the impedance setting.

Distance relays may be built on electromagnetic or induction principle for their operation. In both types, the torques created by current and voltage coils are mechanically compared. The voltage torque acts as a restraining torque (T_r) and the current torque is the operating torque (T_0). when a fault appears in the protected zone, the current rises and the voltage at the relay location drops. The relay operates when $T_0 > T_r$ or $K_1 I > K_2$ or $V/I < K_1/K_2$. V/I represents the impedance seen at the relay terminal.

The characteristic of a non-directional distance relay with regard to zone of protection may be represented by circle on a complex quantity plane as shown in Fig. 8.5(a).

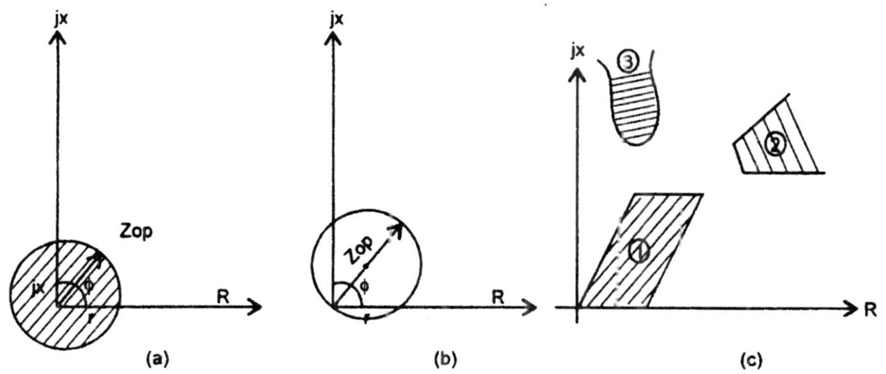

Fig. 8.5 Distance relay characteristics and zone of protection

It is evident that the impedance of operation is not dependent on the phase angle ϕ.

Directional feature can be in built in the operating characteristic by combining voltage and current of the circuit in the operating coil. This makes the operating torque a function of voltage, current and phase angle between voltage and current. The operating characteristic is then a circle passing through the origin as shown in Fig. 8.5 (b). This is a more practical version with better discrimination and is generally used. Short-time transients such as due to transformer charging current in a traction system can be dealt with through use of sufficient time lag in the operation of the relay. An inbuilt time lag of about 100 m.sec (0.1 sec) would suffice as the transient current decays very fast. Although oscillographs of typical in rush currents indicate values as high as 25 times load current at 0.01 sec point, the current falls to approximately 12 times at 0.1 sec. point, indicating sharp decay pattern. An alternative technical solution could be use of distance relays with parallelogram characteristic. Static semiconductor type relays can generate such a characteristic zone, which excludes load current and transformer in-rush current zones, viz. zones 2 and 3 (see Fig 8.5 (c)).

The overcurrent relay is of instantaneous type and its setting caters for permissible overloads of a traction system. The setting of overload relay is 200% or more and operating time 10 msec.

Apart from above, whenever the feed of adjoining zones is extended up to a failed feeding-point (FP), drivers are expected to lower their pantographs while passing the failed FP. Should they not do this either due to an omission or system failure, phase coupling takes place which calls for a "wrong-phase-coupling" relay.

When feed is extended to cover the entire zone of a failed FP, there is a possibility of voltage at the neutral section falling below 17.5 kV which may be injurious for working locomotive auxiliary machines especially compressors. This calls for a "low-voltage" relay to detect this abnormality and terminate the feed extension arrangement for the entire zone.

Lightning protection: An efficient lightning protection which clears a lightning surge without its resulting in an earth fault detectable by the distance relay is key to a reliable traction power supply system. It follows that open spark gap lightning protection should be meticulously avoided and gapless lightning arrestors adopted in lieu. Positioning of lightning-arrestors at a feeding-post may be seen in Fig. 8.1.

REMOTE CONTROL CONCEPT: SIGNIFICANCE OF AUTO RECLOSING FEATURE

To permit monitoring of the power supply system, remote control centres are established from where the circuit breakers and interrupters located at the feeding/sectioning/sub-sectioning posts can be remote controlled to enable isolation of a faulty section or restore power in the event of a transient tripping.

Since quite a few faulty conditions are transient in nature, an auto-reclosing feature is a good idea and results in lessening the overall duration of no-power condition. This feature consists in reclosing of the circuit breaker after 0.5 sec. of its tripping and further tripping subsequent to reclosing resulting in locking of the circuit.

Modern SCADA Systems

Modern Supervisory Control and Data acquisition (SCADA) systems are based on minicomputers or microprocessors.

Earlier, remote control systems were based on selectors and electromagnetic relays. They had limited data acquisition capability and called for spacious remote control centre, which had to be air-conditioned to achieve required degree of reliability. In sharp contrast, state-of-the-art remote control centres based on mini-computer or microprocessor which provide artificial intelligence and eliminate the need for electromechanical equipment. This makes for compactness in respect of space requirement and calls for less frequent maintenance, which is mostly replacement of failed modules.

System Configuration

Computer/Microprocessor-based SCADA systems consists of master-station equipment at the remote control centre (RCC) which with suitable communication channels interact with remote terminal units (RTUs) located at controlled stations viz. traction substations, feedings posts, sectioning and subsectioning posts. The block diagram presented in Fig. 8.6 illustrates various sub-systems of a typical modern SCADA system.

The master-station consists of microcomputers with man-machine interface to provide uptodate network data, data-processing, data-storing mechanisms etc. The system is provided with main and standby computer, operator workstations, front-end processor modems, printers, uninterrupted power supply (UPS), surge arrestors etc. The front-end processor, receives commands from the computer and after conditioning transmits the same through communication sub-system to RTU and also receives data from the controlled devices.

Workstations for operators have color VDU's, keyboards, mice etc.

The RTU's at controlled stations are microprocessor-based sub-system. Transducers are used to convert measurands (e.g. voltage, current) from P.T.'s and C.T.'s to low-level analog signals, which get subsequently digitised for transmission to master station.

RTU receives commands from master station and transmits data back through modem and communication subsystem.

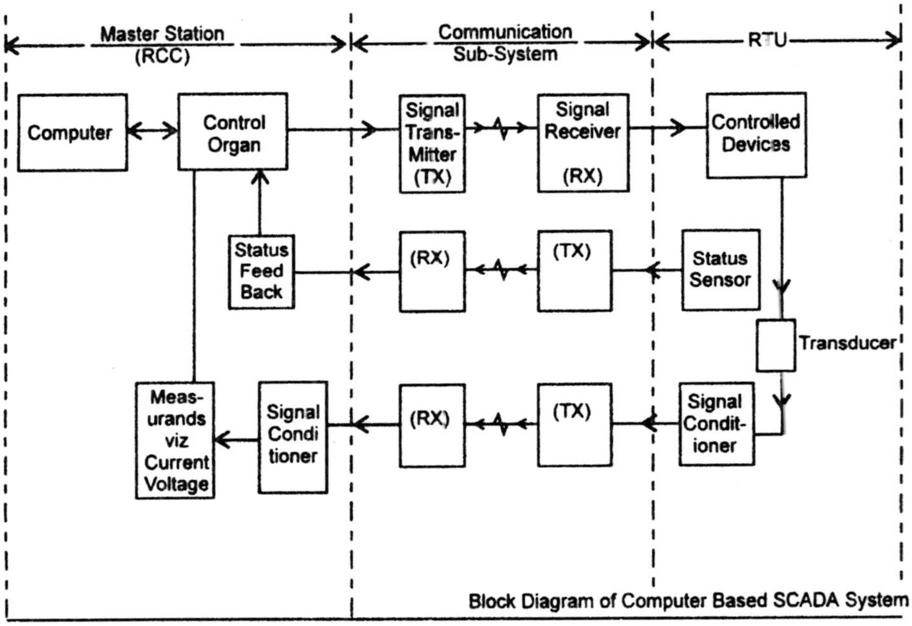

Fig. 8.6 Block diagram of computer-based SCADA system

The communication subsystem may consist of ordinary telephone cables, optical fibre cables or radio channel; time division multiplexing (TDM) or frequency division multiplexing techniques are employed to multiply transmission capability of each channel. Audio-frequency transmission is employed and repeaters at intervals of approximately 50 km with a gain of 20 dB boost signal level. The master station continuously scans all RTU's in a predetermined cyclic sequence to update-status of equipment and measurands. Whenever the operator sends a command, cyclic scanning is interrupted till the command gets executed.

Computer/Microprocessor Based SCADA Systems

These are a powerful tool for controlling traction power. However, the following points must be kept in view while designing new systems or changing over from now obsolete electromechanical systems:

(i) Radio transmission of signals is not a very reliable alternative for traction power control as these signals have a tendency to fade during heavy rains or fog when the need for remote control is often most pressing.

(ii) The average time taken for isolation of faults must be kept within 3 min. by suitable design of software and control strategy

(iii) Rate of obsolescence of electronic equipment is fast and would call for planning of lifetime spares and key repair techniques.

(iv) The plus points of modern SCADA systems, viz. reduced space at RCC and small work-force for operation and maintenance should be fully exploited to make them financially attractive.

A typical centralised supervisory remote control system is illustrated in Fig. 8.7.

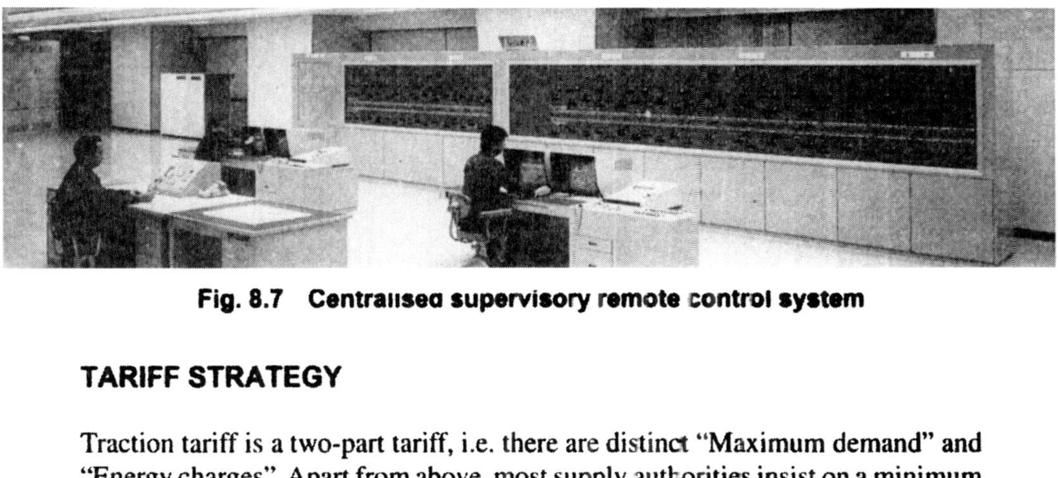

Fig. 8.7 Centralised supervisory remote control system

TARIFF STRATEGY

Traction tariff is a two-part tariff, i.e. there are distinct "Maximum demand" and "Energy charges". Apart from above, most supply authorities insist on a minimum power factor (P.F.) clause which is of the order of 0.85 and minimum energy consumption clause which is based on a load factor of 30% and P.F. of 0.85.

It follows that there is need for close monitoring and control of maximum demand (M.D.). This can be made possible by controlling some trains in the event of bunching in the system and would call for close coordination between the traffic and traction power controller.

It is also desirable to ensure that there is no mixed traction on electrified routes which give rise to the actual energy consumption falling below the minimum consumption clause which is a function of M.D., P.F. and load factor.

It is a good strategy to take bulk power from the grid at a few points and distribute it to different feeding points through Railways over transmission system to achieve better load factor and reduced maximum demand.

CHAPTER 9

Current Collection Gear, Power and Auxiliary Equipment (Excluding Traction Motors)

CURRENT COLLECTION GEAR

During early days of electric traction, the supply of electric power to the moving vehicle was arranged through a conductor rail (called 3rd rail) laid on insulators parallel to the track at a distance of 0.3 to 0.4 m. The schematic arrangement is given in Fig. 9.1.

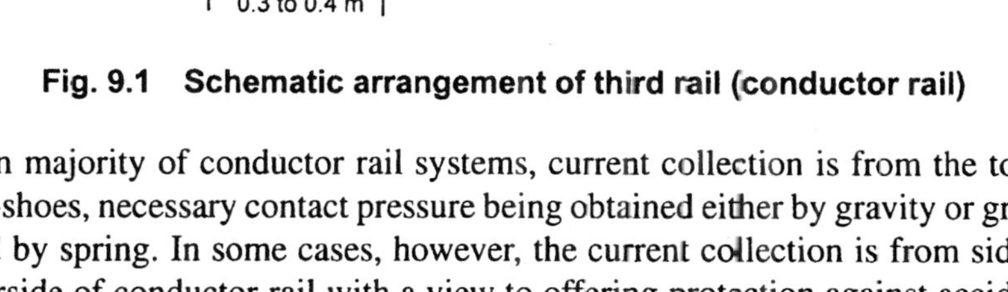

Fig. 9.1 Schematic arrangement of third rail (conductor rail)

In majority of conductor rail systems, current collection is from the top by steel-shoes, necessary contact pressure being obtained either by gravity or gravity aided by spring. In some cases, however, the current collection is from sides or underside of conductor rail with a view to offering protection against accidental contact.

Conductor rails are required to have low resistance and hardness. To reduce voltage drop at joints, copper bonds are provided either by riveting or welding.

The conductor rail system suffers from the disadvantage of possibility of accidental contact and unsatisfactory quality of current collection at higher speeds. Hence it has found limited patronage and is confined to medium voltage metro systems working at 650-700 V.

It has been conclusively established both experimentally and theoretically that current collection from a flexible conductor is better in all respects. Hence for all main line electrification, suburban systems other than metros and tramways, current collection is by means of a bow/wheel trolley collector or pantographs.

Pole Collector

For tramways, grooved gunmetal wheel trolley attached at the end of a long pole kept in raised condition by spring is a common arrangement. The pole can swivel about its support which enables horizontal separation between the tram car/trolley bus and the track/road way. The contact force is of the order of 10 kg. This system is suitable for speeds up to 30 kmph.

Bow Collector: For speeds beyond 30 kmph in tramways, bow collector consisting of two poles with bow-shaped contact strip at the end is used. This gives better current collection possibility for tramways at higher speeds. However, this system is not suitable for trolley buses due to lack of manoeuvrability.

Pantographs

This is one of the most important subsystem of a locomotive or EMU. The purpose of pantograph is to maintain a link between the overhead system and power circuit of the locomotive at speeds which may vary from 100 to 250 kmph and collect power of the order of 2000 to 6000 kW depending upon the rating. A positive upward pressure has to be maintained between the pantograph strip and the contact wire. Further, this pressure should be minimum consistent with the current collection duty without sparking or overheating such that wear at the contact wire is kept down.

For 25 kV A.C. locomotives, the contact pressure of the pantograph is 6.5 kg (min.) and 9 kg (max.). The strips are of steel. In case of D.C. locomotives, the contact wire is heavier and so is the current collected. Hence contact pressures vary between 10 and 15 kg.

Initial designs of pantograph were symmetrical and diamond-shaped, as shown in Fig. 9.2.

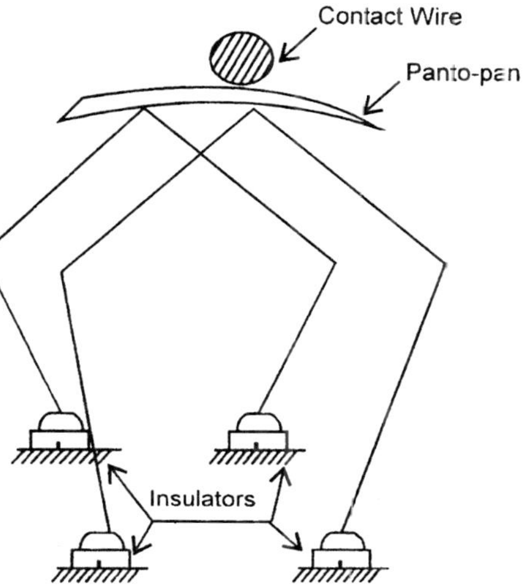

Fig. 9.2 Diamond-shaped pantograph

To ensure light construction with low inertial forces the latest designs developed by Faively (France) have fewer members and are asymmetrical as shown in Fig. 9.3.

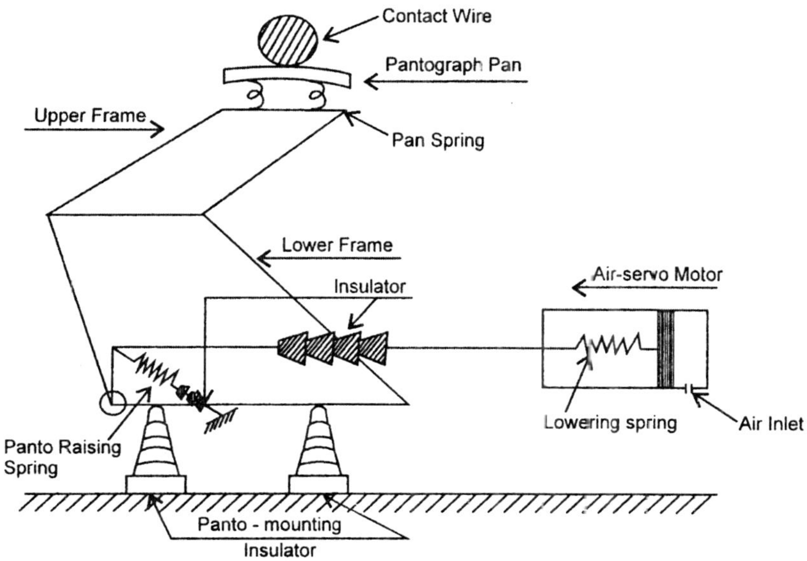

Fig. 9.3 Faively pantograph (schematic view)

For stability of contact pressure, Pantographs are invariably kept in raised condition by springs which maintain the required contact pressure. They are also kept in lowered position by springs of an air-operated motor. Admission of air in the air servomotor compresses the lowering spring and releases the pantograph mechanism to raise itself.

Important Engineering Features of Current Collection Gear

Contact Strip

To ensure minimum wear of the contact wire and realise maximum possible life from a given cross-section, it is necessary to ensure that the pantograph strip wears during the rubbing process rather than the contact wire. Silico-manganese steel strips with suitable lubrication by graphite grease have been found to be a good material and better than cu-strips. For longer life of contact wire, however, it may be advisable to use metallised carbon strips which have self-lubricating properties, and hence do not suffer due to deficiency in lubrication. The 25 kV A.C. locomotives in India are fitted with Faively pantographs and use silico-manganese steel panto strips.

Contact Pressure

This is an important parameter and directly linked to quality of current collection and contract wire/panto-strip wear. The contact pressure in Faively pantographs used on 25 kV A.C. locos is maintained between 6.5 and 9 kg in static condition. It has been experimentally established that less than 5 kg pressure does not give satisfactory current collection whereas increase beyond 9 kg does not give any better performance while aggravating wear.

At higher speeds, aerodynamic pressure gets developed which usually adds-up to the static pressure. However, it is advisable to keep this variation to the minimum by proper aerodynamic design of the locomotive body and positioning the pantograph suitably on the roof.

Behaviour under Dynamic Conditions

Due to upward pressure exerted by the pantograph pan on the contact wire, the latter gets lifted. The lift at mid-span (h) is given by the following equation:

$$h = \frac{P.L}{4\,(T_1 + T_2)}$$

where P = contact pressure
L = length of span
$T_1\ T_2$ = Tensions in contact and catenary wires respectively.

Under dynamic conditions the mid-span lift is somewhat higher than given by the above equation and increases with speed. When the pantograph passes away, the contact wire-catenary drop to their original position and overshoot the same due to inertia and elasticity of the system. Thus the OHE tends to vibrate in a vertical plane which deteriorates the current collection process.

The natural frequency of vibration is given by the following relationship:

$$f = \frac{0.435}{L}\sqrt{\frac{T_1 + T_2}{m}} \text{ cycle/second}$$

where m is mass per unit length of OHE.

If the frequency of vibration generated by a moving vehicle coincides with the natural frequency of the system, the current collection may deteriorate remarkably.

To impart greater stability to the system for current collection, it is necessary to keep the lift h to minimum and the natural frequency large. This is possible by selecting optimum values for T_1, T_2 and reducing length of span or avoiding it being unduly large. It also follows that the pressure P should be kept at minimum consistent with current collection.

In EMU's or double-headed operation of locomotives, the rear pantographs encounter the disturbance created by the front one and may exhibit poor current collection.

Resilient Pantograph Design

Even with the best possible design of the OHE, vertical undulations in contact wire level and hard spots are inevitable. It is, therefore, necessary to design the pantograph in such a manner that it can quickly respond to changes in contact wire level to maintain good contact with least sparking.

The resilience is built in two stages:

(a) Resilient mounting of panto pan; The panto pan must be mounted on spring supports so that it is able to adopt itself to minor undulations in contact wire level quickly.

(b) The panto-frame should have minimum mass consistent with a sturdy design so that it can respond to major changes in contact wire height under the designed contact pressure.

Increased contact pressure can also help to maintain contact in the face of undulations. However, due to other adverse effects, e.g. wear, lift in contact wire etc., of contact pressure value should be carefully selected.

Hence an effective strategy of design is to make use of all the available alternatives in a coordinated manner to cater for the maximum permissible speed of the locomotive.

POWER CIRCUIT EQUIPMENTS (OTHER THAN TRACTION MOTOR)

The main constituents of the power circuit spread out between the pantograph and the traction motors are: Main circuit breaker, Earthing switch, Power transformer tapchanger, Rectifier, Smoothing reactor, Reverser, Line/shunting contactors. We will briefly discuss their functions and main features.

Arrangement of Power Circuit

The circuit diagram shown in Fig. 9.4 brings out the position of different equipments with a view to illustrating their role.

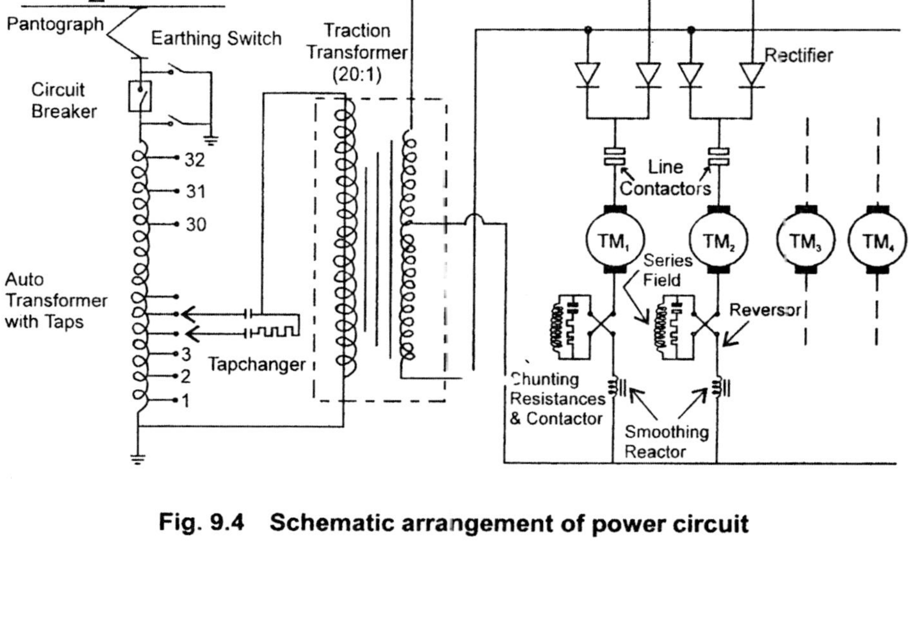

Fig. 9.4 Schematic arrangement of power circuit

Earthing Switch

It is a two-pole isolating switch which can be operated only after pantograph gets lowered and earths the entire power circuit on 25 kV side. The entry to various high tension equipment cubicles is possible only after earthing switch is closed.

Circuit Breaker (Air Blast or Vacuum Type)

All protective relays of the power and auxiliary circuits have their interlocks on the maintaining coil of the circuit breaker which ensures its opening in case of fault. The rating of the circuit breaker should be such that it can open the power circuit under fault conditions.

A recent development is to use vacuum circuit breakers in lieu of air blast circuit breakers with a view to reducing contact wear.

Tap Changer

For controlling speed-torque characteristics of the traction motors, a variable voltage supply is required. In D.C. locomotives series-parallel combinations of traction motors coupled with use of resistances to drop the voltage is the prevalent technique. Apart from being energy-inefficient the method suffers from the disadvantage of large jump in voltages and voltage transfer to the slipping motor in the event of loss of adhesion.

Hence in A.C. traction, advantage is taken of the possibility of on-load tap changing to enable having all motors in parallel.

Larger the number of steps, better the control. In fact a stepless control as achieved by thyristors would be ideal but for the harmonics generated on account of chopping of the sine wave.

In tap-changer locomotives, two strategies are possible, viz.

(a) Control of voltage on the H.T. side by having an autotransformer with the required number of tappings.
(b) Control of voltage on the secondary side.

The latter possibility has not been found popular due to the large amount of current required to be handled by the tap-changing gear. Hence voltage control on the H.T. side is more popular.

The I.R. locos which were designed by the French Railways (SNCF) used two types of tap changes, viz. N40 having 40 steps and N32 having 32 steps. The latter version is now used universally on all CLW built locomotives.

Tap changing is done by a tap-changer operated by an air-servomotor. Rollers move from one tap to another after the adjacent taps are shorted through a resistance to equalise the voltage such that the roller may move with minimum sparking. The schematic arrangement depicted in Fig. 9.4 illustrates the point.

Power Transformer

The auto and fixed ratio (20:1) traction transformers are mounted in the same tank. The transformer is force-cooled by circulating the oil through a radiator which is cooled by a blower. The transformer is the heaviest sub-assembly of a locomotive and is mounted as close to the centre line as possible and in the lowest possible position consistent with track clearances. The oil in the transformer entails a fire potential in the event of leakage of oil or a fault in the winding or tapchanger.

Rectifiers

Initially ignitron-type mercury-arc rectifiers were used. Soon after they gave place to excitrons. Both types were mercury-arc rectifiers.

Towards early seventies, silicon-diode rectifiers became universal as they offered simpler rectification gear with least possible maintenance.

Some locomotives of I.R., as also elsewhere, have thyristor control which makes the tap changing redundant. However, this system was soon given up around mid-eighties due to problems arising out of harmonics in the rectified D.C. Most silicon rectifier systems are air-cooled using blowers.

Smoothing reactor: This is an air-cooled reactor for suppressing ripples in the rectified D.C.

Reversers: These are essentially required to change the connection of the field with respect to armature to reverse direction of movement. Reversers are operated at no load by an air motor.

Line Contactors: The traction motor circuit requires contactors for sectionalising and isolation. These contactors are operated at no-load and are electropneumatic devices. Besides line contactors, there are shunting contactors and resistances for weak-field control of traction motors.

AUXILIARY CIRCUIT EQUIPMENT OF A LOCOMOTIVE

The auxiliary circuit of the locomotive is an essential accompaniment of the power circuit and consists of Arno Converter, battery, auxiliary compressor, D.C. generator coupled to Arno or battery changer, traction motor blowers, rectifier blowers, transformer blower, oil pump, main compressors, exhausters (in case of vacuum-braked trains).

These equipments are fed by an auxiliary winding of the main transformer and are located inside the HT compartment of the locomotive, side by side with the H.T. power circuit equipment which are enclosed from safety angle.

A special features of these equipments is their functioning in ambient conditions which are different from the normal atmospheric conditions in two ways:

(a) The locomotive is fitted with body side filters which filter out dust while preventing entry of rain water. Hence inside the locomotive there is a depression of the order of 10-20 mm water gauge as different coolingblowers suck air from inside. The design of auxiliary equipment must cater for this depression while giving their rated performance.
(b) The ambient temperature inside the locomotive is 10-15°C higher than the outside atmosphere due to constant heat dissipation from the various equipment. Hence all the equipment, including power circuit equipments must cater for a higher ambient temperature than normally prevalent at any place.

The arrangement of auxiliary circuit equipment is shown schematically in Fig. 9.5.

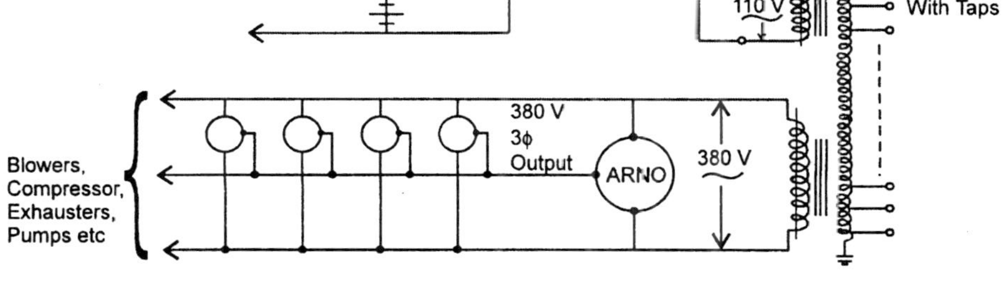

Fig. 9.5 Auxiliary circuit of a locomotive

Another special feature of the auxiliary equipment is the variable voltage supply. The voltage of OHE though 25 kV nominally, varies from 19.0 to 27.5 under designed conditions of the feeding arrangement, and could have 17.0 kV and 30 kV as extremes for short durations. Hence, in their design, all the equipment must cater for this level of voltage variation.

The Arno Converter

To enable use of 3-phase induction motors for driving the various auxiliary circuit machines, a phase convertor fed by a single phase supply on the input side and giving 3-phase output is essentially required. This strategy is technically superior to the possibility of using single phase motors or D.C. motors for the auxiliaries.

Arno converter is a rotary machine which works as a single phase induction motor on the input side and gives a three phase output. The rotor is like a squirrel cage induction motor rotor. The arrangement is schematically illustrated in Fig. 9.6.

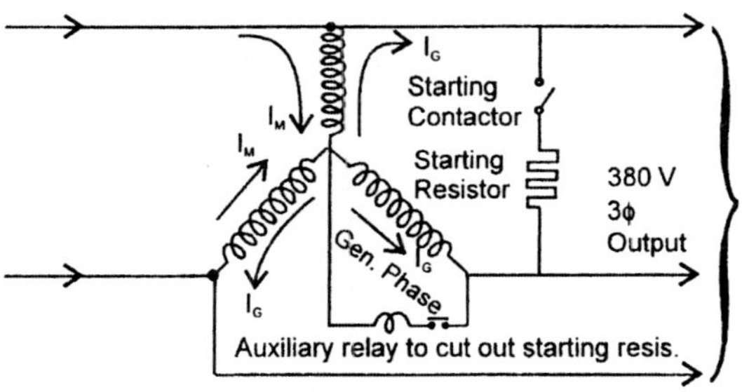

Fig. 9.6 Arno-converter

The machine resembles a 3-phase induction motor. At start, two phases are given single phase supply from the auxiliary transformer directly and the third phase, called the 'generating phase', is connected through a starting resistance enabling start as a split phase induction motor. As soon as a speed of the order of 90% of synchronous speed is picked up, the starting resistance is cut out by a sensing relay connected across the generating phase. The machine then pulls into synchronism and gives a 3-phase output. Since two phases work as motor as well as generator, the voltage drop in them is less. The third phase—the generating phase—is provided with 20% more turns to compensate for the higher voltage drop.

It is obvious that the voltage output from the Arno is inherently unbalanced.

The maximum unbalance occurs under no-load condition when the generating phase gives 20% more voltage and the other two phases have maximum drop due to absence of generated current.

Hence the design of an Arno converter is critical in respect of voltage unbalance which may not be allowed to exceed 5% under any load condition.

Static Phase Converters: Fundamentals

A voltage unbalance of the order of 5% in the 3-phase supply derived from Arno converter would give rise to a current unbalance of the order of 30 to 40% in the driven auxiliary machines. Their design, therefore, must cater for this. Usually a higher rating and frame size is adopted as compared to industrial grade machines of identical duty.

This drawback has led to the development of static phase converters using controlled diodes. On 25 kV A.C. locomotives, a static phase converter would be a combination of rectifier and inverter units with a D.C. link to enable single-phase to 3-phase conversion. The inverter could be of two types, viz. (i) Square wave 3-phase output, (ii) Sinusoidal wave 3-phase output. The latter alternative is preferable from the point-of-view of harmonics but would call for PWM control. This would make the sinusoidal output phase-converter costlier.

On Indian Railways both alternatives have been tried out. The 6000 H.P. ASEA locomotives are fitted with static3-phase converters with square wave output. Although the cost of these phase converters is lesser, the failure proneness of auxiliary-machines is comparable to Arno converter-fed systems. This is due to the fact that the square wave output, though overcoming the problem of unbalance, gives added thermal loading due to the harmonics. On AC/DC locos of BHEL manufacture, phase converters of sinusoidal wave output have been provided. The performance of auxiliary machines on these locomotives is comparatively better due to elimination of unbalance as well as harmonics. However these phase converters are distinctly costlier.

In either case, application of voltage pulses could damage motor insulation due to surge effect and would call for improved surge-withstand capability. Standard Specifications of National Electrical Manufactures Association (USA) NEMA 1-31/1-30 recognises this necessity and prescribes a higher surge-withstand capability in respect of peak value as well as rise time.

Hence, the choice between Arno and static phase converter should be based on an analysis of life cycle costs. While Arno converters cost approximately one fifth as compared to static converters they are repairable and call for regular maintenance. Static phase converters, on the other hand, have limited codal-life and call for only occasional replacement of failed modules.

Battery

On all electric locomotives a battery of approximately 80 to 100 ampere-hour capacity is essentially required. During initial starting of a locomotive, the battery runs a baby compressor to create air pressure for raising of the pantograph and closing of the circuit breaker. It also gives power to the control circuits involved in the initial starting operation. The battery is kept under trickle charge by a generator mounted on the Arno shaft or a separate static battery charger.

Batteries can be of alkaline or lead-acid type. Alkaline batteries are costlier though more rugged. Most I.R. locomotives use lead-acid batteries which are mounted on the outside to avoid damage to contacts etc. due to acid fumes.

Main Compressor

Compressed air requirement of a normal vacuum train brake locomotive is of the order of 1000 liters per minute at 7 kg/cm^2 pressure. The compressed air is stored in cylindrical reservoirs mounted on the under-frame where it also gets cooled and caters to the requirements of pantographs, tap-changer, circuit breaker, electro-pneumatic contactors, reversers, horns, wipers, locomotive air brake etc. In air braked trains, the requirement of air goes up to 2000 to 2500 litres per minute. There is always a leakage in the air circuit of the loco and train.

To cater for these requirements one or two reciprocating or rotary air compressors are provided which have intermittent duty and start when the pressure falls to 5 kg/cm^2 and cut out when it reaches 8 kg/cm^2. The air pressure in the reservoirs is controlled by an air-pressure governing switch.

Vacuum Exhauster

In Indian Railways some trains are vacuum braked. The current trend is to switch over to air braked trains with a view to reducing the braking distance at higher speeds both for passenger and freight stock. In vacuum braked train locomotives, two vacuum exhausters are provided. The induction motors running the exhausters are two-speed type to enable their operation at higher speed to permit quick evacuation of the vacuum circuit after a brake application. After initial evacuation, only one exhauster runs at lower speed which should be adequate for maintaining the vacuum level. Usually, the vacuum level maintained is 50 cm in freight trains and

55/56 cm in high speed passenger trains (atmospheric pressure corresponding to 74 cm Hg).

Blowers for Cooling

For cooling the traction motors and transformer, blowers required are of large output and are usually of centrifugal type. Smaller blowers, viz. smoothing-reactor, silicon rectifier blowers are axial fans. In some designs integrated cooling air circuits are used to reduce the multiplicity of blowers.

The TM and transformer blowers which dissipate a large amount of heat suck filtered air from inside the H.T. compartment and discharge it to outside atmosphere. Hence these blowers must cater for adequate suction head and be capable of meeting the rated performance in partly choked condition of body side filters and minimum OHE voltage.

D.C. Generator/Battery Charger

D.C. generators coupled directly to the arno shaft or static battery charger taking power from a 110 V auxiliary winding of the main transformer are used for trickle charging of locomotive battery and supply of 110 V D.C. power to control circuits. In lead acid batteries the voltage varies from 1.8 to 2 V per cell from fully discharged to fully charged condition. The voltage output of the generator of BA-charger must be stable and cater for the load variation from discharged to fully charged state of the battery.

Oil Pump

For cooling the transformer oil, it is necessary to circulate the oil in the transformer tank through a radiator where blowing air can cool the oil. This calls for a pump of appropriate capacity.

CHAPTER 10

Protection of Electric Locomotive Equipments and Circuits: Safety Considerations and Monitoring

INTRODUCTION

The equipments of an electric locomotive are subjected to certain typical working conditions and the locomotive as a whole is expected to give a high degree of reliability. It is, therefore, necessary to design the protective circuits in a manner that would cater for the above two broad objectives. Besides an electric locomotive is a moving high-tension mechanism that gets handled by a large number of operating and maintenance personnel. Hence basic safety considerations must get inbuilt in the design. In this chapter, these aspects will be dealt with in some detail to enable a grasp of the basic principles and underlying approach.

BROAD STRATEGY FOR PROTECTION

This can be outlined as follows:

(a) Surge protection against internal switching surges and external surges including lightning.
(b) Overload protection of key equipment and circuits.
(c) Earth fault protection.
(d) Protection from overvoltage and undervoltage.
(e) Differential current protection of TM circuits to detect wheel-slipping.
(f) Protection against low air pressure and high air pressure.
(g) Bucholz relay protection for transformer.
(h) Temperature monitoring to prevent fires.
(i) Monitoring of ventilation system of key equipments.

(j) Protection against accidental contact between circuits of different potentials running side by side in the cable trench.
(k) Protection against fires.

The most common protection through overload relays is not practical for the auxiliary machines working under condition of heavy voltage fluctuation. Against a nominal voltage of 25 kV, the overhead line voltage varies from 17.5 to 27.5 kV. Correspondingly the Arno output voltage varies from 270 to 460 V. Then the 3-phase voltages are unbalanced and direct on-line starting is the prevalent control technique.

Hence overload protection becomes impractical as a safe setting for the relay to cater for all the eventualities may not serve the purpose of protection at all. Hence an alternative protection through earth fault detection and functional monitoring has to be conceived to avoid burnouts. Should a single phasing fault develop, the 3-phase machine will fail to start which will get detected through functional monitoring. A failure of insulation at any point will be sensed through earth fault before it gives rise to a burnout.

SURGE PROTECTION

Overvoltages beyond the insulation level of equipment mounted on a locomotive may arise from the following sources:

(a) Direct lightning strokes or electrostatic induction (indirect strokes)
(b) External switching surges from the transmission line and grid system.
(c) Internal switching surges within the locomotive.

Direct Lightning Strokes

A direct lightning stroke on the overhead lines may cause a potential of many million volts and discharge current of several kilo-amperes. The resulting overvoltage in the system may shatter insulators and damage structures until the energy gets dissipated through paths formed to earth. Fortunately such direct strokes are rare. Indirect strokes result from electrostatically induced charges on the conductors due to passage of charged clouds over them and are quite frequent.

The voltage acquired by a conductor at any point travels along the line like a travelling wave whose velocity is $1/\sqrt{LC}$ where L and C are inductance and capacitance per unit length.

The wave is usually specified by its peak value and time t_1 and t_2 representing time of rise to the peak value and its fall to half of the peak value shown in

Fig. 10.1. It has been observed that t_1 varies from 1 to 10 μ sec and t_2 from 10 to 100 μ sec. The discharge current varies from 10 to 400 kA and is equal to the surge voltage divided by surge impedance, i.e. $\sqrt{\frac{L}{C}}$.

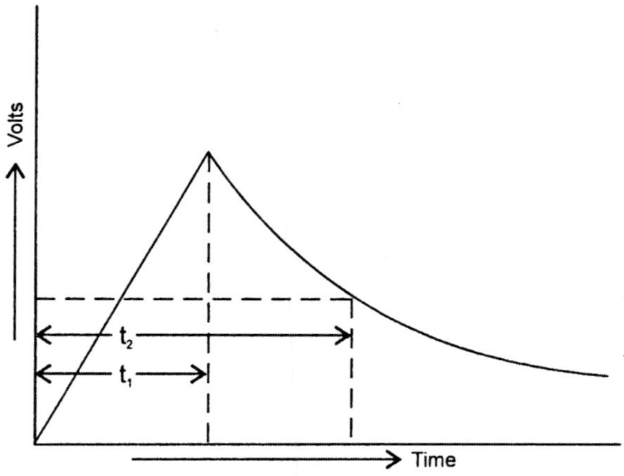

Fig. 10.1 Surge voltage wave

The overhead traction line running all along a track is vulnerable to lightning strokes, direct or in direct. The best strategy for protection would be to plan for sensitive installations individually and build the required surge-withstand capability in the line.

While HV transmission lines may be shielded by means of a ground wire, in traction lines this adds to the cost and is not essential. Trees and structures higher than the OHE along the route act as effective shield and serve the purpose to a great extent. This precludes direct strokes and reduces its probability to an almost negligible degree.

Locomotives are protected against lightning surges by spark gaps (rod or spherical type) or gapless lightening arrestors positioned as shown in the schematic circuit in Fig. 10.2.

In initial designs of locomotive rod or sphere gaps were provided. The performance of these gaps is adversely affected by climatic variations, swarms of insects and dust. Besides, when these gaps break, the follow up current from the OHE system gets interrupted only through tripping of the feeder circuit breakers. The rod gap settings also get vitiated due to melting and globule formation. Hence latest designs provide gapless lightning arrestors of appropriate design which discharge the surge without interrupting the circuit and are not affected by variations in atmospheric conditions.

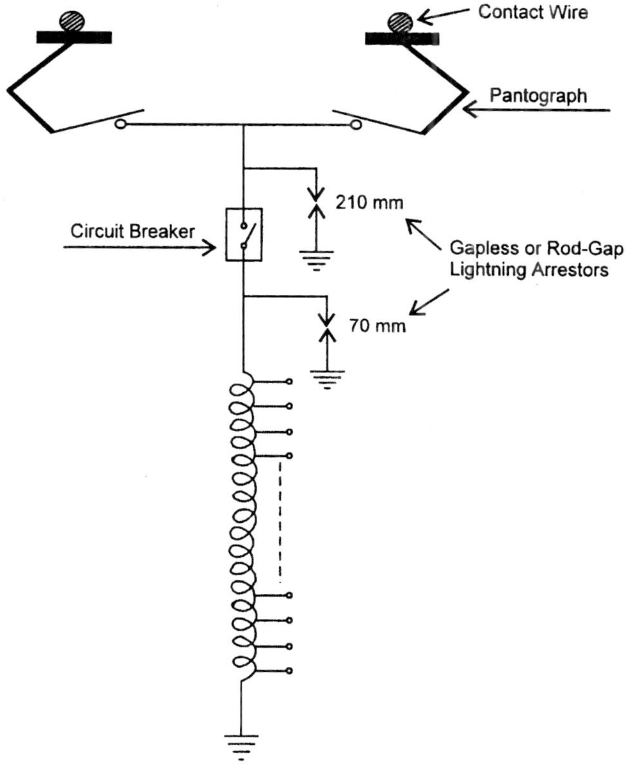

Fig. 10.2 Protection of locos against lightning surges

The lightning arrestors shown in the above circuit (Fig. 10.2) also protect the locomotive from all external surges from the transmission system. The breakdown voltage of the surge arrestor should be approximately 20% lower than the impulse-voltage withstand level of the protected equipment including insulators.

Switching Surges

Within the locomotive, switching surges get generated especially when circuits get interrupted through a tripping of the system under fault or no power conditions. The energy stored in the inductive circuits of transformer, smoothing reactor, traction motor armature/field and induction motors causes a surge voltage which gets reflected at the open ends and travels to and fro giving rise to voltage doubling effect and stressing the insulation system till the energy gets discharged through ohmic resistance of the system.

The strategy adopted for protection against switching surges is to connect (R-C) networks, which reduce the steepness of the wavefront and also help to absorb the energy in the resistance. The (R-C) networks are connected as shown in the schematic circuit diagram of Fig. 10.3. There is evidence to suggest that sometimes surges of the transmission system could find their way to the traction and auxiliary circuits through capacitive coupling at the bushings. These surges also get absorbed by the R-C network. A precaution often required to be observed in connecting R-C networks is to avoid use of unduly long leads in an attempt to find a suitable location for their placement. In principle, the inductance of the lead should be negligible compared to the capacitance or else it should get adequately compensated.

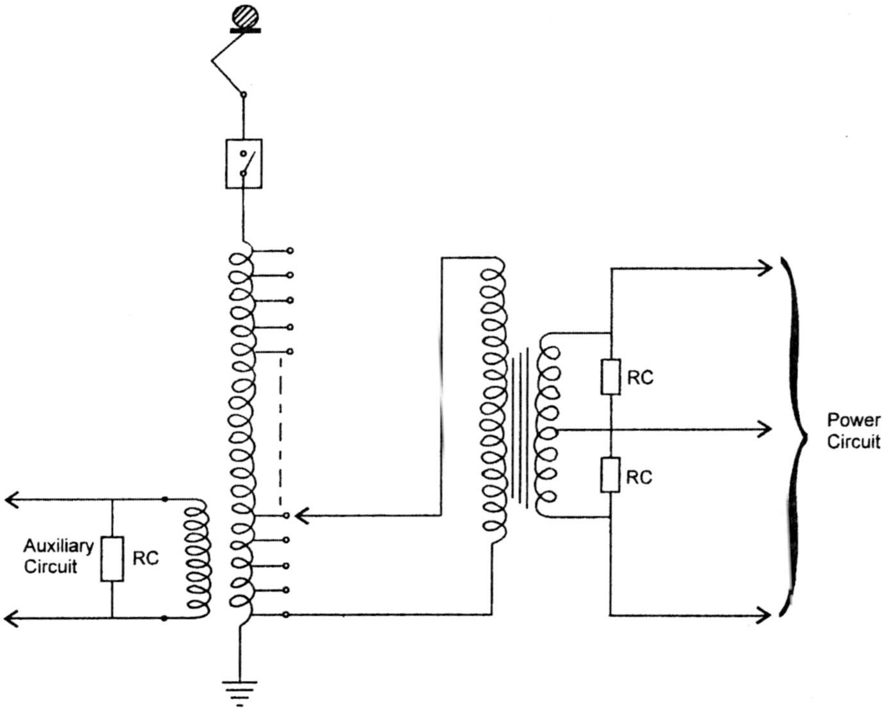

Fig. 10.3 RC network for protection against switching surges

Possibility of 110 V Control Circuits Assuming Higher Voltage

The control circuits of a locomotive are powered at 110 V nominal and are extensively spread out. The operating personnel are in close vicinity of 110 V circuits while carrying out locomotive operation and control. Although precautions are taken during cable layout and design of individual equipment, possibility of an accidental contact between control circuit and high voltage circuits cannot be altogether ruled out. This would call for a suitable protection which could either be relay actuated or based on breaking of a gap both of which would open the control circuit and be self-setting in case the contact is transient.

OVERLOAD PROTECTION OF MAIN POWER CIRCUITS

Shorting of a segment of transformer windings, failure of diodes of the rectifiers, flashover of traction motors and shorting of power circuits due to cable insulation breakdown are some of the eventualities that may give rise to dangerous levels of current flow from the power system which better gets detected fast leading to isolation of the defective locomotive from rest of the system to enable uninterrupted functioning. This calls for overload protection through relays, which trip the main circuit breaker of the locomotive.

The schematic diagram presented in Fig. 10.4 illustrates the placement of main overload relay and two overload relays for the traction circuit subgroups. The traction circuit of the locomotive has two subgroups, each of which is protected by a separate overload relay such that in the event of a fault, the locomotive may operate at half power. The main as well as traction subgroup overload relays trip the main circuit breaker.

EARTH FAULT PROTECTION OF POWER OF AUXILIARY CIRCUITS

Detection of any earth fault in power, auxiliary circuits and control circuits of the locomotive is a very important element of the protection strategy. Since earth fault occurring at any one point would not lead to a dangerous condition till another fault occurs, this protection may be provided with facility of isolation such that the locomotive is not in capacitated in the very first instance while a note is taken for trouble shooting and rectification of the fault at the earliest opportunity.

There are two earth fault relays for the two traction subgroups. The connection scheme for one of the subgroups is illustrated in the schematic diagram of Fig. 10.4. When any earth fault occurs in the traction circuit, a fault current flows

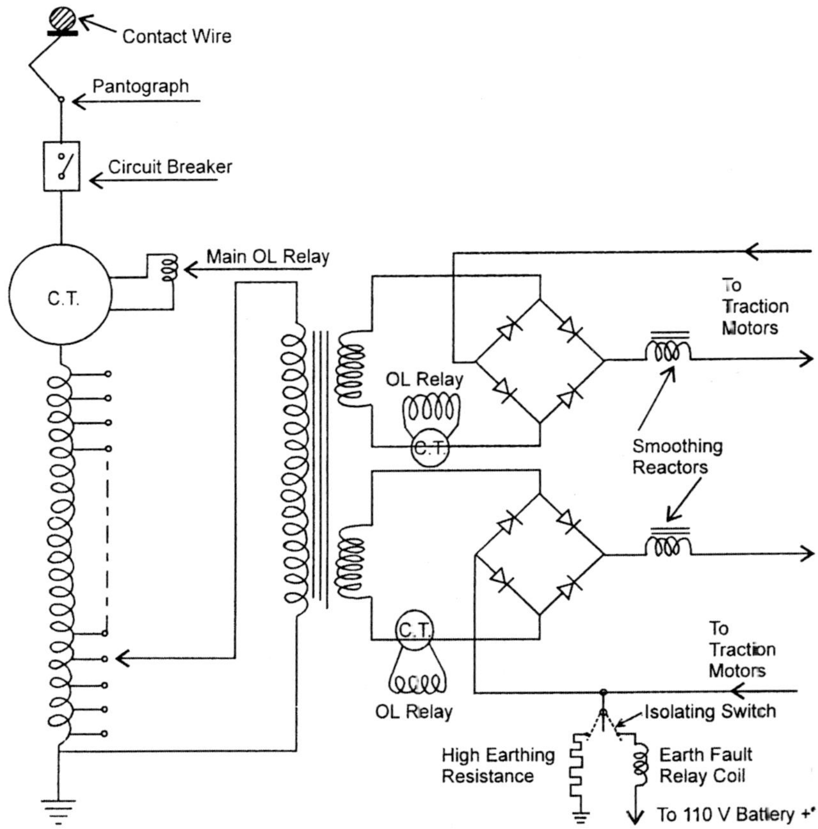

Fig. 10.4 Schematic illustrating placement of main and traction circuit overload relays

through the relay coil as the battery negative is also earthed. This trips the main circuit breaker. The relay can be temporarily isolated by connecting the faulty traction circuit through a resistance to earth. Unless another earth fault occurs in the same traction circuit, no problem would arise. Hence in isolated condition of the relay, cautious approach on the part of driving crew is called for.

The protective relay for monitoring earth fault in the auxiliary 380 V circuit is connected to the star point of the Arno as shown in Fig. 10.5, An earth fault occurring anywhere in the 380 V auxiliary circuit gets monitored by the relay which acts to trip the main circuit breaker. Since earth fault at anyone point alone is not dangerous, the locomotive can be worked temporarily by isolating the relay which connects the star point to earth through a high resistance.

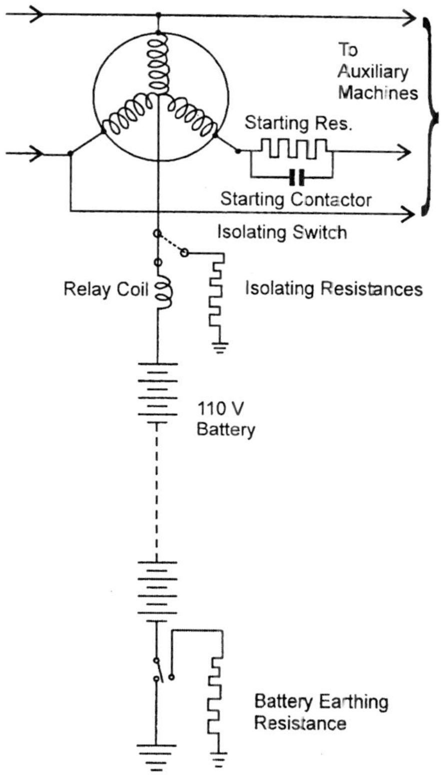

Fig. 10.5 Relay connection for monitoring the earth fault in the auxiliary 380 volt circuit

Earth Fault in 110 V Control Circuit

The battery negative terminal is earthed through an isolating switch as shown in Fig. 10.5. Should an earth fault occur in the 110 V circuit, which has a potential difference with respect to earth, the resultant fault current is sensed by the main battery fuse or protective breaker. In this case also isolating facility exists by injecting a resistance in the earthing circuit to enable operation till detailed trouble shooting gets done.

The earth fault protection of different circuits is a key strategy in the overall protection scheme of the locomotive. Any failure of insulation gets detected as soon as it occurs. This does not incapacitate the locomotive straight away due to the inbuilt isolation facilities. However, caution on the part of the driving crew becomes necessary to detect any further fault, which will exhibit through smoke emission. Besides, maintenance intervention at the earliest opportunity becomes necessary to detect the singular earth fault and repair the same.

PROTECTION FROM OVERVOLTAGE AND UNDERVOLTAGE

Voltage lower than 17.5 kV may not be desirable for efficient working of auxiliary circuits as Arno may not start after a tripping and auxiliary machines starting under load may behave erratically and fail to deliver the desired output. This situation usually develops near neutral sections in the event of a feed extension. A better strategy, therefore, is to get low voltage at the neutral sections monitored through a relay triggering an alarm, which enables the power controller to react and take corrective measures. Since there is no immediate danger, the locomotive is not provided with undervoltage protection.

High voltages in traction circuits are controllable through tap changing; hence only an alarm needs to be provided through an overvoltage relay which attracts the attention of the crew.

As a measure of protection, a no-voltage relay is provided which trips the circuit breaker and calls for resetting of the power and auxiliary circuits to their starting mode such that upon resumption of power, unsafe conditions do not arise.

DIFFERENTIAL CURRENT PROTECTION OF TRACTION CIRCUITS

This is a key protection device. Traction motor behaviour under condition of slipping of wheels upon loss of adhesion does need monitoring. Apart from damage to the wheels and rails, wheel slipping can result in damage to the brush gear, trigger flashovers and damage the armature bandings in a D.C. traction motor. Hence a relay QD is provided to compare the current flowing in two different traction motor circuits. Should a differential higher than normal (due to difference in characteristics and wheel diameters) arise, this relay would cause notching down of the tap changer and thereby reduce voltage applied to the traction circuit till the wheel slipping gets arrested.

PROTECTION AGAINST HIGH AND LOW AIR PRESSURE IN THE COMPRESSED AIR CIRCUIT

High pressure in the air circuit may be detrimental to the various elements constituting this circuit and can also cause damage to the compressor due to its working against a higher back pressure. A safety valve fitted in the compressed air circuit protects the compressed air system against excessive pressure.

Low air pressure can arise due to a leakage in the air circuit. Before the air pressure falls to a level that would result in locked circuit breaker, it is necessary to trip the circuit breaker. This is done by a relay monitoring the air pressure available at the circuit breaker air reservoir.

TEMPERATURE MONITORING

Temperature monitoring of critically loaded electrical equipment can be a key strategy in prevention of fires. The temperature-sensing device can trigger an alarm, which attracts attention of the crew.

It is a common practice to monitor the transformer oil temperature where fire potential is maximum. The concept of temperature monitoring can be extended to other critical equipment of a design, as fire potential gets pinpointed in actual working.

PROTECTION OF TRANSFORMER BY BUCHOLZ RELAY

This is a universally accepted transformer protection and is provided in locomotive transformers too.

Monitoring of Ventilation System of Key Locomotive Equipment

All locomotives have a set of blowers for cooling the power circuit equipment, viz:

(i) *Transformer oil cooling blower*: Oil is circulated through a radiator by an oil pump where the blower cools the oil.

(ii) *Traction motors*: Minimum air pressure in the commutator chamber is correlated to the rating of the motor. This is achieved by a blower for each group of TMs of a bogie.

(iii) *Silicon rectifiers*: Since the junction temperature of diodes is a critical operating parameter, all silicon rectifiers are provided with a cooling blower which blows air over the diode fins. Working of the blower is critically related to the rating.

(iv) *Smoothing reactor*: This suppresses ripples of the rectified D.C. for better commutation. To achieve a manageable size of the reactor which can be accommodated on a locomotive, it is force-cooled by a blower.

All the above blowers are monitored through flow relays fitted on the output side of the blower duct. Should a relay monitoring the flow not pick up within a few seconds of closing of the blower switch or drop during the course of its working, the relay triggers the main circuit-breaker-opening circuit, with a time lag which distinguishes this protection from the overload and earth fault protections which are instantaneous in their response. The oil pump of the transformer is also fitted with a flow relay which interacts with the circuit breaker in a similar fashion.

PROTECTION AGAINST ACCIDENTAL CONTACT WITH H.T. EQUIPMENT

All locomotives have one or two corridors running through the H.T. compartment and communicating between the two driving cabs. These corridors are either central or on the two sides along the length and permit access to the equipment and panels for maintenance and monitoring during operation.

To prevent the possibility of accidental contact with the operating or maintenance personnel in charged condition, all equipment at voltages exceeding 400 V (nominal) are enclosed by expanded metal frames which are fitted with locks and doors at suitable locations. These locks are opened by keys which get released after operation of the main earthing switch to 'Earth' position, which, in turn, becomes possible only after pantographs get lowered.

A similar locking arrangement also exists for releasing the ladder which is required for going on the locomotive roof. Of course, in this case, a permit to work is also needed from the traction power controller.

PROTECTION AGAINST FIRES

A key drawback of electric locomotives is their proneness to fire. This is primarily due to the following reasons.

(i) Presence of a large number of joints in electrical circuits, arcing contactors, possibility of inter-turn shorts in machines and transformers.
(ii) Presence of oil in the transformer and tapchanger and leakage of oil or oil vapour inside/outside the locomotive and its deposition on cables, bogies etc.
(iii) Absence of overload protection for auxiliaries.

While the design of the locomotive ensures that all materials used are fire-retardant and all potential circuits are well protected or functionally monitored, there is need for a meticulous care during operation and maintenance. Negligence can cost a locomotive due to fire damage which quite often is irreparable.

In the matter of locomotive fires, a strategy for prevention is decidedly better than planning for the cure. Very often, the place where a fire is detected is inaccessible by road and not easily or promptly accessible to fire fighting by rail. Fire extinguishers provided on the locomotive have limited capacity and can give only marginal help in the event of early detection of the fire.

Fire Prevention Strategy

Regular cleaning of body side filters, oil deposit in cable ducts or equipment/bogies, preventing oil leakage, tightening of loose joints in control/auxiliary/power circuits, checking correct setting of relays and ratings of fuses, monitoring condition of transformer oil for dielectric strength, preventing continued overcharging of batteries, checking arc-chutes for proper securing, replacing cables with aged insulation in due time, are some of the preventive measures which help.

Early Detection: During operation, an alert driving crew can detect fires in the very initial stages and control the same with the help of fire-extinguishers provided on the locomotive. Following the principle that "there can be no fire without smoke", fitting smoke detectors at sensitive locations in the vicinity of transformer/tapchanger/compressor/exhauster such that an early alarm is triggered for the crew to verify and act, could be a good strategy.

Fire Fighting: Every locomotive must carry two to four fire extinguishers of adequate capacity and type that can deal with electrical fires. Besides, rail-based fire fighting vehicles should be planned at nominated depots from where they can cover every location within 30 to 45 min.

CHAPTER 11

Preventive, Corrective Maintenance; Reliability and Condition Monitoring

INTRODUCTION

Electric Locomotives and overhead equipment including power distribution system, the two main constituents of electric traction, are acquired at considerable capital investment. Hence, maximising their availability for optimum exploitation and reducing maintenance costs are key strategies towards making a success of electric traction over alternative modes of haulage.

Besides, in a widely spread out network such as Indian Railways, it is probable that a locomotive picking up a train near Calcutta ends up at Bombay and fails to turn up at its base maintenance depot in time for a preventive checkup. The maintenance strategy chalked out should cater for this eventuality without seriously jeopardising reliability.

While corrective maintenance may need a positive down time necessitating temporary withdrawal of a working asset, it should be possible to plan preventive maintenance in a manner that matches with the working cycle and avails inbuilt idle periods in the best possible manner. This may call for judicious utilisation of monitoring techniques and trained personnel to execute the work in least possible time.

In this chapter, an attempt will be made to discuss all relevant aspects of an effective maintenance strategy to conform to the objectives outlined above.

TYPES OF MAINTENANCE AND THEIR OBJECTIVES AND MAINTAINABILITY

B.S. 3811: 1974 defines maintenance "as a combination of actions carried out to retain an item in or restore it to, an acceptable standard for the designated activity." Recently a new term "Tero-Technology" has been coined from the Greek word "Terein" which means, "to look after". It has been defined as "a combination of managerial, financial, engineering and other practices applied to physical assets in pursuit of economical "life cycle costs". Thus tero-technology brings in other allied aspects of maintenance to make it cost-effective and achieve right balance between initial cost, modifications, maintenance and replacements.

The recognised objectives of maintenance are:

(a) To extend the useful life of assets.
(b) To ensure optimum availability.
(c) To ensure reliability and operational readiness.
(d) To ensure safety.

Maintenance Activities

To achieve the above objectives, the following types of maintenance activities are involved:

(i) Preventive maintenance: Checks and adjustments set out in manufacturer's manual which ensure timely lubrication, topping up of consumables, adjustments for correct functioning, correcting alignments, replacement of fast wearing items, cleaning etc.
(ii) Corrective maintenance: This includes general overhaul as a result of wear and tear in service. This would involve replacement of major sub-assemblies or their repair, detection of cracks or deterioration in highly stressed components undergoing service fatigue and their repair, corrosion repairs, replacement of cabling, painting, rewinding or rebanding of machines etc.
(iii) Emergency (including breakdown) maintenance: failures that may occur due to unforeseen circumstance leading to immobilisation of the asset in spite of regular maintenance.

Cost of Maintenance vis-a-vis Reliability

The relationship between cost of maintenance and its degree is illustrated graphically in Fig. 11.1

As the degree of planned maintenance is increased, the emergency maintenance comes down but the total cost of maintenance, which drops initially, increases. Hence, there is an optimum level of planned maintenance at which breakdown maintenance is at a reasonable level, availability is optimum and maintenance cost minimum.

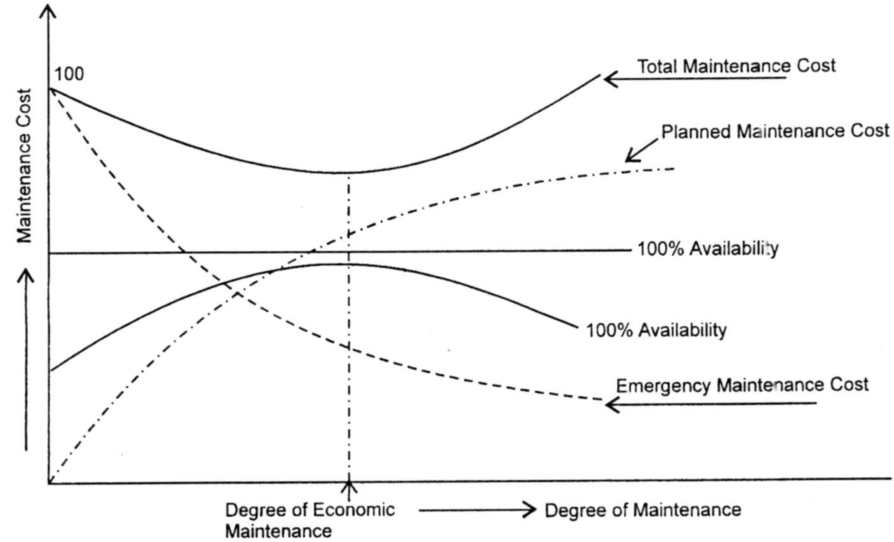

Fig. 11.1 Relationship between degree of maintenance, cost and availability

The optimum level of planned maintenance, therefore, should be judiciously defined for a given set of service conditions and tendency towards overmaintenance checked.

Workmanship Errors: Human Reliability

Studies indicate that nearly 25 to 50% of equipment failures result from human errors of which 50 to 80% are attributable to poor workmanship. Although it is possible to contain workmanship errors through proper training, it is evident that the optimum level of maintenance should be designed keeping this factor also in view. The recent trend in tero-technology is in favour of condition monitoring of major equipment and their need-based maintenance, rather than frequent interference for preventive check up which tends to disturb a stabilised assembly through human error and entails inherent destabilization in the process of check up. This aspect will be dealt with in greater detail in the later part of this chapter.

SPECIAL FEATURES OF ELECTRIC TRACTION ASSETS HAVING BEARING ON MAINTENANCE STRATEGY

By virtue of a keen competition from diesel-traction alternative and high initial capital investment, it is imperative that the maintenance strategy of electric traction assets be chalked out with the following objectives in view:

(i) An availability level of 90 to 95% for electric locomotives should be aimed at by resorting to short-duration maintenance or inspection schedules which can be fitted into the idle periods of the utilisation cycle such that the need or major corrective maintenance is brought down to minimum.

(ii) For all major assemblies, the necessity for corrective maintenance should be need-based and linked to actual condition to the extent possible.

(iii) Need for workshop repairs should be brought down drastically by making better use of running depot facilities and unit exchange spares.

Overhead equipments or traction distribution assets are required round the clock for uninterrupted movement of trains. They are, however, available for maintenance during short interruptions in the train running schedule or when track is under maintenance. Hence a maintenance strategy availing such time slots is best suited.

The electric locomotives become available for short durations during crew changing which often gets combined with dropping of a load in a yard and before picking up of a fresh load which is either ready or getting ready elsewhere in a departure yard.

Passenger trains which often run in a bunch according to a time table which has to match best arrival or departure time for key stations, leave sufficient margin in their linkage which can be utilised for most of the running maintenance schedules except major corrective maintenance.

The above specific features of electric traction assets merit consideration while chalking out the maintenance strategy of traction assets.

ATTENTION TO MAINTAINABILITY ASPECTS AT DESIGN/ CONSTRUCTION STAGE

Considering that the best strategy for maintaining electric traction assets is to make use of inbuilt idle time slots in their utilisation pattern or working in conjunction with other elements of the system, it follows that the "corrective attention" should be widely spaced and most of the attention should get covered in "preventive maintenance" or "servicing schedules" which should be of smaller duration and capable of fitting into the available time slots of one to two hours duration.

This brings us to the aspect of 'maintainability' which is inbuilt in a design and could be realised through proper "specification".

A generally accepted definition of maintainability is as follows:

"Maintainability is the probability that a system will be restored to operational effectiveness *within a given period of time* when the maintenance action is performed in accordance with prescribed procedures.

Optimum maintainability can be aimed in the design of an equipment through attention to following factors.

(i) Design for minimum maintenance skills and tools.
(ii) Design for minimum need for periodical adjustments.
(iii) Use of standard parts/components.
(iv) Divide the system into identifiable subsystems.
(v) Provide for visual inspection.
(vi) Provide trouble-shooting indicators, overload indicators, alarms etc.
(vii) Plan for modular replacements, plug-in-rather than solder-in modules.
(viii) Make parts and components easily accessible.

Besides, to ensure that appearance of a fault does not lead to immobilisation, adequate redundancy may be provided for key subsystems.

The corrective maintenance schedules involving repairs or replacements are either depot or POH workshop based. Their frequency should be minimum say at intervals of 90 to 100 days for depot based schedules and 7-10 years for workshop based schedules with some degree of flexibility between actual and due dates.

From the foregoing it is clear that design can play a key role in realising maintainability of the required degree through proper specification by the user.

MAINTENANCE OF OVERHEAD EQUIPMENTS

The overhead equipment which distributes power along the track, consists of contact wire suspended at a uniform height with respect to the track with inbuilt stagger by a catenary and dropper system. Automatic regulation is achieved by tensioning weights in every tension length which keeps the contact wire practically free from sag due to temperature variations.

Apart from the above, there are bracket assemblies and masts which support the overhead equipment through insulators. Section insulators, sectioning switches, jumpers, lightning arrestors, auxiliary transformers, neutral sections, interrupters etc. form an essential part of the overhead system.

The maintenance work required falls into the following broad categories:

(i) Ensuring that the key parameters affecting current collection properties, viz. height, stagger, tension are maintained within specified tolerances.
(ii) Ensuring that the fastening arrangements of the various components, conducting or non-conducting are not slackened in the course of service as it may result in faster deterioration of the key parameters and accelerated wear and tear.
(iii) Ensuring cleanliness of insulators especially in critical areas where deposit of dirt/dust may vitiate insulating properties.
(iv) Monitoring wear pattern of contact wire and taking timely action to check abnormal wear and arrange timely replacements.
(v) Locating wear and tear of droppers, jumpers, insulators through visual inspections and arranging timely replacements.
(vi) Monitoring healthy condition of lightning arrestors, auxiliary transformers, interrupters and switches etc. and arranging timely replacements.
(vii) Guarding against bird nesting and infringement from vegetation along the track.

The schedules usually resorted to are:

(i) Patrolling of OHE by trained staff to detect developing faults.
(ii) Periodical cleaning of insulators and tightening of fasteners.
(iii) Periodical measurement of key parameters and their restoration.
(iv) Periodical maintenance of automatic tensioning device.

Inspections by patrolling staff coupled with monitoring of current collection properties of locomotives and monitoring of height/stagger etc. through a high speed tower car can be done to pin-point defects without need for taking power block and shutting down the line. This may be possible through adequate training of patrolling staff and use of gadgets e.g. telescope, temperature sensor etc.

The need for cleaning insulators in most cases can be avoided by using insulators of longer creepage distance in critical areas such that seasonal rains are sufficient to wash the insulators and keep them clean.

In general, OHE at curves and turn-outs needs more frequent attention and adjustment than the one on straight track. Hence graded schedules should be organised to save on maintenance time and manpower input.

The maintenance blocks should be clubbed with track maintenance. The work done by individual workers should be clearly laid down for a block duration of 2 hr. and meticulous record keeping done to pin-point accountability.

To minimise the need for frequent contact wire replacements, following strategies may be adopted:

(a) Location showing higher wear pattern should be staggered through use of stop boards in the vicinity of relevant signals.
(b) A higher size of contact wire should be used initially and all new systems planned with pantograph strips which are self-lubricating and give reduced wear.

'Fit and forget'-type fasteners should be adopted to the extent possible.

MAINTENANCE OF ELECTRIC LOCOMOTIVES

An effective maintenance strategy for electric locomotives, which by very nature of their duty move over long distances, would consist in:

(a) Rational sub-division of maintenance work between running depots, locosheds, i.e. (base depot) and workshops such that most servicing, adjustment and preventive maintenance gets done in running depots through schedules which are kept within 2 hr duration or less.
(b) The visits to loco-sheds (for corrective/preventive maintenance), which are built on the pattern of minor workshops are to be at intervals of 60 to 90 days with sufficient flexibility in the time of visit and actual materialisation of the schedule. Execution of this schedule should not take more than one-day withdrawal through judicious use of unit exchange spares.
(c) The visit to a major repair or POH shop is to be at not less than 7 to 8 yr. interval. This schedule should not take more than two weeks to execute.
(d) A proper system of accountability should be established for running depot maintenance as they may fall over different administrative zones of the system.

Assuming that the running depot maintenance is clubbed with crew changing and picking up of fresh loads and hence does not result in effective withdrawal of a locomotive from service, the execution of the other two schedules in loco-sheds and POH shops will give an availability of the order of 98%. Allowing a 2 to 3% for emergency maintenance, an availability of 95% becomes possible.

Types of Preventive and Corrective Maintenance Work on Electric Locomotives

The various maintenance requirements of a locomotive can be broadly classified into the following categories:

Servicing Schedules

These schedules require planned attention at regular intervals and relate to the following operations:

(i) Topping up oil/grease in suspensions/axle box bearings.
(ii) Topping up oil in gear cases.
(iii) Topping up oil in compressors/exhausters
(iv) Topping up oil in auxiliary machine bearings.
(v) Renewal of brake blocks
(vi) Renewal of pantograph strips and checking their adjustment for contact pressure.
(vii) Changing of carbon brushes of traction motor.
(viii) Topping up distilled water in batteries
(ix) Checking and repair to leakage in air/vacuum circuits.
(x) Checking proper securing of arc-chutes.
(xi) Adjustment of pressure governors, battery charging current and other similar equipment undergoing drift in their settings due to vibration.
(xii) Cleaning of body side filters or their replacement by cleaned set.
(xiii) Cleaning filters in compressed air system and draining out accumulated water in compressed air reservoirs.
(xiv) Renewal of silica gel of transformer breather.

Inspections Coupled with Minor Corrective Maintenance

These may consist of:

(i) Inspection of circuit breakers, pantographs, tap-changer, transformer including monitoring of oil-condition through dielectric tests.
(ii) Inspection of vibration-level and terminal connections of auxiliary machines and correcting alignments.
(iii) Tightening connections which exhibit looseness.
(iv) Checking and adjustment of relay settings.
(v) Inspection of commutator for ovality.
(vi) Inspection of wheels for profile/cracks including ultrasonic testing.
(vii) Inspection for incipient cracks in bogie and couplers.
(viii) Checking adequacy of ventilation on equipments provided with forced cooling etc.

Corrective Maintenance and Overhauls

These involve aspects such as: wear and tear occurring in highly stressed parts, correcting out-of-squareness of bogies and replacing worn out parts of brake gear, reprofiling of wheels, thorough inspection of traction motors including banding, insulation and reprofiling of commutators, checking condition of rotors, changing of gaskets which show aging, checking and renewing contacts of switch gear, desludging of transformer tank, checking contacts of main circuit breaker and its adjustment, checking condition of springs and replacing those showing fatigue, checking condition of cables and replacing those showing aging, painting of body, replacing pipes and components showing corrosion etc.

These operations would need schedules extending over 10 to 15 days even with the best possible availability of unit exchange spares.

From a scrutiny of the above list which, though not exhaustive, is fairly representative of the type of maintenance work involved, one may come to the conclusion that the objectives listed out earlier and can be served by posting trained personnel at running depots located in yards and loco-sheds. These staff should be trained on multiskilling principle limiting the highly specialised skills to fewer areas only.

Particular care may be necessary in designing inspection pits in the running depots such that quick access is possible to undergear and overhead equipments to make best possible use of the available time slot.

Positioning unit-exchange spares and drilling the maintenance staff in prompt replacements can go a long way in reducing the overall time cycle.

A system of maintaining job-cards which indicate who has done what, is the best strategy for ensuring quality work through a sense of accountability.

CONDITION MONITORING TO ACHIEVE NEED-BASED MAINTENANCE

One of the key objectives of a successful maintenance strategy lies in monitoring the condition of key equipments usually in off-line mode without dismantling and preferably *in situ* such that major interventions requiring removal and dismantling get linked to physical condition. The importance of this technique in an electric locomotive is obvious.

The key equipments of a 25 kV locomotive which attract application of this technique are:

(i) Circuit breaker main contacts.
(ii) Transformer windings.
(iii) Tap-changer taps and rolling contacts.
(iv) Main rectifier diodes.
(v) Traction motor windings, banding, commutator and bearings.
(vi) Axles and armature shafts (for cracks).

(vii) Suspension bearings (for wear)
(viii) Gears (for wear and pitting).
(ix) Bogie frame (for deformation and cracks).
(x) Main centre-buffer couplers (for cracks).

The condition monitoring techniques already in use are:

(i) Testing of transformer oil for breakdown voltage
(ii) Measurement of commutator ovality *in situ* by dial-gauge or ovality-graph plotter
(iii) Monitoring bearing noise by shock-pulse meter
(iv) Ultrasonic testing of axles
(v) Meggaring of windings for insulation level.

Almost all of these fall in off-line category.

While these techniques serve their stipulated purpose, the need for periodical dismantling of major equipments on yearly, 3 yearly or 5 yearly basis remains.

Recent Developments and Trends

Recent developments in non-destructive testing, transducer technology and data acquisition systems have led to evolution of ON-line and OFF-line condition monitoring systems. Judicious application of these techniques to failure-prone equipment can minimise the need for frequent preventive check-ups and dismantling. The techniques which have been found useful are briefly discussed in the following:

DGA Test on H.V. Transformers: Abnormal generation of fault gases, viz. C_2H_2, C_2H_4, CO and CO_2, as evidenced by levels present in the oil can be interpreted as per guidelines framed in IEC or I.S. standards. Experience has proved that impending failures and major breakdowns can be prevented by timely intervention.

Remnant Life of Transformer Insulation: This can be assessed by measurement of degree of polymerisation of paper, furan content in oil and rate of CO or CO_2 formation in oil.

Residual Life of Insulation in Traction Motor and Rotating Machines: This can be assessed through tan δ measurement and determining the rate of its change in addition to absolute values. Some guidelines are available in VDE 530 which can help in assessing aging and deciding about rewinding.

Condition of Circuit Breaker and Tap Changer Contacts and Operating Mechanism: Time of interruption and condition of contacts are two most important parameters. While the former can be measured and compared, the latter can be monitered through millivolt drop as contacts are not readily accessible for temperature monitoring or visual inspection.

Silicon Diode Condition Monitoring: This may be possible through monitoring of its blocking property as quantified by flow of leakage current. This principle can be used in development of ON-line or OFF-line monitoring kits.

Monitoring Armature Banding: Armature banding is susceptible to premature failure either due to abnormal settling of the winding in service which is a manufacturing defect or frequent slippings due to loss of adhesion when the motor tends to race. In OFF-line mode, permanent lift in the end-winding as indicated by widening of the gap between armature head and end winding is a tested technique. ON-line monitoring of vibrations as in the case of power-station generators is also technically feasible.

Monitoring Bearings of Rotating Machines: The conventional method consists in monitoring of bearing temperature and noise. The latest development is measurement of shock-pulses by a shock pulse metre (SPM) which detects the shock pulses generated when free rolling gets interrupted due to some damage to bearing elements.

Ultrasonic testing of axles: Ultrasonic testing of axles which are subjected to stresses and are susceptible to fatigue failures which may have serious consequences, is a key strategy. This is possible without dismantling the axle from the bogie through special probes that can be fixed to the axle end-faces.

This technique of non-destructive testing can also be applied to traction motor armature shafts (whenever they are dismantled for other attention), bogie frames, pins and bushes of brake gearing and suspension, sleeve-type suspension bearings etc. to determine serviceability.

Cracks on Bogie Frames and Couplers: Visual inspections should be supplemented by magnaflux or other nondestructive testing techniques to detect developing fatigue cracks during visit to the depots for schedules. The sensitive points meriting this check may be defined through experience and stress analysis of the failure-prone subassemblies.

From the foregoing deliberations, it may be observed that there is enormous scope for applying condition monitoring and non-destructive testing techniques with assured advantage of avoiding dismantling just for a check up and ensuring condition-based attention. OFF-line techniques which can be used *in situ* and without dismantling are more useful and simpler than ON-line ones which may not be called for in most cases. The basic approach should be to examine application of condition monitoring techniques in failure-prone situations where prescribed check is not possible without removal/dismantling with a view to economising on maintenance down time and ensuring timely attention.

HUMAN RESOURCE DEVELOPMENT: TRAINING OF ARTISANS AND SUPERVISORS

Reliability of all mechanisms in general and traction assets in particular is closely linked to 'human reliability' or 'workmanship errors', It has been universally experienced that "Human performance is highly reliable and dependable once a job is learnt". Hence all technical establishments must develop a system of "Human resource development".

Electric traction assets require a large number of skills during manufacture, installation, operation and maintenance. These specialities or skills may fall under civil, mechanical, metallurgical, electrical or electronic disciplines when looked upon from the angle of syllabii prevalent in engineering institutions. Hence to reduce the number of personnel deployed to the bare minimum level and ensure expeditious attention, it is necessary to plan training facilities which will result in 'multi-skilling' without compromising with the quality of workmanship.

A good strategy based upon experience is to recruit skilled artisans with intimate knowledge of the most predominant skill and train them for the other allied skills in the desired proportion. Kinship to the basic engineering process is a good motivation for learning the other allied skills to generate better resourcefulness and efficiency at work. It is clear that such a training is not possible at the level of engineering institutions which lay emphasis on basic skills.

Considering the nature of work involved in maintenance of overhead equipments, power supply installations, remote control system and electric locomotives, the following basic skills may be called for:

(i) Electric fitters
(ii) Mechanical fitters
(iii) Electronic fitters
(iv) Switch gear fitters

Apart from the above, armature winders and welders may also be needed in the base sheds and workshops.

The multiskilling training to be imparted after recruiting the artisans/diploma holders for the above basic skills should be based on the maintenance requirements of specific equipment as per manuals furnished by the manufacturers. Such an orientation training would need approximately a year in training centres attached to major depots.

The supervisory staff possessing diplomas/degrees should also be trained in the maintenance of the specific equipments and should be good enough to impart on-job training to the artisans exhibiting weaknesses in execution.

Well-laid out inspection charts and repair process sheets go a long way in improving the level of skills. A system of job cards should help in pinpointing specific responsibility and inculcating a sense of accountability.

Based on review of trend of workmanship errors, refresher courses should be planned to upgrade skills and also update knowledge about new technologies and innovations.

CHAPTER 12

Railway Signalling

INTRODUCTION

The purpose of a railway signalling system is to "control the passage of trains" such that they may run at any "desired speed" in "safety". This becomes possible if presence of another train is signalled well in advance to permit braking.

BLOCK SECTION CONCEPT: AUTOMATIC BLOCK SIGNALLING

The running section of railway track may be divided into several block sections of convenient length say 5 to 10 km. At the end of every block section, there is a station where signals and other block working gadgets are located. These stations have "Distant/warning" signals at the approach end, followed by stop signal governing entry into the station premises usually called "Home signal" and departure signals at the other end of the station usually called "Starter signal". The stations are manned and actuating signal circuits/lowering of signals is done manually after required conditions of safety are met.

A quicker method of signalling could be to divide the entire length of the track into smaller block section of 1 km to 1.5 km length. Signals located at the junction point of these block sections can have multiple aspect indicating number of sections free of obstruction ahead. These aspects may be triggered by relays actuated through track circuits automatically. A schematic diagram of the above two concepts is given in Figs. 12.1 (a) and (b).

TRACK CIRCUITS

In both the concepts of signalling a train as described above, the least requirement of safety is ensured by a track circuit, which detects presence of train or vehicle on the running track and restricts the signal aspect when required. In

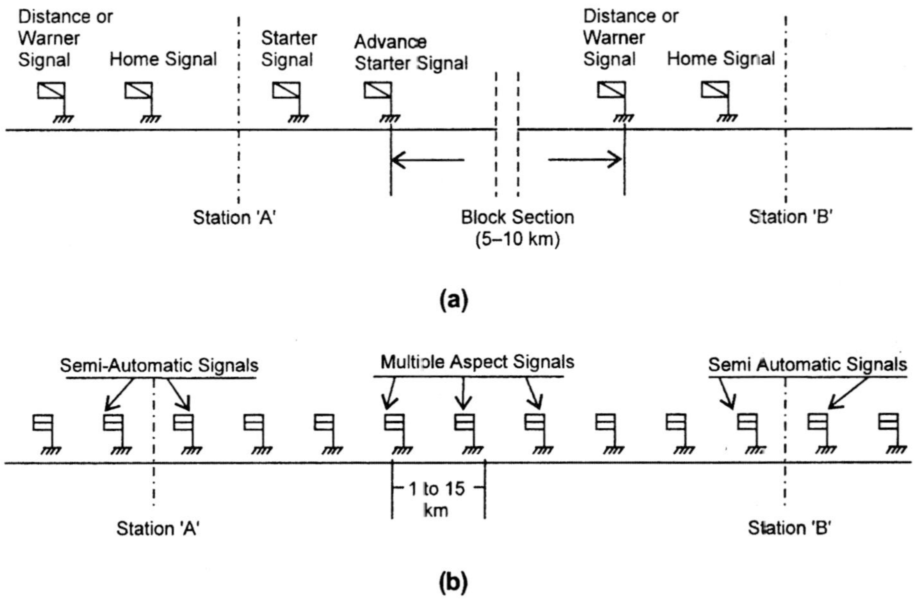

Fig. 12.1 (a) Schematic diagrams of manually operated block section and (b) automatic-block signalling

block section concept, these track circuits are located within the station limit on the main or loop line where a train is to be received.

In automatic block signalling, the entire length of the running-track is track circuited and the signal aspects are governed by occupancy or otherwise of the track sections ahead.

Track circuit concept

A track circuit is an electrical circuit formed by a section of the track isolated electrically from adjacent rail section by insulated joints. While ordinary rail joints are bridged by metallic bonds for better connectivity, the joints at the track circuit boundary are electrically insulated.

For a track circuit to be formed, it is essential that the sleepers on which the track is laid do not conduct, i.e. they are either wooden or of concrete with insulating pad. Metallic sleepers will bridge the rails and would not permit formation of the track circuit.

D.C. Track Circuit

A typical D.C. track circuit is illustrated in the schematic diagram given in Fig. 12.2. The ballast resistance is a critical variable. Ordinarily under dry condition the ballast resistance is of the order of 14-20 ohms/1000 m but under wet conditions, this may fall to a value as low as 0.5 ohm/1000 m.

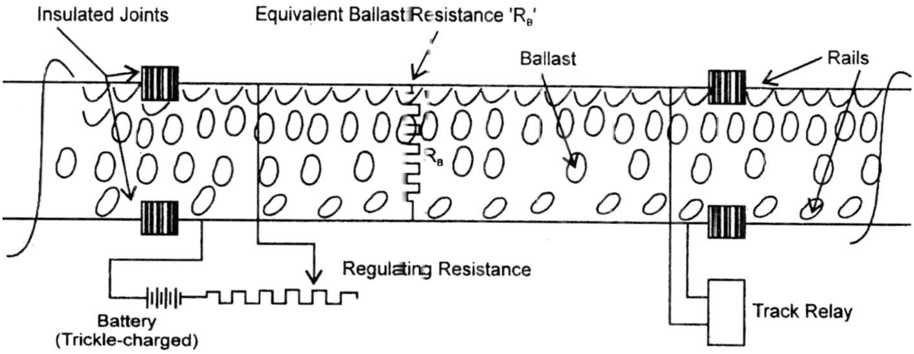

Fig. 12.2 D.C. track circuit (schematic)

When track is laid on concrete sleepers, insulated pads and fixing arrangement is used at the support points.

Normally the D.C. track relay is in energised (picked-up) condition. When a train stands on the track circuited rails, the axles act as shunt and cause the relay to drop which corresponds to occupied track condition.

For proper discrimination, relay drop-out voltage is 68% of pick up voltage.

Wet ballast can also cause relay to drop. To reduce sensitivity of the track circuit, the length is restricted such that the shunting resistance is higher than 2 ohms.

Fail Safe Principle: All signalling gear is designed on "Fail Safe" principle, i.e. if any failure occurs, the signal aspect should become restrictive. In the track circuit, this is ensured as any failure would cause relay to drop.

D.C. track circuits work satisfactorily in A.C. traction areas. It is, however, necessary to ensure that the track relay is immunised against false operation by A.C. traction currents.

A.C. Track Circuit

A capacitor-fed A.C. track circuit is illustrated in the schematic diagram given in Fig. 12.3. The advantage of a capacitor-fed track circuit is that there is no path for D.C. traction currents into the relay circuit. The track relay is an induction type relay one coil of which is connected to the mains which helps to reduce the power requirement from the track circuit.

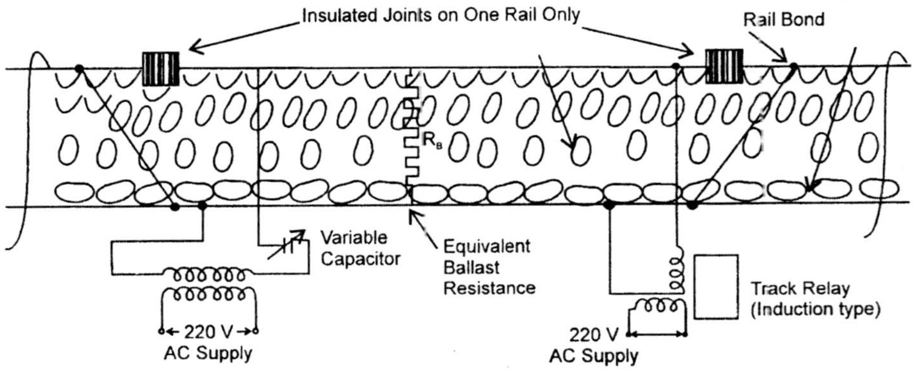

Fig. 12.3 A.C. track circuit (schematic)

A.C. track circuits are installed in D.C. traction areas.

Impedance Bonds: On A.C. electrified lines where both rails are used for traction return current, impedance bonds are provided at insulated rail joints which offer low impedance to traction currents but high resistance to track circuit currents. This is illustrated diagrammatically in Fig.12.4.

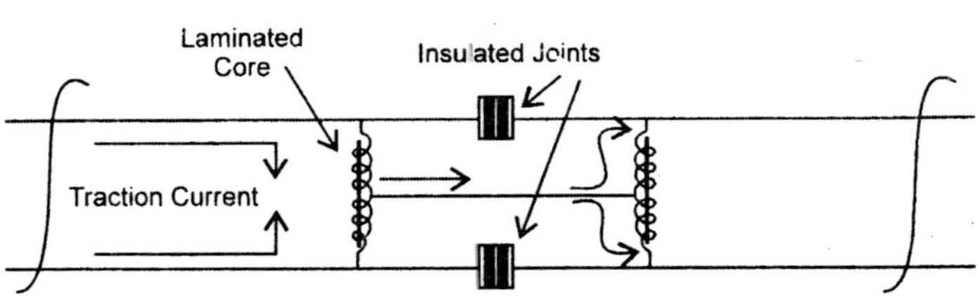

Fig. 12.4 Impedance band (schematic)

Balanced traction currents give zero effective m.m.f. in the laminated core which results in low impedance.

Electronic Track Circuits (Audio Frequency Track Circuits)

In certain areas, a track circuit has to work on D.C. as well as A.C. electrified sections contiguous to each other. Track circuits using transmitters (transistor oscillators) and receivers tuned to carrier frequency of around 1500 to 2000 Hz (but avoiding multiples of 50 Hz) have been designed, a schematic of which is shown in Fig.12.5. These track circuits are of longer length, say 2 to 2.5 km, than normally permitted for conventional D.C. or A.C. track circuits and can become cost effective in Automatic signalling areas. These track circuits can be jointless and become the only option on longwelded or continuous welded rail track.

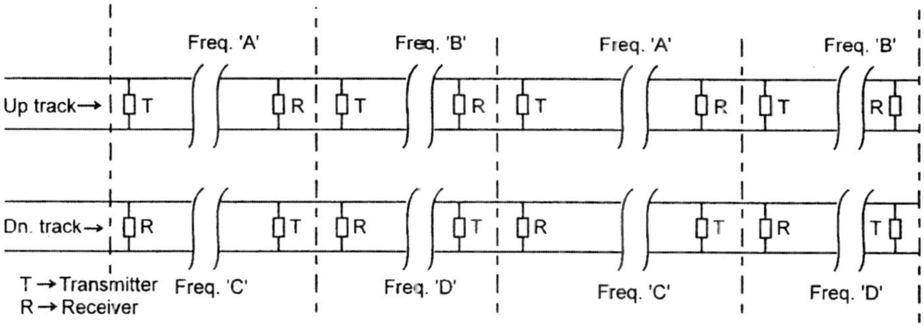

Fig. 12.5 Electronic track circuit (schematic)

Axle Counter Track Circuits

In track layouts where it is not possible to use normal track circuits and traffic density as well as speeds are low, axle counter track circuits may become cost effective. Axle counters may become the only option where rust formation on the rail or wheel surface may cause poor shunting resistance of the axle. This may be so when disc brakes get used extensively. The axle counters are installed at both ends of a track circuit. The system works on the principle of 'axle in = axle out'. Hence this system may fail where the movement is unbalanced due to movement of motor trolley, inspection carriages and slip coaches etc.

COLOUR LIGHT/SEMAPHORE SIGNALS AND INTERLOCKING PRINCIPLE

The movement of the train is governed by trackside signals, which can be lowered or made permissive if conditions for passage or reception of trains are satisfied, viz.

(a) Track is clear: This is verified by a track circuit
(b) The points for movement are correctly set and locked
(c) There is no other conflicting route set for movement.

The latter two aspects are verified by point-detectors and interlocking of concerned levers at the lever frame as well as through the mechanism of track circuit relay ensures safety. This is called Interlocking.

The signals can be with *mechanical arms* called *semaphore signals or colour light type.* The latter is universally adopted on electrified as well as high-speed routes as distance at which such signals can be installed and fed electrically presents no constraint.

The colour light signals usually have four aspects, which permit indication of the condition of block-sections ahead well in advance. The four aspects are:

Green
Double yellow
Yellow
Red

TRAIN SPEED AND SIGNALLING

For ensuring safety, it is necessary that a driver becomes aware of a stop-signal at a distance which is adequate for braking of his train. High-speed trains running at 150 kmph or more may have braking distance of the order of 2.5 to 3 km or even more with modern air/dynamic brakes. Therefore a driver should be able to know about presence of a red signal at 3 km distance or more. This becomes possible by multiple aspect colour light signals.

SOLID STATE INTERLOCKING

This is a recent trend. The basic purpose of interlocking in station areas and yards is to ensure that before a signal gets lowered, all points are set and locked and there is no conflicting route set. Besides there are no vehicles present on the signalled route. In conventional signalling interlocking is obtained by electromechanical relays.

Though the electromechanical system is a proven one it becomes complicated due to multiplicity of relays at large station and yards where a number of movements are to be controlled centrally. This has led to the development of computer-based interlocking system. It look long time to develop a computer based system which could conform to "Fail Safe" principle. Basically either of the following two strategies are adopted to ensure failure-free system, viz.

(i) Redundant software system
(ii) Redundant hardware system

Both systems are provided with diagnostic features to stall a possible failure through timely attention.

In India this system is still in an experimental stage and is yet to establish its usefulness in our situation.

AUTOMATIC WARNING SYSTEMS

Where speeds increase beyond a certain level, drivers may experience fatigue due to quick succession of signal aspects. Besides their delayed response can become disastrous.

It then becomes necessary to install an Automatic Warning or Automatic Train Stop system (AWS or ATS) to ensure safety. This is done by track-magnets, which actuate the warning or brake system in the driver's cabin, should a driver not react to the approaching restrictive signal aspect in time.

CAB SIGNALLING

Normally signals are located on trackside and have to be viewed by the driver either through the front lookout glass or the side windows. At higher speeds, such viewing becomes impossible. Further, visibility of signals also gets governed by rains or fog. Hence for higher speeds above 160 kmph, cab signalling becomes inescapable. The signal aspect gets displayed in the cab and this is done through track magnets.

SIGNALLING AT LEVEL CROSSINGS

One of the most vulnerable locations for railway accidents is the level crossing where rail borne trains interact with road traffic. While the best and foolproof arrangement would be to construct road over bridges which flyover the rail track, it is a very costly proposition and could merit adoption only at extremely busy locations.

A satisfactory way of signalling at manned as well as unmanned level crossings could be detection of an approaching train approximately 1 km in advance and actuating a flasher light for the road user at the crossing.

CHAPTER 13

Diesel Electric Traction and Excitation Control

INTRODUCTION

Diesel electric traction is achieved through a self-contained power unit, i.e. locomotive which carries the diesel engine driven D.C. generator or alternator. Since there is no need for transmitting electrical power along the track as in the case of electric traction, this system of traction, which is more efficient than steam traction and as good as electric traction in some respects, can be installed with reduced capital cost and greater degree of flexibility than available with electric traction.

The inherent limitations of this system are higher axle load for the same H.P. output, limited H.P. output due to diesel engine rating and need for a mechanism called torque converter to convert almost constant H.P. and constant torque output of the diesel engine into a variable torque constant H.P. output.

Mechanical and hydraulic torque conversion systems employing a variable gear ratio or a fluid coupling employing an impeller pump and turbine were employed initially but soon proved to be a limiting factor in realising the full capability of this system of traction. Hence a rational growth of diesel traction became possible only after Electrical Transmission system got developed. In this system, the diesel engine is coupled to a generator or alternator and the power output is utilised to drive D.C. motors.

CHARACTERISTICS OF DIESEL ENGINE

To be able to appreciate the salient features of Diesel Electric Traction (DET) it is essential to understand the relevant features of a diesel engine and its characteristics.

Diesel Engines are special type of heat engine in which chemical energy of fuel combustion is released inside the engine cylinder while in other group of heat-engines viz. steam engine or turbine, the energy generated by combustion of fuel is first transferred to steam which works the engine or the turbine.

In Germany, the birthplace of diesel engines, it is simply called as 'combustion engine'.

The main characteristic of diesel engine, which distinguishes it from other combustion engines, is the method of igniting the fuel. In diesel engine, the fuel is injected into the cylinder in the form of a fine spray, where it comes into contact with hot compressed air and ignites. Hence no external means of ignition is required. The usual compression ratios of diesel engines vary from 12:1 to 19:1. With lower compression ratio than 12:1 there is a danger that the temperature of compressed air may not be high enough to ensure ignition of the fuel especially when the engine is started from "cold".

Another important characteristic of diesel engine is that it produces a torque, which is more or less independent of speed. As the amount of air admitted during the suction stroke is limited, so is the fuel it can burn and thrust it can generate upon ignition. The torque being a function of the thrust and its leverage about the crankshaft, therefore, is independent of speed.

The rated horsepower of the engine is function of the torque and rated speed; hence the maximum horsepower is obtained at the maximum speed and is also fixed. Diesel engine is more or less a constant H.P. engine with overload capacity of 10% or less.

The maximum speed of a diesel engine is limited due to the reciprocating motion between the piston and the crankshaft and presence of sliding friction between the piston and the cylinder. Most diesel engines have rated speeds of the order of 1000 rpm and the maximum is around 2000 rpm.

Diesel engine has higher thermal efficiency than other heat engines due to the fact that the heat energy of combustion is directly converted into mechanical energy without another intervening stage.

Diesel engines are of two-stroke or four-stroke types. The main difference between two-stroke and four-stroke engines is in the method of removing the burnt gases and filling the cylinder with fresh charge of air. In a four-stroke engine, these operations are performed during exhaust and suction strokes of the engine. In a two-stroke engine these operations are performed near bottom dead centre by means of a separate air pump or blower.

Supercharging: This consists in pushing air compressed by a separate pump or blower rather than leaving the engine to cater to its air requirement through natural aspiration from the atmosphere. As greater amount of air so admitted can burn larger quantity of fuel, supercharging increases the power developed by an engine of given piston displacement and speed.

Governing: The purpose of governor is to keep the engine running at a desired speed regardless of the changes in the load carried by the engine.

The diesel engine governors sense the speed of the engine and regulate the fuel supply to suit the load fluctuations of a limited magnitude.

Diesel Engine Characteristic

Typical torque-speed and H.P.-speed characteristics of a diesel engine are as shown in Fig. 13.1. Rated H.P. output is realised at the maximum rated speed.

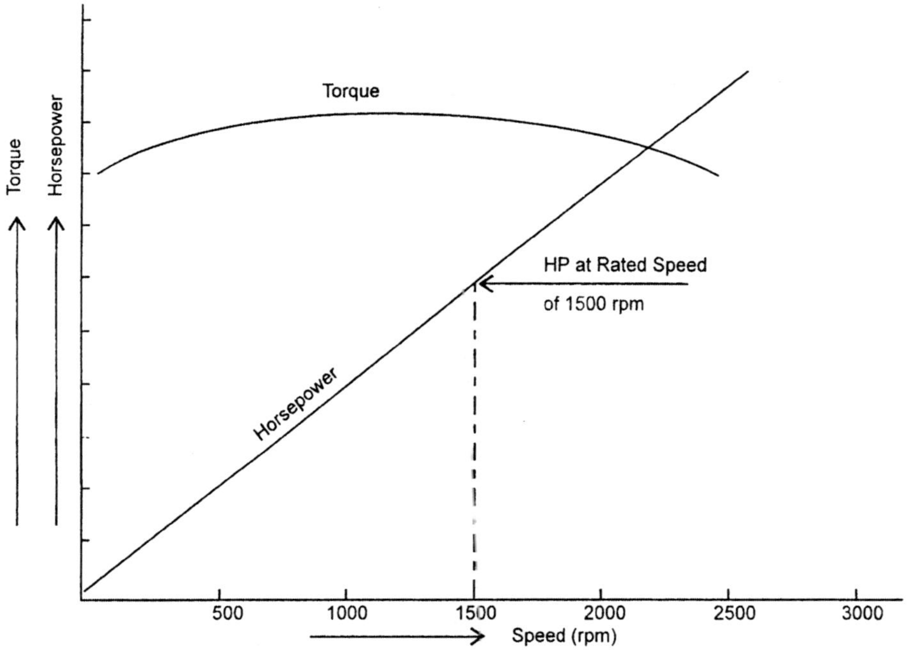

Fig. 13.1 Speed-torque and horsepower-speed characteristic of a diesel engine

Diesel engines do not have starting torque. Hence a means of starting them.

either by compressed air-motor or using the generator as motor powered by a 'starting battery', has to be provided.

USE OF DIESEL ENGINE FOR TRACTION DUTY

Traction duty demands a high torque at start so as to overcome the static friction of the trailing load as well as giving a residual accelerating torque. The running torque required is approximately inversely proportional to speed for any particular setting of the control.

Since the speed at starting is zero, the horsepower required is negligible. The requirement of H.P. builds up as the load accelerates and is maximum just before the finish of acceleration period. After finish of the acceleration period the H.P. required settles down at a level necessary for overcoming the train resistance due to friction and aerodynamic drag.

Torque Converter

In sharp contrast to the above characteristics of a traction load, the diesel engine is primarily a constant speed, constant power unit.

Hence the diesel locomotive essentially requires a mechanism for converting constant torque at full engine speed into a variable torque (T) at the locomotive wheel which is inversely proportional to the train speed (N) such that ($T \times N$) is constant and corresponds to the constant H.P. output of the diesel engine. This exactly is the function of torque converter, which converts fixed H.P. of the diesel engine into a variable tractive effort at different train speeds including starting.

Hence it will be seen that while a diesel locomotive is capable of a high tractive effort at starting and low speeds, its tractive effort at higher speeds would reduce sharply.

The diesel locomotive is, therefore ideally suited for hauling heavier loads at lower speeds.

ELECTRICAL TORQUE-CONVERTER OR POWER TRANSMISSION SYSTEM

Torque-Speed Curve of D.C. Series Motor

A D.C. series motor is idealy suited for traction duty as its torque-speed characteristic corresponds to the traction requirement of high torque at low speed and reducing torque at higher speeds. In a D.C. series motor

$$T \propto I . \varnothing \propto \varnothing^2$$

where I is armature current and $\varnothing$ field flux.

and $\quad V \propto N . \varnothing$

where N is speed of rotation.

or $\quad \varnothing \propto \dfrac{V}{N}$

$\therefore \quad T \propto \dfrac{V^2}{N^2}$

At a given voltage, therefore, torque is inversely proportional to N^2 and drops sharply as the speed increases. The curve of torque vs speed is hyperbolic as evident from Fig. 13.2 (a).

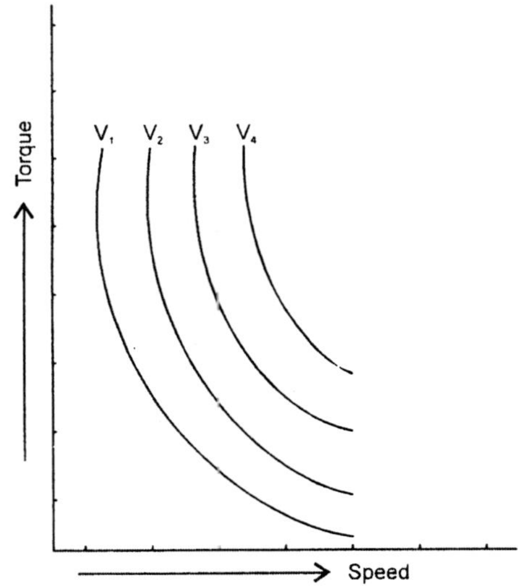

Fig. 13.2 (a) Torque-speed curve of a D.C. series motor at different voltages

D.C. Generator Characteristic to Match Diesel Engine Output

Speed-torque characteristic of D.C. series motor is closest to the diesel engine characteristic, though not ideally suited. An ideally suited speed-torque characteristic for diesel engine would have the following relationship:

$$T.N. = \text{H.P.} = \text{Constant}$$

whereas in a D.C. series motor $T.N^2 \propto V^2$; hence torque-speed curve is different for different voltages but some what similar to diesel engine *T-N* curve at any particular voltage.

From the curves in Fig. 13.2 (b) it would appear that if the voltage applied to the traction motors is varied in suitable steps, different combinations of train speed (*N*) and torque (*T*) can be found which have intersection points falling on the ideal curve conforming to the diesel engine characteristic and traction load *T-N* curve requirements. The varying voltages applied to the traction motor can be achieved through excitation control of the D.C. generator.

It follows from the foregoing discussion that there is a need for designing a generator system whose output voltage can be varied and matched with the diesel engine output curve. Such a generator would serve as a flexible power link between the diesel engine running at a fixed speed and constant H.P. and the traction motors.

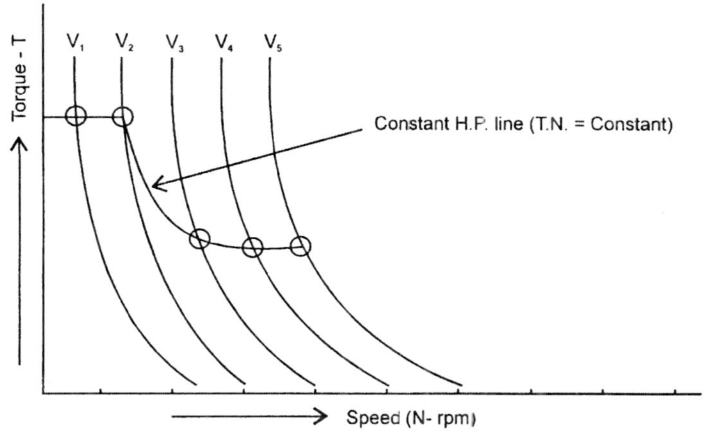

Fig. 13.2 (b) Matching of diesel engine and traction load TN curve by voltage control of the series motor

Therefore, essentially the problem reduces to developing a system wherein the output of the D.C. generator corresponds to the diesel engine power curve.

Referring to Fig. 13.2 (c) the ideal *V.I* curve of a generator to correspond to fixed diesel engine output would be DC' B. On this curve *V.I* is constant.

As against the above requirement, the nearest shunt generator output *V.I* curve is ABCDE.

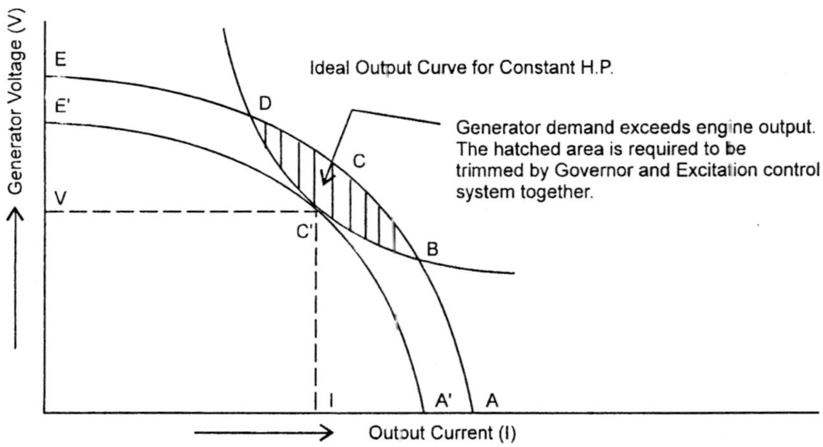

Fig. 13.2 (c) Matching of generator and diesel engine characteristic through excitation control of the generator

If the hatched portion is to be completely avoided, it is possible to have a generator characteristic corresponding to A' C' E' which will give the rated output of the diesel engine only at one point, viz. C'.and would underload the engine at all other points. This will under-utilise the diesel engine for most part of the working range.

Such an arrangement is very simple and could be utilised in shunting services. For main line locomotives, it is necessary that the full capability of diesel engine gets utilised over a wide working range of the generator.

A well designed generator excitation system working in conjunction with the engine governor can alter the *V.I* curve of the generator such that it matches with the engine output curve over a wide working range. The generator is to be provided with a regulating winding which ensures the required degree of drop in voltage with increasing current. Such a mechanism could be actuated in one of the following ways:

(a) Governor actuated servomechanism,
(b) Magnetic amplifier actuated field control,
(c) Transistorised excitation control system.

ELECTRICAL TRANSMISSION UTILISING 3-PHASE ALTERNATOR IN CONJUNCTION WITH A SILICON DIODE RECTIFIER

Around 1965, a new type of transmission system based on 3-phase alternator combined with a silicon-diode rectifier became commercially available. This development was impelled by the following limitations of the D.C. generator system:

(a) Use of commutator in a D.C. machine limited the maximum peripheral speed of the generator and led to an increased size or unfavourable weight: power ratio.
(b) Commutator and brush gear called for expensive maintenance.
(c) Higher efficiency to the tune of 2 to 3% is achievable in the alternator-based transmission system as compared to D.C. generator-based system.

The system, however, has a disadvantage, as the D.C. generator is no more available to perform the starting duty.

Use of silicon controlled rectifier (SCR) or thyrister in place of diodes further simplifies voltage control system.

ELECTRICAL TRANSMISSION USING GTO CONVERTER-INVERTER SUPPLYING INDUCTION MOTORS

As in the case of electric locomotives, 3-phase induction motor drives powered by variable voltage and frequency power-source have become a commercially viable proposition from around 1985.

The alternator output is rectified by a GTO thyristor bridge to a suitable link voltage which is then inverted into VVVF power supply which, in turn, is fed to the 3-phase squirrel cage motors working as traction motor. PWM control of the GTO thyristors helps to produce a sinusoidal waveform free from dangerous harmonics.

This system of transmission has the advantage of using maintenance-free squirrel cage motors which are much lighter and compact than D.C. series motors and capable of working at higher speeds. Induction motors also have a very steep *T-N* characteristic which is a distinct advantage in traction duty.

Besides the above advantages, regeneration during braking becomes less complicated. This feature helps to save energy to the tune of 20 to 25% in electric traction especially where severe gradients or frequent stoppages are involved. In case of diesel engines, energy saving is much less than electric engines as regenerated power can only cater to the auxiliary load which is around 10%.

CHAPTER 14

LEM-Propelled Traction: Recent Trends

INTRODUCTION

Electric traction using rotary electric motors (REM) has been dealt with in the previous chapters. The torque produced by REMs is converted to pull via gears (mounted on motor shafts and driving axles) and the wheel-rail interaction (between the driving wheels and the track rails). In this transformation, the wheel-rail interaction, i.e. the adhesion between the driving wheels and the track, plays an important role. This is so because it decides the maximum torque at driving wheel-rim that will be converted to pull along the track, for moving the locomotive/EMU and the trailing coaches. As has been discussed in Chapter 3, this transformation is dependent upon many factors and there are methods for improving it.

The present chapter deals with linear electric motor based electric traction which is independent of adhesion between the wheel and the rail and hence the associated problems. In fact, in this system there are no driving wheels. The wheels only perform the function of suspension and lateral guidance. Thus by suitably integrating a levitating system with a linear electric motor-propelled vehicle we can obtain a wheel-less drive.

LINEAR ELECTRIC MOTOR

A linear electric motor (LEM) is obtained by cutting-open a rotary electric motor and laying it flat as shown in Fig. 14.1. In this process the mechanical torque and speed in revolutions per minute at the shaft of the rotary electric motor become mechanical force and speed in meter per sec at the flat secondary/primary member of the linear electric motor. In this way, depending upon the application, a linear version of all types of rotary electric motors can be obtained. It has been found

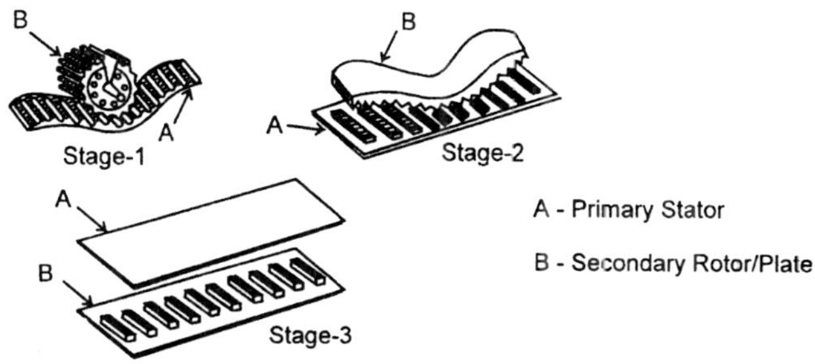

Fig. 14.1 Evolution of linear induction motor from rotary induction motor

that for traction applications the linear induction motor (LIM) is most convenient to apply and economical to maintain.

Linear synchronous speed of an LIM is expressed as:

$$V_S = 2\tau_P f \text{ m/s}$$

where τ_P is the pole pitch in m, and f is the frequency of supply in Hz. From the above equation it is evident that altering the pole-pitch and/or the supply frequency can change the synchronous speed. Since there is no limit on the pole-pitch, the synchronous speed can be changed to any value. Thus for a linear synchronous speed of 400 kmph the pole-pitch for 50 Hz operation will be:

$$\tau_P = (400 \times 1000)/(3600 \times 2 \times 50) = 1.1 \text{ m}$$

Note: In rotary induction motor at 50 Hz, the maximum synchronous speed corresponding to two poles is 3000 r.p.m.

LINEAR INDUCTION-BASED TRACTION SYSTEM

In its simplest form a LIM-based traction system will have the primary member fixed to the underside of the vehicle and the secondary member fixed on the track between the two rails as shown in Fig. 14.2. LIM's can be used for traction purposes in many other ways also as shown in Figs. 14.3 and 14.4.

Arrangements described in Figs. 14.2 and 14.3 have a distinct advantage as the mechanical clearance, between the primary member and the secondary member along the track length, can be conveniently maintained at its minimum. In case of the arrangement shown in Fig. 14.3 the problems associated with the cur-

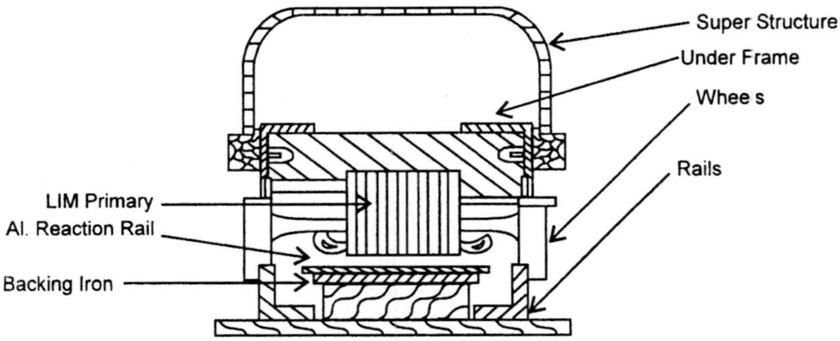

Fig. 14.2 Moving-primary fixed-secondary single-sided LIM

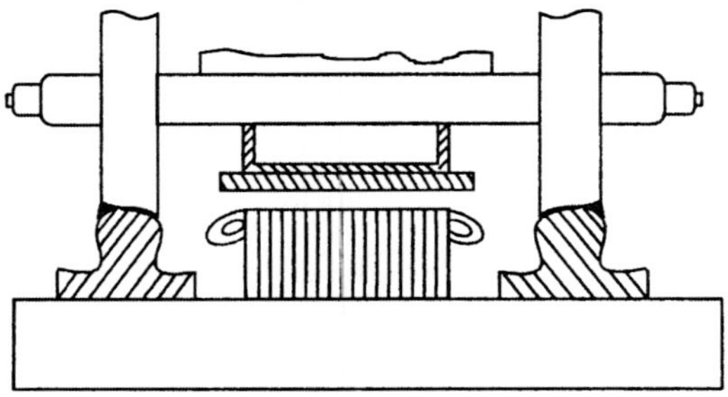

Fig. 14.3 Moving-secondary fixed-primary single-sided LIM

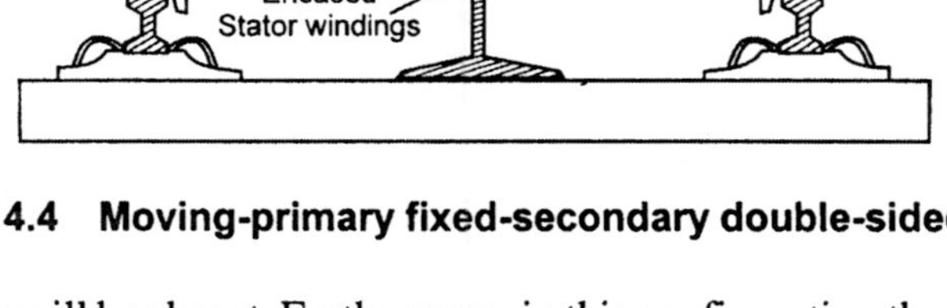

Fig. 14.4 Moving-primary fixed-secondary double-sided LIM

rent collection will be absent. Furthermore, in this configuration the motor-weight of the secondary member attached to the moving vehicle will be much lower as compared to the motor-weight of the primary member attached to the moving vehicle in the arrangement of Fig. 14.2. This feature of the arrangement of Fig. 14.3 increases the value of the pay-load-to-tore-load ratio and hence the specific energy consumption. However, the track cost will be much higher because expensive primary member with its copper winding will have to be laid all along the track. For this reason the system can be advantageous only when the utilisation factor of the track is very high, that is, at all instants of time, most of the primary member along the track sees a secondary member below the vehicle. In majority of the traction applications this is not possible and hence a major portion of the length of the primary member does not see a secondary member and this affects significantly the performance of arrangement shown in Fig. 14.3.

In the system shown in Fig. 14.4 the secondary aluminium reaction rail faces a primary on either side. These primaries are so connected that the opposite poles are formed in the primary members along the length on either side of the secondary member and the travelling field is produced so that propulsive forces are produced in the same direction. Contrary to the system shown in Fig. 14.2, there is no need for a backing-iron along the track as the laminated core used in each primary also plays the role of backing iron for improving the magnetic circuit for the other primary. However, the problem of maintaining a uniform mechanical clearance between the secondary aluminium plate and the two primaries (on either side) all along the track becomes complex, particularly at points and crossings. It also increases the risk of accidents that may occur as a result of changes in the gap due to sudden production of lateral forces on the moving vehicle. Considering these disadvantages of Fig. 14.4 in which although the force-to-weight ratio of the reaction rail is higher, the system shown in Fig. 14.2 is normally preferred for traction applications.

STRENGTHS/WEAKNESSES OF LIM-PROPELLED RAILWAY TRACTION

Historically electric traction using linear electric motor is as old as the rotary electric motor traction itself. In 1845 a trolley was moved using a linear version of rotary electric motor. However, certain major drawbacks did not permit the adoption of this technology for traction application. In this section the strengths and weaknesses of the LIM-propelled traction have been discussed. The discussion is important because it would help to appreciate the reasons for adoption of this technology for underground Metro Rail transport system.

Strengths of LIM-Propelled Railway Traction System

LIM-propelled railway traction system has the following advantages over its rotary electric motor counterpart and the D.C. traction motor based system:

(a) In LIM-propelled system the pull produced for propelling the system is independent of adhesion between the wheels of the motorised coach and the rail. In fact, the system has no driving-wheel and hence no associated adhesion problem. This feature permits negotiation of steeper gradients.
(b) The two wheels fixed to an axle can rotate independent of each other and hence the curve negotiating property improves.
(c) The system does not require gears as the pull is directly produced in the moving vehicle through the linear force developed in the primary member attached to it. This results in reduction in the associated noise level and also the cost of maintenance.
(d) In case of levitated system, linear electric motor propulsion is the only possibility.
(e) The floor height above the rail level is substantially reduced. Thus without altering the height of the coach-ceiling above the floor-level, the total height of the coach-ceiling above the track-level's reduced. This will result in corresponding reduction in the height of bridges and the diameter of tunnels along the route.
(f) Since high speeds can be achieved without gears and adhesion it can be used for high speed levitated trains.

Weaknesses of LIM-Propelled Railway Traction System

The major weakness of the LIM propelled traction system are discussed in the following.

(a) The system requires laying of a reaction rail consisting of aluminium plate backed by mild steel plate all along the route. This considerably adds to the cost of the track.
(b) Since the aluminium is relatively an expensive material, it is prone to pilferage and hence disruption of service due to this reason.
(c) The air-gap in LIM, for mechanical reasons, has to be kept at a value many times higher than that conveniently possible for RIM. This leads to deterioration of motor power factor that also contributes to motor losses.
(d) Since there is discontinuity in the magnetic and electric circuits at the entry and exit ends of the motor, it leads to production of corresponding losses and hence the motor efficiency becomes poorer. However, at low and medium speeds this problem is not so serious as it would be for high-speed applications.
(e) Three-phase linear induction motor would necessitate a suitable on-board power-conditioner, in the form of an inverter, for operation from a single-phase a.c. or d.c. power distribution along the track.

PRACTICAL POSSIBILITIES OF LIM-PROPELLED TRANSPORTATION

The LIM-propelled modes of transport systems have enormous amount of flexibility in their design and topology and, therefore, these are compatible with other modes of transport. These systems can operate from lowest to highest desirable speeds.

Table 14.1 gives a classification of transportation systems based on requirements excluding air and sea travel. The criteria for classification are based on journey-distance, speed-of-operation, and type of suspension. The table also includes a brief discussion of each type of transportation system from the point of view of its usefulness.

In Table 14.2 some technically feasible LIM-propelled transport systems have been listed. The table also highlights the most suitable fields of application for each type.

It is evident that in comparison to the existing transportation technologies, a reliable and comparatively maintenance-free transportation system may be obtained by integrating an LIM-propulsion unit, having 100% transmission efficiency, with the well established and proven steel-wheel-on-steel-rail suspension-cum-guidance system.

However, it must be borne in mind that the aluminium secondary plate laid all along the track is vulnerable to theft and this factor alone would limit the adoption of this technology in most countries for traction applications.

INPUTS/MODIFICATIONS FOR ADOPTION OF LIM PROPULSION IN THE EXISTING SYSTEM

Advantages of LIM-based traction system can be best exploited if the complete system (track, vehicle, current-collection etc.) is designed, manufacture and installed from scratch. However, the technology can be adopted in a phased manner also if the existing railway track and vehicles are suitably modified as discussed in detail.

Track Modification

Case A: If it is already electrified and can be made available for LIM-propelled system.

Table 14.1 Need-Based Classification of Surface Transport systems

Criteria	Types	Remarks
Journey distance	(a) City Centre Service—upto 5 km (b) In-city service—5 to 15 km	For movement of pedestrians in the city centres along straight/circular platforms
	(c) Suburban service—15 to 30 km (d) Urban service—30 to 60 km (e) Intercity service—60 to 500 km (f) Interstate service—500 to 1000 km (g) International—above 1000 km	Along high-density routes.
Speed of operation	(a) Walking speed—5 to 10 kmph	Using moving-platforms/people mover system.
	(b) Low speed—30 to 80 kmph (c) Medium speed—80 to 250 kmph (d) High speed—250 to 700 kmph (e) Ultrahigh speed—above 700 kmph	Using lightweight coaches with/without levitation, surface, underground and overhead systems.
Suspension	(a) Steel-wheel on steel-rail	For low and medium speeds.
	(b) Rubber-tyre wheel on rail (c) Air cushions (d) Magnetic cushions	For high and ultrahigh speeds.
	(e) Water surface	For waterways along pre-defined route and for crossing rivers.

Table 14.2 Classification of Some Technically Feasible LEM-Propelled Transport Systems

Criteria	Types	Remarks
Number of sides	(a) Single sided (b) Double sided sandwiched secondary (c) Double sided sandwiched primary	For surface, underground and overhead transportation. For surface transport modes only. For overhead transportation.
Relative size of Pri. & Sec.	(a) Long primary/Short secondary (b) Short primary/Long Secondary	Primary utilisation poor. Preferred when track utilisation is high. Primary utilisation 100%. Has a current collection problem.
Stationary/ Moving	(a) Fixed primary/moving secondary (b) Fixed secondary/moving primary	For high traffic-density/utility-factor. For low and medium traffic-density/utility-factor.
Direction of return path of flux	(a) In direction of motion—longitudinal flux (b) In direction 90° to the direction of motion—transverse flux	For low and medium speed without levitation, force/weight and Force/power ratios high. For high-speed application. Can behave like magnetic-river producing levitation, lateral-guidance and propulsion forces. Force/weight and force/power ratios low.
Suspension	(a) Steel wheel on steel-rail (b) Rubber-wheel on road (c) Flat surface on water (d) Air Cushion (e) Levitation	Best choice with motor propulsion having100% transmission efficiency. Same as for type (a) but has about six times more frictional losses. For crossing rivers and for travel along the length of the river. Proposed but dropped. Useful for wheel-less travel along pre-defined routes with exclusive right of way.
System	(a) Surface (b) Overhead (c) Underground (d) Trolley bus (e) Ropeways (f) Waterways (g) Moving platform (h) People mover	(i) Type (a), (b), (c), (g) and (h): Can be without or with levitation. (ii) Type (a): For any transport system. (iii) Type (b) and (c): For in-city/city-centre travel. (iv) Type (b) and (e): for hilly areas. (v) Type (f): For crossing river and for moving along the length of river. (vi) Type (c): For moving between fixed points. (vii) Type (h): For circular routes in city-centres.

Modification required for Case A: A reaction rail consisting of aluminium sheet backed by MS sheet should be laid between the existing steel rails.

Case B: If the track is not electrified.

Modifications required for Case B: (i) The track should be electrified, (ii) Modifications similar to Case A.

Vehicle Modification

(i) Axles to be redesigned with wheels of reduced diameter mounted on roller bearings such that the two wheels of the same axle rotate independently.
(ii) The primary member to be mounted between axles of each bogie.
(iii) Matching modifications in existing mechanical braking.

Voltage and Speed Control

Depending upon the power available from OHE there should be a suitable converter/inverter (along with a transformer for a.c. supply and an inverter alone in case of a d.c. supply) to give three-phase VVVF a.c. supply to the on-board primary members. Features that will make regenerative braking possible should be incorporated.

LIM-PROPELLED UNDERGROUND METRO RAIL SYSTEM

In Table 14.2 technically feasible LIM-propelled transportation systems were discussed. Of these the most promising application of this technology is for underground Metro Rail transportation. This section elaborates upon the factors that make it best suited for underground Metro systems in the present-day technological scenario.

Factors Influencing Adoption of LIM for Metro Rail

Earlier we have discussed the strengths and weaknesses of LIM propelled Railway system. We will now analyse, point by point, the features of Metro Rail System, which make LIM propulsion an ideal choice.

(a) In conventional Metro rail system the energy used for traction is approximately 25% of the total energy consumed as compared to approximately 80% in case of surface rail system. For this reason the motor efficiency does not significantly affect the total energy consumption used in Metro rail system. On the other hand, the reduced diameter of the tunnel reduces energy consumption for air conditioning substantially.

(b) With the development of variable voltage variable frequency (VVVF) drives for rotary induction motors, the possibility of LIM based transport system has improved phenomenally. VVVF controllers enable single-phase power distribution and give a smooth starting and continuous speed control features. These controllers also improve the system power-factor and energy-efficiency. The improvement in energy efficiency is for two reasons, first through regenerative braking which reduces the total energy consumed for traction purposes and secondly through significant reduction in energy consumed in air conditioning as the heat produced due to mechanical braking gets minimized.

(c) As shown in Fig. 14.2, since LIM primary fixed on the coach axles is a flat coil, the coach floor can be brought down and the wheel diameters reduced. Studies conducted have concluded that with LIM propulsion, the underground Metro tunnel diameter can be easily reduced to approximately 75% of the existing tunnel diameter resulting in reduction of the tunneling cost to about 60%.

(d) With the reduction in tunnel diameter the total volume of air requiring air conditioning will also reduce and hence there will be a corresponding reduction on air-conditioning load.

(e) It is evident that adhesion is not a limiting feature in LIM-propelled system. Hence track can be laid with steeper gradients. Also the wheels fixed to an axle can rotate independently thereby improving the curve negotiating property of the vehicle. With these two features the track alignment can tolerate sharper curvatures and steeper gradients. This may help to reduce the track length between two points thus permitting reduction in the specific energy consumption even if it is considered that energy consumed for hauling the load remains unaltered.

(f) There is a vertical force of attraction between the primary laminated iron and the backing iron in the reaction rail. It acts as a stabilising force, thereby reducing the chances of derailment. However, if backing-iron is eliminated from the secondary member then a force of repulsion will be produced due to eddy currents in the secondary-conducting rail.

(g) The only moving part in the system is the wheel fixed via bearings to the axles. Therefore wear-and-tear of the motor-rotor and the gears is eliminated. This also reduces noise inside the tunnel considerably.

(h) In the conventional traction system employing rotary electric motor, the tractive effort (required to haul the train) is produced at the contact surface between the driving wheels and the steel rails. Thus the stresses produced at any point on the track is a function of tractive effort divided by the contact surface area. In case of LIM-propelled system however, the forces are produced directly in the primary and secondary members throughout the surface area facing each other. Also since each coach is expected to have at least two primaries fixed on each bogie the force per unit area produced on the track will be considerably lowered. This feature when exploited while designing the track could lead to saving in cost of laying the track and the cost of material used.

(i) In Metro application the expensive reaction rail material is inside the tunnel and not exposed to general public. Therefore, the possibility of reaction-rail pilferage gets eliminated. This is an important point that makes LIM propulsion easily adaptable in underground Metro application.

(j) Another feature of the Metro system that ideally suits LIM propulsion is the high frequency of service. This improves the utilisation factor of the investments on reaction-rail.

(k) The complete arrangement is such that the maintenance of motors and gears gets almost eliminated.

The net effect of the above-mentioned features is to reduce the cost of Metro-rail construction and operation. Thus it could lead to a financially viable Metro-rail system for the cities and the metropolis.

International Scenario

The potential of LIM-propelled system, with VVVF inverters, in underground Metro rail systems is being widely appreciated. In Japan, studies have led to the conclusion that new subways may employ LIM propulsion technology almost universally. Based on the experiences gained on LIM-propelled wheel-on-rail systems, levitation technologies when developed at reasonable cost, could be integrated to have levitated coaches propelled by LIM's. Table 14.3 gives a summary of these developments at the international level.

Layout of a Typical System for Metro Applications

Figure 14.5 illustrates schematically the layout of a typical underground Metro rail system propelled by LIM. The figure also shows a cut-section of the tunnel and the coach on a platform and a similar section inside a tunnel. The two LIM primaries are fixed between the two axles of each bogie. Since the axles are non-rotating, direct fixing of primary members becomes possible. The primary and secondary suspensions between the coach and the bogies will be more or less similar to the suspensions used in the conventional system. The figure also shows a section of the track. It is similar to the existing track except that it has a reaction-rail consisting of aluminium plate backed by a mild-steel U-shaped channel.

Table 14.3 International Scenario of Linear Motor-based Systems

S.No.	System	Application	Particulars	Status
Air-Cushion/Rubber-Tyre/wheel-on-Rail				
1.	Duke University at North Carolina,USA	Shuttle Service	LIM (Short primary), Air Cushion, 2-km Dual Guideway	Operating since 1981
2.	Wedway People Mover System, Houston Airport, USA	Airport People Mover	LIM (Short Primary). Rubber Tyre	Operating since 1983
3.	Scarborough, Canada	Urban Transit	LIM (Short primary), Steel Wheel-on-rail, 7.1-km Track	Operating since 1985
4.	Advanced LRT, Vancouver, Canada	Urban Transit	LIM (Short Primary), Steel Wheel-on-rail, 24.5-km Track	Operating since 1986
5.	Detroit People Mover, Detroit, USA	Urban Transit	LIM (Short primary), Steel Wheel-on-rail, 4.7-km Track	Operating since 1987
6.	Osaka Line # 7, Japan	Mini Subway	LIM (Short primary), Steel Wheel-on-rail 5.2-km Track	Operating since 1990
7.	Tokyo Line # 12, Japan	Mini Subway	LIM (Short primary), Steel Wheel-on-rail, 43-km Track	Operating since 1997
MAGLEV Slow Speed Systems				
8.	Birmingham people Mover, UK	Airport People Mover	LIM (Short primary), Attraction (EMS), 600 m long	Operating since 1984
9.	M-Bahn, Berlin	Urban Transit	LSM (Long primary), Attraction (Permanent Magnet) 1.6 km long	Completed and removed
10.	Yokohama Exposition '89, Japan	Demo track	LIM (Short primary), Attraction (EMS) 600 m long	Completed and system removed
11.	Nagoya, Japan	Urban Transit	LIM (Short primary), Attraction (EMS) 7 km long	Under construction
MAGLEV High Speed Systems				
12.	Miyazaki (Linear Express), Japan	Test Track	LSM (Long primary), Repulsion (EDS)	Many prototypes tested
13.	EMSLAND, Germany (Transrapid)	Test Track	LSM (Long primary), Attraction (EMS) 31.5 km	Many prototypes tested
14.	Tokyo-Osaka high speed corridor on Maglev	High Speed Trains	LSM (Long primary), Repulsion (EDS)	50 km under construction for trials

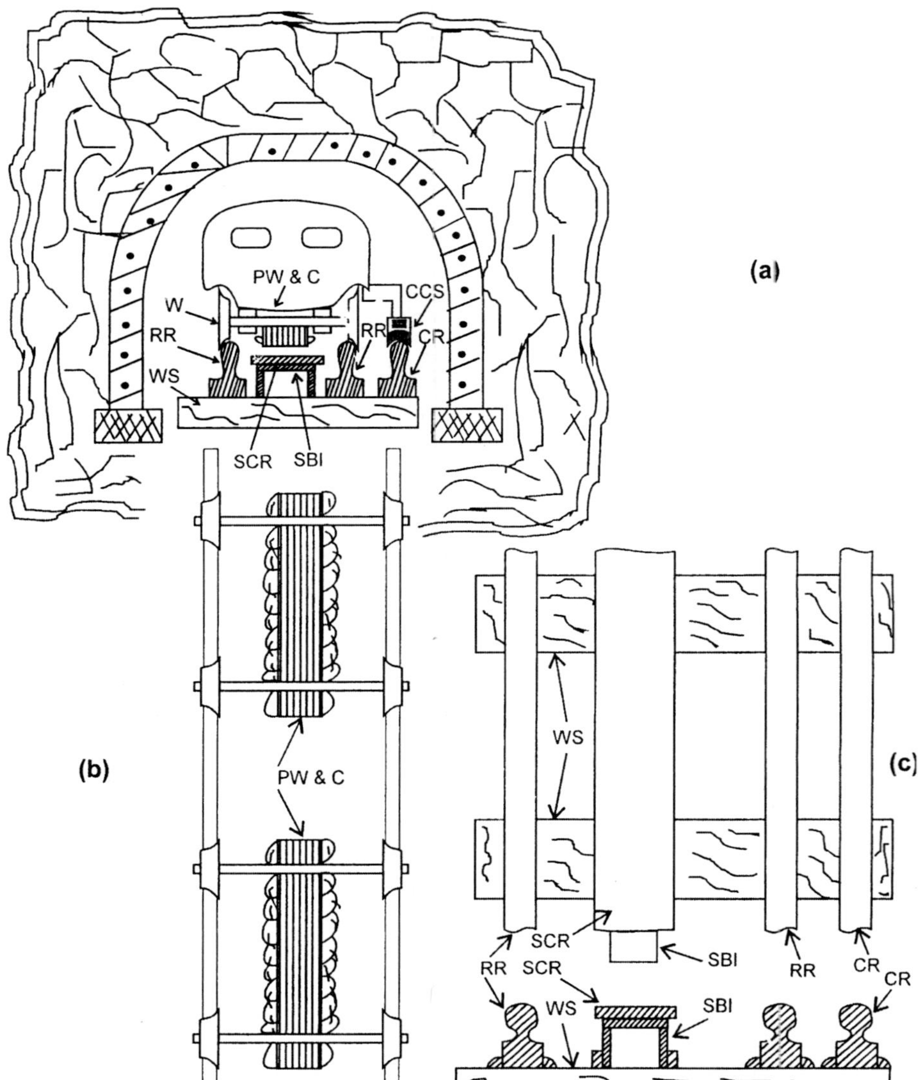

Fig. 14.5 Schematic diagram of LIM propelled Metro-rail system: (a) Cross-section of tunnel with LIM propelled coach; PW & C: Primary winding & core; SCR: Secondary conducting rail; SBI: Secondary backing-iron; CCS: Current collection shoe; CR: Current rail; RR: Running rails; WS: Wooden sleepers; W: Wheel; (b) Fixing position of primary member on the bogies; and (c) Track with reaction-rail and backing-iron

WHEEL-LESS TRACTION

Wheels play an important role in the transportation world. They provide suspensions and lateral guidance to the moving vehicles. The driving wheels, in addition, contribute towards conversion of motor-torque to linear-pull due to adhesion between the periphery of the wheel and the track.

One of the most significant modifications in the design-methodology of LIM based traction system is the consideration that the pull is independent of adhesion between the wheel and the rail. The implication of this major change in the design methodology of traction systems is especially important for transportation systems operating at high speeds when the coefficient of adhesion becomes poor and hence also the motor-torque to pull ratio. The permissible discrepancy in the level between one rail and the other for the conventional freight and commuter trains, as per the Federal Rail Administration (FRA) standards, is given in Table 14.4.

Table 14.4 Permissible Discrepancy between the Levels of the two Rails

Speed in kmph	Permissible discrepancy in mm
120	32
180	13
250	4

Thus satisfying standards for high-speed services is not only very difficult but it is also very expensive.

The problems associated with high-speed traction can be summarised as:

(i) Insufficient adhesion between the driving wheel and the rail.
(ii) High maintenance-cost due to increased wear-and-tear.
(iii) Stringent track standards.
(iv) Increase in the level of environmental noise pollution and vibration due to rubbing action of steel-wheel on steel-rail.

With wheel-less traction most of the problems discussed above will be reduced/eliminated. This can be achieved by employing a suitable levitation scheme. Table 14.5 compares wheel-on-rail system with levitated system.

Levitation Schemes

The main objective of various levitation schemes is to nullify the gravitational force acting on the moving vehical and provide vertical force so that the vehicle

Table 14.5 Wheel-on-rail Suspension System versus Levitation System

S. No.	Parameter	Wheel-on-rail system	Levitation system
1.	Contact Pressure	Point contact. Typical contact pressure around 70,000 psi	Large support area. Contact pressure of the order of 1-1.5 psi
2.	Propulsion	Through wheel-rail adhesion	Contactless-propulsion through on-board jet or linear motor
3.	Upper speed	Limited by wheel-rail adhesion limits	Limited by aerodynamic force
4.	Noise level	Medium to high	Low to medium
5.	Wear-and-tear/ Maintenance	High maintenance. Highly variable for rail and flanged wheel	Low wear-and-tear and maintenance. Hence long guideway life.

can move without any physical contact with the stationary track. In addition, the levitation scheme should be integrated with a lateral guidance scheme to keep the levitated vehicle on the track while in motion.

Based on the mechanism employed for levitating the vehicle in air the technically feasible levitation schemes can be classified as follows:

(i) Aerodynamic system
(ii) Permanent Magnet system
(iii) Electromagnetic Repulsion (EMR) system
(iv) Electromagnetic Attraction (EMA) system

Figure 14.6 compares these levitation schemes with wheel-on-rail system. Of the various forms of levitation schemes, the air-cushion scheme is considered to be complex as compared to its magnetic counterpart. Hence the current research on advanced ground transportation (AGT) is based on two forms of magnetic suspension, viz.

(a) Electro-magnetic/Electro-dynamic (super-conducting) repulsion (EMR) system; and
(b) Electromagnetic (ferromagnetic) attraction(EMA) system

Both the systems are technically suitable for high-speed intercity links but the latter can also used for low-speed urban transportation. However, because of inherent instability of the electromagnetic system, a significant part of its design concerns with suspension stability. For this, the influence of feedback of air-gap length, air-gap flux, vertical velocity and acceleration need to be considered for passenger-carrying vehicles.

PRESENT SCENARIO

LIM-based systems, though visualised as a technical possibility long ago, have

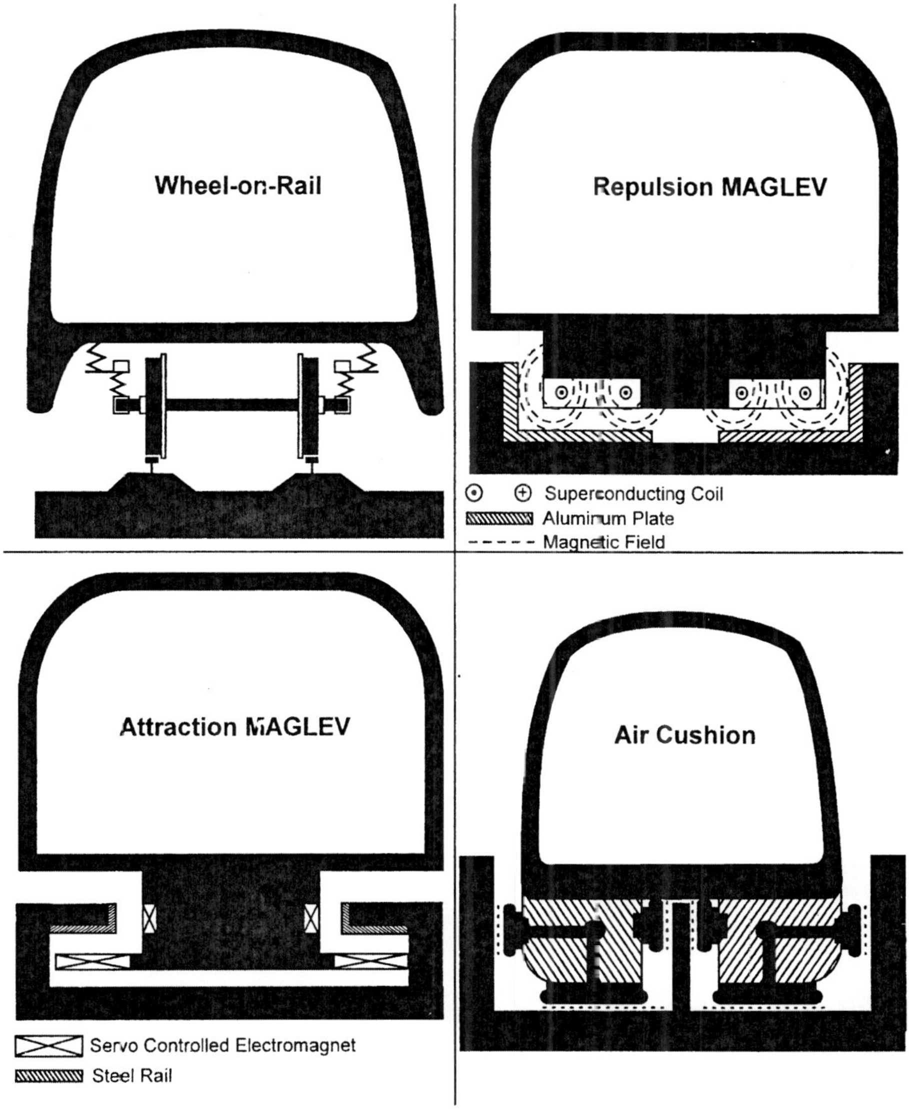

Fig. 14.6 Comparison of different types of levitation systems with wheel-on-rail system

gathered momentum with the developments in the fields of VVVF three phase drives in mid-eighties. Though LEM is the only option in case of levitated transport systems, three-phase linear induction motor drives have proved to be a valuable strategy for Metro systems based on wheel-rail interaction. Application of linear induction motor in such systems reduces vehicle height and brings down diameter of the tunnel, which yields substantial reduction in the cost of tunneling. Besides, the operational and maintenance costs also come down appreciably which improves the financial viability of the LIM-propelled Metro rail system.

As regards levitation, presently Japan and Germany are deeply involved in R&D related to development of magnetically levitated transportation system. It is expected that the rise in fuel cost will open new markets worldwide. The National Research Council of Canada conducted a detailed study for Toronto-Montreal corridor (approximately 600 km). In this study various transportaion modes were evaluated. It has been found that the specific energy consumption for the present short-haul turbo-jet aircraft (DC-9) would be seven times higher than the magnetic levitation system and that for the advanced version B-757 it would be 3.8 times higher. This conclusion points towards techno-economic feasibility of levitation system for high-speed long distance travel.

CHAPTER 15

Application of Computers in Management of Electric Traction

INTRODUCTION

Application of computers to achieve efficient management of electric traction system right from the design stage can help to achieve an overall reduction in costs and break-even traffic-density level. Since the main drawback of electric traction lies in the high initial capital cost of the infrastructure, i.e. OHE and power-supply installations, strategies that reduce the initial investment, enhance availability of assets and reduce operational and maintenance cost are relevant. Since computers can help to achieve these objectives, traction engineers must become conversant with the areas where use of computers can improve efficiencyand reduce costs, which would make electrification cost-effective. Computers should not be thought of merely for reducing clerical staff but as an effective device for efficient management of the system.

COMPUTERS' CAPABILITY RELEVANT TO ELECTRIC TRACTION MANAGEMENT?

Computers have entered all fields of present-day activity in a big way. Computers can do arithmetical and data processing at a very fast speed and with unfailing accuracy. Another thing that computers can do very well is record keeping or data storage.

What computers cannot do fall in the categories of judgement, imagination, intuition, creativity etc.

Computers work according to a programme that, in turn, is a product of human intelligence.

Thus, in situations where there is necessity for data keeping, processing stored data to establish correlationships which aid management efforts and do computations at a fast speed, computers can be a real good asset.

The above capabilities of computers are ideally suited to management of traction system, which consists of a large number of sub-systems widely spread over geographically, viz. overhead installations, power supply and sectioning installation, electric locomotive moving over different zonal railways and receiving attention at several out-station depots, key equipment of locomotive whose behaviour needs compilation in the form of history and to serve as an aid for major maintenance interventions, driving staff (performance, training and driving aspects) etc. All activities listed above involve record keeping and manipulation of stored data.

Monitoring of the above activities and their key parameter may result in:

(i) Energy saving through better driving.
(ii) Preventive/corrective maintenance based on condition of subsystem/equipments.
(iii) Better coordination of maintenance that gets executed at different points and accountability for workmanship.
(iv) Improved availability and reliability of assets.
(v) Saving of expenditure on staff and paper work.

It must, however, be clearly understood that fruitful application of computers is only possible if the system fundamentals are clearly understood to permit selection of correct software, design of appropriate database and devising new programmes that are not covered by standard software.

AREAS OF COMPUTER APPLICATION IN TRACTION SYSTEM MANAGEMENT

We will now briefly, discuss areas where computers have been and can be successfully applied in management of traction systems.

Optimisation of OHE and Power Supply Installation Designs

Design of OHE

Leaning of masts is a common occurrence and is mainly attributable to inadequate design of foundations to suit local soil conditions. The approach to apply thumb-rules in this regard results in installation of masts with reduced span to cut down load coming on the foundation. Average spacing of masts may be as low as 70% of the optimum permissible value from the point of view of sag. Thus there is scope for reducing initial as well as recurring maintenance costs by designing foundations optimally to suit local soil condition. This can be best done by computers with the assistance of appropriate software.

Design of Power Supply Installations

Considerable savings are possible in terms of initial costs and tariff if feeding posts are optimally spaced and the installed capacity matches the growth of load through a modular approach. Spacing of feeding points is mainly governed by voltage drop considerations. Working out of the loading pattern for a given traffic level is a tedious exercise involving complex calculations. To avoid this manual effort, often thumb-rule calculations are made which result in closer spacing of feeding points with excess of installed capacity.

It is also often forgotten that traffic on an electrified route builds up over a period of time following electrification. The prevailing system of traction, which is mainly diesel-electric, takes time to wind up on account of inertia and sometimes operational limitations imposed at change-over points. A liberal assessment of maximum demands and installed capacities could result in high tariffs which is counterproductive. It may be a better strategy to place the initial maximum demands at 10 to 15% lower than the calculated value and depend on short time rating of electrical equipment for a while. A modular design approach can take care of future build-up of load through suitable expansion at an appropriate stage.

Computer-aided Locomotive Designs

Use of computers for designing locomotive subsystems can be very useful particularly where stress analysis is involved. While this is a domain belonging to the expertise of individual manufacturers, an obvious area for application is rationalisation of equipment layout to cater to the following objectives:

(a) Adequate accessibility for maintenance including removal for replacement.
(b) Minimum length of cabling.
(c) Location of vibration generating auxiliaries away from control panels.

Computer Aided Design (CAD) systems with graphic display of the layout can be useful towards evolution of rational designs to cater to the above objectives.

Monitoring of Maximum Demand

The old generation of supervisory remote control systems employing electromagnetic devices and mimic diagrams are almost universally getting substituted by computer based SCADA systems (Supervisory control and DATA acquisition systems). These control systems require much lesser space for their installation and offer means for more efficient management of power. Apart from features of auto-reclosing of circuit breakers which helps to reduce power-off period attributable to transient trippings, these systems possess self-diagnostic features which can be programmed to avoid errors attributable to human judgement.

The SCADA system offers opportunity of continuously monitoring and controlling maximum demand. When the maximum demand at a feeding point tends to approach the contracted value, if may be possible to control unimportant movements or even switch off few load centres for a few seconds. This may reduce tariff without jeopardising traffic flow. However, coordination between traction and operating wings to develop understanding and achieve optimum results is essentially called for.

Energy-saving Driving Approach

The best energy-saving strategy for long distance train operations consists in:

(a) Acceleration to the "booked speed" promptly;
(b) Running at the "booked speed" to maintain the time table negotiating short up-grades by momentum and down-grades by acceleration to maximum permissible speed without braking;
(c) Coasting without power before application of brake at stoppages or speed restriction locations.

This situation may often get disturbed by bunching of trains causing frequent braking and re-starting, which, in turn, results in energy wastage.

Computers can be used to analyse situations that could give rise to bunching on a large scale. Quite often such bunchings are caused due to speed restrictions in critical sections whose inter-station running time is near maximum. Periodical review of such restrictions can help to establish the required coordination between maintenance and operating wings and chalking out of priorities. It would not be out of context to mention that bunchings arising out of abnormalities affecting running can be best dealt by re-starting movement after the disruption has been cleared and conditions for free flow re-established.

Another energy-saving strategy could be to work out the optimum booked speed for a given set of speed restrictions and suggest the same to drivers for guidance.

The expected energy consumption for a run can also be worked out for goods, passenger and express trains and drivers encouraged to generally conform to the same with the help of energy meters installed on their locomotive while maintaining the running schedule.

Training of Drivers on Simulators

Simulators can be effective for training drivers in good driving practices and route learning. A well-designed simulator system can train drivers for the following essential requirements:

(a) Route learning using route-films on videotapes,
(b) Time table adherence,
(c) Energy conservation measures,
(d) Traction and braking control,
(e) Passenger comfort and sopping accuracy,
(f) Systematic and planned response to failure and accidents.

The basic components of a simulator are:

(a) Replica cab,
(b) Instructor console,
(c) Data Base,
(d) Matching computer model with necessary degree of sophistication,
(e) A visual display system giving impression of driving a real train with images of trackside signals and other visual events.

Although the purpose of simulation is to create an illusion, the degree of sophistication in this regard can be reduced to an economic level. Overemphasis on simulating vibration and noises is not always necessary.

Most advanced railway systems are adopting simulators for training of drivers on an increasing scale. Indian Railways have also installed simulators for training drivers on an experimental scale.

Aiding Drivers and Maintenance Depot through On-Board Computers

Use of on-board microprocessor/computer is being made increasingly in modern locomotives to cater for the following objectives:

(a) Traction and braking control, especially for high-speed trains.
(b) Monitoring conditions of key equipments/systems, primarily through temperature rise-based diagnostic data, to aid maintenance.
(c) Aiding drivers in trouble shooting.

History of Locomotive and OHE Equipment

The conventional system of maintaining history of locomotives and overhead equipment in registers, cards or charts is cumbersome and calls for lot of clerical effort. This function can be easily taken over by a computer. Apart from enhancing the integrity of such records, there is an added advantage of being able to call for an information processed in a manner that helps decision making for major interventions or preventive measures.

Usually, a history card is maintained for every locomotive and key equipment like bogies, traction motor, transformer, tapchanger, pantograph, circuit breaker, rectifier etc.

For overhead equipment and power supply installations, similar records are maintained for contact-wire wear, operation of interrupters and trippings due to operation of distance relays etc.

Failure Analysis

By classifying failures of locomotive or key equipment under certain groups, viz. mechanical system failures, brake equipment failures, electrical equipment failures, control system failures, failure of traction motors due to commutator, bursting of bands etc., application of computers can be made through suitable software to pinpoint repetitive causes. This may give vital clue to developing trends due to unexpected wear/tear pattern or fatigue arising out of aggravation in the service conditions.

For overhead equipment, compilation of failures elementary section-wise and recording contact wire wear for those sections can pinpoint the need for major intervention as well as give vital clue regarding need for preventive action. For example, evidence of accelerated contact wire wear at certain locations could be due to frequent stopping and restarting of frames from there and some stagger in exact stopping point could reduce the wear rate to an acceptable level conforming to the general pattern.

Monitoring Execution of Trip-Inspection Schedules of Locomotives

An important area of monitoring is execution of trip-inspection schedules at running depots located near crew-changing points. For greater availability of locos and flexibility in their utilisation, it is desirable that this schedule is made to cover all servicing and minor attention in such a manner that postpones the need for a main base depot attention to two or there months interval. By the very nature of locomotive operation over different zonal railways, this maintenance may be getting done at different places. For proper accountability, details of servicing done or minor attention given together with code names of workers, need recording and storage. This can be best done through multi-terminal PCs with facility for networking to enable access for the base depot to the data stored at different execution points.

Inventory Control

An effective material inventory control may consist in watching the stocking levels of key stores such that procurement action gets initiated well in time. Besides, periodical monitoring of consumption trends may give vital clues to deterioration in operating condition of an equipment or a subsystem. For example increased consumption of carbon brushes could either be attributable to poor commutation or poor quality of brush. Increased consumption of gear-case oil may indicate increased leakage or theft.

Such monitoring of inventory can be best done by a computer. Appropriate and timely intervention by the managerial level on the basis of computer feed back can be of immense help both financially and technically.

POSSIBLE OTHER AREAS FOR COMPUTER-CONTROLLED MONITORING

The list of activities enumerated above where computers could be used fruitfully and in a cost-effective manner is illustrative only and not exhaustive. There can be several other areas where field managers may find computers a useful management tool.

A typical set-up for an Electric Traction Division could be a common computer for electric locos and overhead installations with multi-terminal and networking facilities.

Each terminal could have a keyboard operator who inputs data to the computer system in prescribed format.

The central processing unit may be manned by a system analyst-cum-programmer who can analyse the data and arrange feedback to different units as required.

An advanced technology PC with Winchester disc in conjunction with appropriate software could, in most cases, serve the purpose.

CONCLUSION

From the foregoing discussions, it is evident that computers could be an effective tool for management of electric traction system to achieve the following objectives:

(a) Cut down initial investment;
(b) Improve operational efficiency;
(c) Restrict staff costs to improve system viability in relation to other modes of traction.

However, the tendency to have PCs installed as a showpiece in a disjointed manner and justified on the basis of saving clerical staff should be discouraged.

CHAPTER 16

Numerical Exercises

The worked out numerical examples given in this chapter are designed to illustrate the principles explained in the preceding chapters. To facilitate correlation, examples pertaining to different chapters have been separately grouped. For further practice, a separate set of exercises have also been given.

ILLUSTRATIVE WORKED OUT EXAMPLES

Mechanics of Train Movement (Chapter 2)

EXAMPLE 1

(a) What is "schedule speed" of a train?

(b) A suburban EMU train has a maximum speed of 65 km/h, acceleration of 1.3 km/h/sec and retardation of 1.2 km/h/sec. Find schedule speed of the train if the distance between two adjacent stations is 3 km and stopping time at the station 30 sec. Assume a trapezoidal speed time curve without coasting.

ANSWER 1

(a) The "schedule speed" of a train takes into account the time of stop at a station and is used for the purpose of time-tabling.

(b) Assuming a trapezoidal speed-time curve, let the time taken for acceleration be t_a, time taken for braking t_b, time of free running t_r, and time of stoppage t_s.

t_a = 65/1.3 = 50 sec. Distance travelled during acceleration is

$$65/2 \times 50/3600 = 0.45 \text{ km}$$

t_b = 65/1.2 = 54.16 sec. Distance travelled during braking is

$$65/2 \times 54.16/3600 = 0.48 \text{ km}$$

Hence distance travelled at maximum speed

= (3–0.45–0.48) = 2.07 km

Free running time at maximum speed

t_r = (2.07/65) × 3600 = 114.6 sec.

Total time including stop

= 50 + 54.16 + 114.6 + 30 = 248.8 sec.

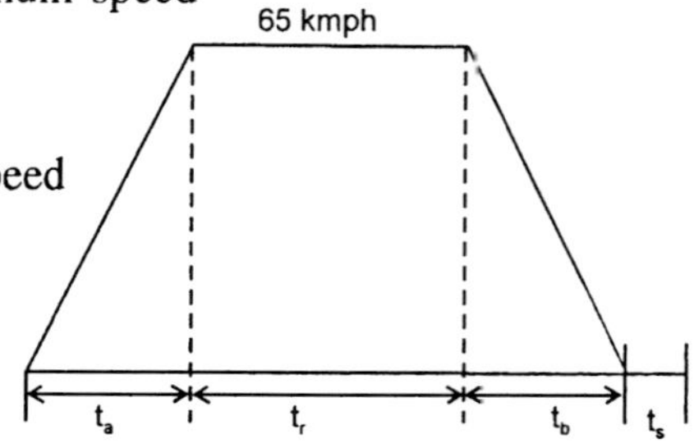

Schedule speed = (3/248.8) × 3600 = 43.4 km/h.

EXAMPLE 2

A train is accelerated at a uniform rate up to a maximum speed of 48 km/h in 24 sec. Then the power is shut off and the train coasts for 69 secs against a constant train resistance.

The train is braked at 3.2 km/h/sec retardation during 11 sec.

(a) Calculate the distance between stations.
(b) Calculate the schedule speed if the stoppage at the stations is 20 sec.

ANSWER 2

The speed-time curve is indicated in the adjoining sketch. There is no time of free running.

Speed V from which the train is braked is

11 × 3.2 = 35.2 km/h

(a) Distance between the stations

= 48/2 × (24/3600) +
69/3600 (48/2 + 35.2/2) +
35.2/2 × 11/3600
= 0.16 + 0.79 + 0.05 = 1.00 km

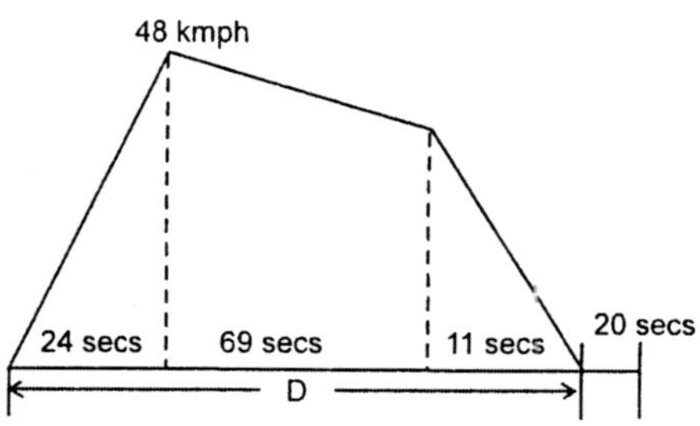

(b) Schedule speed = 1 x 3600/(24 + 69 + 11 + 20) = 29.03 km/h

EXAMPLE 3

An EMU train unit with a trailing tonnage of 254 t is equipped with four motors. It takes 20 sec to attain a speed of 40 km/h on a one per cent gradient. If the gear ratio is 3.5, gear efficiency 0.95%, wheel diameter 91.5 cm, train resistance 44, NW/tonne and rotational inertia 10% of the dead weight, find the torque developed by each motor.

ANSWER 3

(i) Tractive effort required to overcome train resistance: 254 × 44 NW = 11,176 Newtons (NW)

(ii) Tractive effort required for acceleration of the dead wt and to cater for rotational inertia = 277.8 × 1.1 × 254 × rate of acceleration in km/h/sec = 277.8 × 1.1 × 254 × 2 = 155, 234.6 NW

(iii) Tractive effort to overcome grade resistance = 254 × 1/100 × 1000 × 9.81 NW = 24,917.4 NW

Hence, the total train resistance or tractive effort to overcome the same is = 191328 NW.

$$\text{Tractive effort at the driving wheel} = \frac{191328}{0.95} \times \frac{0.915\,(\text{m})}{3.5 \times 2}$$

= 26,325 NW-m.

Torque developed by each motor = 26325/4 = 6581 NW-m

EXAMPLE 4

A 250-tonne train with 10% rotational inertia effect is started with a uniform acceleration to reach a maximum speed of 50 km/h in 25 sec on a level track. After free running at 50 km/h, the train is braked at 3 km/h/sec to reach the next station located at a distance of 2.4 km. Find specific energy consumption assuming an overall efficiency of 85% and train resistance of 5 kg/tonne on level. Assume a simplified trapezoidal speed-time curve.

ANSWER 4

(a) Distance travelled

(i) Distance covered during acceleration = 50/2 × 1000/3600 × 25 m = 173.6 m

(ii) Distance covered during braking = 50/2 × 1000/3600 × 16.67 m = 115.7 m

(iii) Free running distance = 2400–(173.6 + 115.7) = 2110.7 m

(b) Tractive effort (T.E.) required

Tractive effort for acceleration = Mass × Acceleration

= 1000 × 250 × 1.1 × 2 × 1000/3600 Newton
= 1000 × 250 × 1.1 × 2 × 0.277 Newton = 152,350 NW

Tractive effort to overcome train resistance = 5 × 250 × 9.81 NW
= 12,262.5 NW

(c) Energy Consumed
(i) During Acceleration

Total T.E. during acceleration = 152,790 + 12,262.5 NW
= 165,052.5 NW

Work done = T.E. x distance

= 165,052.5 × 173.6 W-sec
= 165,052.5 × 173.6/(1000 × 3600) kWh = 7.959 kWh

(ii) During freerunning

Work done = T.E. × distance

= 12262.5 × 2110.7 W-sec
= 12262.5 × 2110.7/1000 × 3600 kWh
= 7.19 kWh

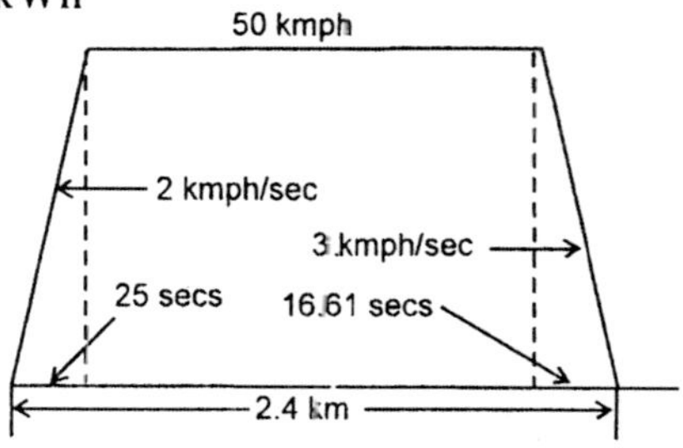

(c) Total Energy consumed
= 7.959 + 7.19 = 15.15 kWh

(d) Specific Energy consumption
= Power intake per tonne-km
= (15.15/0.85) × 1/(250 × 2.4)
= 0.0297 kWh/tonne-km = 29.7 WH/tonne-km

Adhesive Weight, Weight Transfer, Coefficient of Adhesion (Chap 3)

EXAMPLE 5

An electric locomotive is required to start a train weighing 350 t (inclusive of locomotive weight) on an up gradient of 1 in 200 with an acceleration of 1 km/h/sec. Determine

(i) The minimum adhesive weight of the locomotive assuming the following:

(a) Train resistance 60 NW/tonne
(b) Coefficient of adhesion 20%
(c) Effect of rotational inertia = 10% of dead weight

(ii) If the front axles are off-loaded by 10% due to weight transfer, what should be the weight of the locomotive to permit start without slipping?

ANSWER 5

(i) T.E. required

(a) T.E. for acceleration:
$= (350 \times 1.1 \times 1000) \times 1 \times (1000/3600) = 106944.4$ NW

(b) T.E. for gradient effect:
$= 350 \times 1000 \times 9.81/200 = 17167.5$ NW

(c) T.E. for train resistance:
$= 350 \times 60$ NW $= 21000$ NW

(d) Total T.E. required = 145112/9810 t = 14.79 t

Minimum adhesive weight of the locomotive = 14.79/0.2 = 73.96 t

This is shared by two bogies equally.

(ii) If the weight of the locomotives is W, Weight normally shared by the front bogie is $W/2$. Since the 10% weight coming on the front bogie is transferred to the rear bogie during start, the effective weight on the front bogies becomes $0.9 \times W/2$.

This should cater for the minimum adhesive weight required to avoid slipping.

$0.9\ W/2 = 73.96/2$

$W = 73.96/0.9 = 82.17$ t

Series Traction Motor (Chapter 4)

Example 6

A locomotive is equipped with four series traction motors mounted on axles with wheel diameters of 900 mm, 925 mm, 1000 mm and 1025 mm. If the currents taken by the motor mounted on wheel with minimum diameter at 60 km/h is 250 A, determine the currents taken by other motors connected in parallel and percentage variation of current from minimum to maximum.

Assume I.R. drop in armature to be negligible and magnetic circuit unsaturated.

Answer 6

(i) The rpm of different axles corresponding to a vehicle speed of 60 km/h are as follows:

$$900 \text{ mm} \quad \frac{60 \times 1000}{60 \times \pi \times 0.9} = \frac{1111}{\pi} = 354 \text{ rpm}$$

$$925 \text{ mm} \quad \frac{60 \times 1000}{60 \times \pi \times 0.925} = 344 \text{ rpm}$$

$$1000 \text{ mm} \quad \frac{60 \times 1000}{60 \times \pi \times 1.0} = 318 \text{ rpm}$$

$$1025 \text{ mm} \quad \frac{60 \times 1000}{60 \times \pi \times 1.025} = 311 \text{ rpm}$$

In a series motor with negligible I.R. drop:

$$E = V = k.\ N.\ I$$

Where N is speed, I current and k a constant.

Since applied voltage is same for all motors, $(N \times I)$ can be taken as constant for the purpose of this assessment. Further, the gear ratio being the same, the axle speeds can be taken to be proportional to armature speeds.

Hence, the current taken by different motors are as:

TM mounted on 900 mm dia.axle	=	250 Amps (354 rpm)
TM mounted on 925 mm dia.axle	=	257.3 Amps (344 rpm)
TM mounted on 1000 mm dia.axle	=	278.3 Amps (318 rpm)
TM mounted on 1025 mm dia.axle	=	284.6 Amps (311 rpm)

(iii) Variation of current:

$$\frac{284.6 - 250}{250} \times 100 = 34.6 \times 100/250 = 13.8\%$$

EXAMPLE 7(A)

A traction motor has the following speed-current characteristic with 100% field.

Arm. current in A :	40	60	80	100	120	160	200
Speed in km/h :	58.1	47.4	40.3	35.8	33.9	29.8	28.5

Deduce the corresponding characteristic with field strength reduced to 66%, i.e. 2/3rd, using a diverter resistance in parallel with the series field.

ANSWER 7(A)

The armature current-speed characteristic of the series motor with 100% field can be plotted approximately as shown in Fig. 16.1.

Consider the point corresponding to 120 A on this characteristic curve. The speed corresponding to this point is 33.9 km/h. If the field strength becomes 2/3rd due to the diverter resistance, the field current would become 2/3 × 120 = 80 A. This would result in the motor speeding up such that the back EMF produced matches the applied voltage. The speed would rise to a value obtaining at 80 A on the plotted curve. The new points corresponding to 66% field would be 'A'.

Let us take another point corresponding to 90 A armature current. The reduced field strength due to diversion is 60 A. Hence the speed at this point would rise and be as at 'B'. Yet another point corresponding to 60 A would be at 'C'.

Hence the new speed-current curve corresponding to 66% field would be passing through A, B and C, and will be as shown in Fig. 16.1 (upper curve).

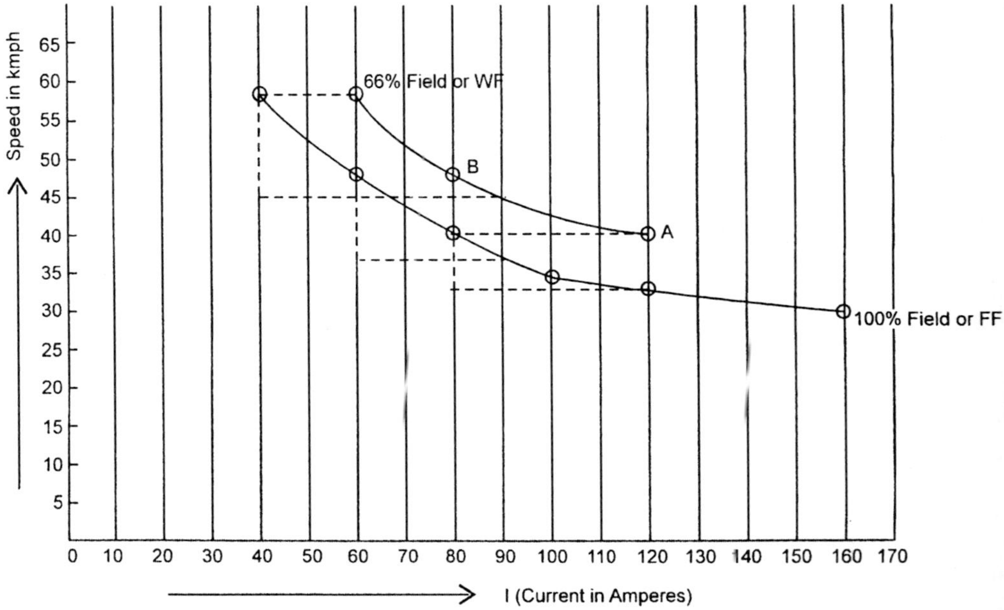

Fig. 16.1 Modification in speed current curve of the motor due to a diverter resistance in the series field (Example 7a)

EXAMPLE 7(B)

If in the above example, T.E. corresponding to different armature currents at full field (FF) is:

Current (A)	:	40	60	80	100	120	200
T.E. (kg)	:	185	440	700	970	1245	2380

Deduce the T.E. at 66% field (WF).

ANSWER 7(B)

$$\text{T.E.} \propto \text{I} \,.\, \phi \propto \frac{1}{N}, \text{ if the voltage is constant}$$

$$\therefore \text{ T.E. at FF} \propto \frac{I_a}{N_{FF}} \text{ and T.E. at } \frac{2}{3}\text{rd Field} \propto \frac{I_a}{N_{WF}}$$

$$\therefore \frac{\text{T.E. (FF)}}{\text{T.E. (WF)}} = \frac{\text{N (WF)}}{\text{N (FF)}}$$

$$\text{or T.E. (WF)} = \frac{\text{T.E.(FF)} \times \text{N(FF)}}{\text{N(WF)}}$$

Since speed at different armature currents gets determined by the curves in (Fig. 16.1), the T.E. can be deduced employing this relationship.

Regenerative Braking (Chapter 6)

Example 8

A 400t train travels down a gradient of 1 in 70 for 120 sec. During this period the speed gets reduced through application of regenerative braking from 80 to 50 km/h. Determine the energy returned to the overhead system if the tractive resistance is 5 kg/tonne, rotational inertia 7.5% and overall efficiency of regeneration 75%.

Answer 8

(i) The kinetic energy stored in a train of W tonne running at V km/h is:

$1/2 \times (1000\ \text{W}) \times (1000\ \text{V}/3600)^2\ (1/3600)$ W-h
$= 0.0107\ \text{W.V}^2$ W-h

(ii) The energy available due to reduction of train speed from 80 to 50 km/h is:

$= 0.0107 \times (400 \times 1.075)\ (80^2 - 50^2)$ W-h
$= 0.0107 \times 430 \times (6400 - 2500)$ W-h
$= 0.0107 \times 430 \times 3900/1000$ kW-h
$= 17.944$ kWh

(iii) T.E. available due to down gradient $= \dfrac{400}{70} \times 1000 \times 9.81$ NW

$= 56057$ NW

Resistance to the train movement is: $400 \times 5 \times 9.81 = 19620$ NW

∴ Net force working on the train:
= 56057 – 19620
= 36437 NW

Distance moved during regeneration = $\frac{(80+50)}{2} \times \frac{1000}{3600} \times 120$

= 2166.7 m

∴ Energy available due to movement of the train on the down grade is:

$$\frac{2166.7 \times 36437}{1000 \times 3600} = 21.93 \text{ kWh}$$

(iv) Total energy available due to reduction of speed and movement of the train on the down gradient is (17.944 + 21.93) kWH = 39.874 kWh

Since regeneration efficiency is 0.75, energy returned to overhead system is:

$$0.75 \times 39.874 = 29.9 \text{ kWh}$$

EXERCISES FOR PRACTICE

Chapter 2

1 It is proposed to put an electric trolley service in a city. The schedule speed is to be 45 kmph. The distance between stops is 2.8 km. The track is assumed to be level. Each stop is of 30 sec duration. Using simplified speed-time curve, calculate the maximum speed assuming the acceleration to be 2 kmphps and retardation to be 3.2 kmphps. The dead weight of the car is 16 tonne. Rotational inertia is 10% of the dead weight and track resistance 40 N per tonne. If the overall efficiency is 80% calculate (a) maximum power output from driving axles (b) the specific energy consumption in watt-hours per tonne-km.

2 An electric train has quadrilateral speed-time curve as follows:

a. Uniform acceleration from rest at 2 kmphps for 30 sec
b. Coasting for 50 sec
c. Duration of braking 20 sec

If the train is moving on uniform up-gradient of 10‰, tractive resistance is 40 N/tonne, rotational inertia effect 10% of dead weight, duration of station stop 15 sec and overall efficiency of transmission gear and motor is 75%, find the schedule speed and specific energy consumption of the run.

Chapter 3

1 Find the minimum adhesive weight of a loco required to start a 2340 tonne (inclusive of loco) on 1 : 150 gradient and accelerate it at 0.1 kmphps. Assume coefficient of adhesion as 0.25, train resistance 4 kg/ tonne and rotary inertia as 8%.

2 A locomotive of 100 tonne can just accelerate a train of 500 tonne with an acceleration of 1 kmphps on up-gradient of 10‰. Adhesive weight of locomotive is 70% of total dead weight, tractive resistance 45 Newton/tonne and rotational inertia 10%. If this locomotive is helped by another locomotive of 130 tonne with 100% adhesive weight, find out:
   a. Trailing weight that can be hauled up the same gradient under same conditions.
   b. The maximum gradient, trailing hauled load remaining unchanged.
   c. Acceleration if gradient and hauled load remain unchanged.

Chapter 4

1. The characteristics of a D.C. series motor when operated at 600 V and driving 107-cm diameter wheels, are as follows:

Current, A	500	400	300	200
Train speed, km/h	35.5	38.7	42	50
Tractive effort, kg	2,580	1960	1,340	860

A motor bogie is fitted with two of these motors. One motor has a pair of wheels of 107-cm diameter and the other of 101-cm diameter. Calculate (a) power input and (b) tractive effort of each motor when (i) the motors are in parallel and their speed is 45 km/h, (ii) the motors are in series and current is 400 A. The resistance of each motor is 0.08 ohm.

Chapter 5

1 An electric train weighing 100 tonne is equipped with four 600-V motors. Each motor draws a current of 400 A during starting and develops a net accelerating tractive effort of 1,630 kg. The resistance of each motor is 0.1 ohm. Allow 10% for rotational inertia. Track resistance is

3.7 kg/tonne. The train speed at the end of starting period is 56 km/h. Determine:

a. Acceleration
b. Duration of starting period
c. Speed during transition
d. Energy dissipated in starting resistance
e. Energy developed by each motor and
f. Total energy input

Chapter 6

1. A 2340 tonne train (including loco) proceeds down a gradient of 1 in 80 for 5 min, during which period, its speed gets reduced from 60 to 36 km/h by application of regenerative braking. Find the energy returned to the line, if the tractive resistance is 5 kg/tonne, rotational inertia 10% and the overall efficiency of the motors during regeneration is 70%.

Bibliography

Books and Handbooks

1. Railway Traction by H.L. Andrews, Elsevier Science Publishers, Netherlands, 1986.
2. Electric Traction by A.T. Dover, Pitman, London, 1963.
3. Electric Traction Systems and Equipment by D.W. Hinde and M. Hinde, Pergamon Press, Oxford, 1968.
4. Electric Traction Engineering by E.A. Benney, Cleaver Hume Press Ltd., London.
5. Electric Drives by M. Chilikin, Mir Publishers, Moscow, 1970.
6. Diesel Engine Operation and Maintenance by V.L. Maleev, McGraw-Hill Book Co., New York, 1954.
7. Reliability Engineering by A.K. Govil, Tata McGraw-Hill Publishing Co., New Delhi, 1983.
8. Protective Relaying in Electric Power System by M. Titarenko and I. Naskov, Peace Publishers, Moscow, Second Edition.
9. Electrical Engineer's Reference Book by M.G. Say and M.A. Langhton, Butterworth International Editions, Fourteenth Edition.
10. Utilization of Electric Energy by E. Openshaw Taylor, Orient Longmans, Bombay, 1962.
11. Electric Traction by H. Partab, Dhanpat Rai & Sons, New Delhi, 1980.
12. Induction Machines for Special Purposes by E.R. Laithwaite, George Newnes Ltd, London, 1966.
13. Propulsion without Wheels by E.R. Laithwaite, The English University Press Ltd., London, 1974.
14. Linear Induction Machines by S.A. Nasar and I. Boldea, John Wiley & Sons, New York, 1976.
15. Linear Motion Electromagnetic Systems by I. Boldea and S.A. Nasar, John Wiley & Sons, New York, 1985.
16. Linear Electric Motors: Theory, Design and Practical Applications by S.A. Nasar and I. Boldea, Prentice-Hall Inc., New Jersey, 1987.

17. Transport without Wheels edited by E.R. Laithwaite, Elek Science, London, 1977.
18. Electromagnetic Suspension—Dynamics and Control by P.K. Sinha, IEE Control Engineering Series 30, Peter Peregrinus Ltd., London, 1987.

Magazines, Periodicals, Reports & Manuals

1. A.C. Drives System for Rolling Stock (Booklet), Hitachi 1997.
2. French Railway Technique, SNCF, France.
3. Hitachi Review, Japan.
4. Railway Gazette International.
5. International Railway Journal and Rapid Transit Reviews, USA.
6. Traction Vehicle Technique System Technology, ABB, Henchel.
7. Three-phase Asynchronous A.C. Traction Motor Systems: Technology Assessment, Association of American Rail Roads (AAR) Report No. R-778 (1991).
8. Railway Electrification Magazine, Published by CORE Indian Railways, Allahabad.
9. ABB Manuals for 3 Phase A.C. Locos, ABB Switzerland.
10. Feasibility Study by Japanese International Corporation Agency (1987) on Railway Improvement Plan in India.
11. IR A.C. Traction Manual, Indian Railways.
12. IR Signalling Manual, Indian Railways.
13. AEG Manual, AEG, Berlin, Eighth Edition.
14. Proceedings of International Workshop on "Lim Propelled Rail Metro System" Department of Electrical Engineering, I.T Banaras Hindu University in January 1999.